Globalisation in Transition

Umair Ghori · Mary Hiscock · Louise Parsons ·
Casey Watters
Editors

Globalisation in Transition

Human and Economic Perspectives

Springer

Editors
Umair Ghori
Bond University
Robina, QLD, Australia

Mary Hiscock
Bond University
Robina, QLD, Australia

Louise Parsons
Bond University
Robina, QLD, Australia

Casey Watters
Bond University
Robina, QLD, Australia

ISBN 978-981-99-2438-7 ISBN 978-981-99-2439-4 (eBook)
https://doi.org/10.1007/978-981-99-2439-4

This Springer imprint is published by the registered company Springer Nature Singapore Pte Ltd.
The registered company address is: 152 Beach Road, #21-01/04 Gateway East, Singapore 189721, Singapore

Chancellor's Foreword

I am delighted to be asked to write the foreword to this monograph in honor of John Farrar.

Emeritus Professor Farrar has, for over 50 years, been an eminent legal scholar active in the UK, North America, New Zealand and Australia. His contribution has been, quite simply, exemplary and extraordinary. The breadth of the impact of his teaching, mentorship and knowledge is well reflected in the range of subjects now covered.

In my view, it is indeed fitting that he be honored by the publication of a Festschrift. It is a tribute to his life and his work in so many areas, including his contribution to Bond University.

I congratulate the various contributors to this book and the editors and wish all who read it, well.

Gold Coast, Australia

Hon Dr. Annabelle Bennett, AC SC FAA
Chancellor

List of Publications for John H. Farrar

Articles, Commentary and Notes

Farrar, John H., and Hawes, Cynthia. Commentary on Sale of Goods. In *Halsbury's Laws of England*, New Zealand Pilot.
Farrar, John H., and Powles D. G. The Effect of s 9 of the European Communities Act 1972 on English Company Law. *Modern Law Review* 36(3): 270–277.
Farrar, John H. 1967. The Taxation of Investment Trusts. *New Law Journal* 117: 286.
Farrar, John H. 1967. The Industrial Reorganisation Corporation. *New Law Journal* 117: 317.
Farrar, John H. 1967. The Finance of Take-over Bids. *New Law Journal* 117: 539.
Farrar, John H. 1969. Thomas More—Lawyer and Judge. *New Law Journal* 119: 679.
Farrar, John H. 1970. Illegality in Take-over Bids. *New Law Journal* 120:401.
Farrar, John H. 1970 Contracting out of Set-off. *New Law Journal* 120: 771.
Farrar, John H. 1971. A Bank's Rights in an Insolvency Situation. *Modern Law Review* 34(2): 211–215.
Farrar, John H. 1971. Mutual Dealings and a Bank's Lien. *New Law Journal* 121:314.
Farrar, John H. 1971. Transfer of a Business to a Company. *New Law Journal* 121:332.
Farrar, John H. 1971. The Authority of a Company Secretary. *New Law Journal* 121:911.
Farrar, John H. 1972. The EEC Draft Convention of Bankruptcy. *Journal of Business Law* 256.
Farrar, John H. 1972. Law as Fact. *Journal of the Society of Public Teachers of Law* 12: 62.
Farrar, John H. 1972. Fraudulent Trading and the Company Secretary. *New Law Journal* 122:13.
Farrar, John H. 1972. Termination of a Partnership on the Grounds of Illness. *New Law Journal* 122: 172.

Farrar, John H. 1973. Illegality—Takeovers and Preacquisition Profits. *Cambridge Law Journal* 32(2): 234–236.
Farrar, John H. 1974. Legal Values in Western Society by Peter Stein & John Shand. *British Journal of Law and Society* 1(2): 210–213.
Farrar, John H. 1974. Abuse of Power by Directors. *Cambridge Law Journal* 33(2): 221–225.
Farrar, John H. 1974. Floating Charges and Priorities. *Conveyancer & property lawyer* 38(5): 315.
Farrar, John H. 1975. Developments in the Law of Receivers. *Journal of Business Law* 23.
Farrar, John H. 1975. Editorial on Reform of Bankruptcy Law. *Journal of Business Law* 86.
Farrar, John H., and Lowe, N. V. 1975. Fraud, Representative Actions and the Gagging Writ. *Modern Law Review* 38(4) 455–462.
Farrar, John H. 1975. Lord Chorley's Law of Banking 6th edition (Review). *Journal of the Society of Public Teachers of Law* 13: 22.
Farrar, John H. 1975. Report of the Committee on the Preparation of Legislation. *Modern Law Review* 38(5): 553–556.
Farrar, John H. 1976. The Crystallisation of a Floating Charge. *Conveyancer & property lawyer* 40(6): 397.
Farrar, John H. 1976. Law Reform Now—a Comparative View. *The International and Comparative Law Quarterly* 25(1): 214–228.
Farrar, John H. 1976. Public Interest Parties and the Active Role of the Judge in Civil Litigation by Mauro Cappelletti and J. A. Jolowicz. *The International and Comparative Law Quarterly* 25(3): 708–709.
Farrar, John H. 1976. Corporate Insolvency and the Law. *Journal of Business Law* 214.
Farrar, John H., and Furey, Nigel E. 1977. Reservation of Ownership and Tracing in a Commercial Context. *Cambridge Law Journal* 36(1): 27–32.
Farrar, John H. 1977. The EEC Draft Convention on Bankruptcy and Winding Up—A Progress Report. *Journal of Business Law* 320–337.
Farrar, John H. 1978. Informal Company Arrangements with Creditors. *New Zealand Law Journal* (4): 71–75.
Farrar, John H. 1978. Alteration of Objects—a suitable case for treatment. *New Zealand Universities Law Review* 8: 164.
Farrar, John H. 1979. The Securities Act 1978. *New Zealand Universities Law Review* 8: 301.
Farrar, John H. 1980. Dr. C J Foster—Canterbury's First Law Teacher. *Canterbury Law Review* 1(1): 5–14.
Farrar, John H. 1980. Fraudulent Trading. *Journal of Business Law*.
Farrar, John H. 1980. Law Reform in New Zealand—The State of Play. *Canterbury Law Review* 1(1): 104–121.
Farrar, John H. 1980. Recent Developments in New Zealand Company Law. *Journal of Business Law* 296.
Farrar, John H. 1980. The Floating Charge on Trial. *Company Lawyer* 1: 83.

Farrar, John H. 1980. Public Policy and the Pari Passu Rule. *New Zealand Law Journal* (5): 100–103.
Farrar, John H. 1982. Commercial Law Notes. All England Reports Annual Review: 19–33.
Farrar, John H., and Aldridge, P. 1983. Crimes Relating to Insolvency. Commonwealth Law Ministers' Conference.
Farrar, John H. 1983. The Bankruptcy of the Law of Fraudulent Preference. *Journal of Business Law* 390.
Farrar, John H., and Russell, Mark. 1984. The Impact of Institutional Investment on Company Law. *Company Lawyer* 5(3): 107.
Farrar, John H. 1985. Some Distinctive Characteristics of New Zealand Insolvency Law. *Insolvency Law and Practice* 1: 68.
Farrar, John H., and Maxton, Julie K. 1986. Social Investment and Pension Scheme Trusts. *Law Quarterly Review* 102: 32–35.
Farrar, John H. 1987. Law Reform in New Zealand. *Oxford Journal of Legal Studies* 7(1): 151–154.
Farrar, John H. 1989. Business Judgment and Defensive Tactics in a Hostile Takeover. *Canadian Business Law Journal* 15(1): 15–42.
Farrar, John H. 1989. Harmonization of Business Law between Australia and New Zealand. *Victoria University of Wellington Law Review* 19(4): 435–463.
Farrar, John H. 1990. Fraud, Fairness and Piercing the Corporate Veil. *Canadian Business Law Journal* 16(4): 474–479.
Farrar, John H. 1990. New Zealand Considers a Personal Property Security Act. *Canadian Business Law Journal* 16(3): 328–331.
Farrar, John H. 1990. The United Kingdom Companies Act 1989. *Canadian Business Law Journal* 17(1): 150–161.
Farrar, John H. 1991. Cross Frontier Mergers. *Canterbury Law* Review 4(3): 429–446.
Farrar, John H. 1993. Corporate Governance, Business Judgement and the Professionalism of Directors. *Corporate and Business Law Journal* 6(1): 1–28.
Farrar, John H., and McCabe, Bernard. 1995. Corporatisation, Corporate Governance and the Deregulation of the Public Sector Economy. *Public Law Review* 6(1): 24–43.
Farrar, John H. 1996. The Idea of a Private University. *Institute of Public Affairs Review* 49(2): 19–22.
Farrar, John H. 1997. The Personal Liability of Directors for Torts of Company. *Australian Law Journal* 71(1): 20–22.
Farrar, John H. 1997. The Personal Liability of Directors for Corporate Torts. *Bond Law Review* 9(1): 102–112.
Farrar, John H. 1998. Towards a Statutory Business Judgment Rule in Australia. *Australian Journal of Corporate Law* 8(3): 237–243.
Farrar, John H. 1998. Reasoning by Analogy in the Law. *Bond Law Review* 9(2): 149–74.
Farrar, John H. 1998. 'Frankenstein Inc or Fools' Parliament? Revisiting the Concept of the Corporation in Corporate Governance. *Bond Law Review* 10(2): 142–163.

Farrar, John H. 1998. Legal Issues Involving Corporate Groups. *Company and Securities Law Journal* 16(3): 184–206.

Farrar, John H. 1999. A Brief Thematic History of Corporate Governance. *Bond Law Review* 11(2): 259–273.

Farrar, John H. 2001. In Pursuit of an Appropriate Theoretical Perspective and Methodology for Comparative Corporate Governance. *Australian Journal of Corporate Law* 13(1): 1–18.

Farrar, John H., and Laurence J. Boulle. 2001. "Minority Shareholder" Remedies—Shifting Dispute Resolution Paradigms. *Bond Law Review* 13(2): 272–304.

Farrar, John H. 2001. Directors' Duties and Corporate Governance in Troubled Companies. *Canterbury Law Review* 8(1): 99–112.

Farrar, John H. 2002. Developing Corporate Governance in Greater China. *University of New South Wales Law Journal* 25(2): 462–485.

Farrar, John H. 2003. Corporate Governance and the Judges. *Bond Law Review* 15(1): 65–101.

Farrar, John H. 2003. Inadequate Boards, Organs and Section 35A of the Companies Act. *Cambridge Law Journal* 62(1): 45–47.

Farrar, John H., and Christoph Pippel. 2004. Piercing the Corporate Veil in an Era of Globalisation and International Terrorism and Emergence of the Lawyer as Gatekeeper and Whistleblower. *Bond Law Review* 16(2): 66–95.

Farrar, John H. 2005. Enforcement: A Trans-Tasman Comparison. *New Zealand Law Review* (3): 383–429.

Farrar, John H. 2006. The Radical Transformation of Company Law—Global Trends and Local Initiatives. *Journal of Malaysian and Comparative Law* 33: 1–25.

Farrar, John H. 2006. Book Review: Legal Reasoning: The Use of Analogy in Legal Argument. *Waikato Law Review* 14: 145–149.

Farrar, John H. 2007. Winds of Change Hit the Legal Profession. *Waikato Law Review* 15: 23–25.

Farrar, John H. 2008. The Governance of SMEs and Unlisted Companies. *New Zealand Business Law Quarterly* 14(4): 213–230.

Farrar, John H. 2008. Salmond and Corporate Theory. *Victoria University of Wellington Law Review* 38(4): 925–934.

John. H. Farrar, Parsons, Louise, and Pieter I. Joubert. 2009. The Development of an Appropriate Regulatory Response to the Global Financial Crisis. *Bond Law Review* 21(3): 1–41.

Farrar, John H. 2009. Reasoning by Analogy in the Law. *Judicial Review* 9(3): 309–330.

Farrar, John H. 2010. The Global Financial Crisis and the Governance of Financial Institutions. *Australian Journal of Corporate Law* 24(3): 227–243.

Farrar, John H. 2010. Living with the Waikato Foundation Principles 20 Years On. *Waikato Law Review* 15: 83–89.

Farrar, John H., and Watson, Susan. 2011. Self-dealing, Fair-dealing and Related Party Transactions—History, Policy and Reform. *Journal of Corporate Law Studies* 11(2): 495–523.

Farrar, John H. 2011. Directors' Duties of Care—Issues of Classification, Solvency and Business Judgement and the Dangers of Legal Transplants. *Singapore Academy of Law journal* 23: 745–761.

Farrar, John H. 2011. Fighting Identity Crime. *Bond Law Review* 23(1): 88–101.

Jessep, Duncan C., Farrar, John H., and Watson, Susan. 2012. Related Party Transactions in New Zealand; An Empirical Study of a Flawed System. *Company and Securities Law Journal* 30(2): 110–142.

Farrar, John H., and Parsons Louise. 2012. Globalisation, the Global Financial Crisis and the Reinvention of the State. *Singapore Academy of Law journal* 24(2): 367–401.

Farrar, John H. 2012. Early Conceptions of the State in New Zealand. *Yearbook of New Zealand Jurisprudence* 13/14: 51–65.

Farrar, John H. 2013. Piercing the Corporate Veil in Favour of Creditors and Pooling of Groups—A Comparative Study. *Bond Law Review* 25(2): 31–55.

Farrar, John H. 2019. Billion Dollars Bonfires—A Comparative Study of Regulatory Failure in the Non-Bank Sector in Australia and New Zealand. *New Zealand Business Law Quarterly* 25(3): 213–223.

Farrar, John H. 2019. William Larnach—Victorian Mastermind, Fraudster or Tragic Victim? *Waikato Law Review* 27: 77–86.

Farrar, John H. 2020. A Conspiracy of Paper? William Paterson and the Mysterious Origins of Banking and Company Law. *Bond Law Review* 32(1): 139–150.

Books

Australian Corporation Law Service—Specialist Contributor (Company Charges)

Farrar, John H. 1974. *Law Reform and the Law Commission Modern Legal Studies Series*. London: Sweet & Maxwell.

Farrar, John H. 1977. *An Introduction to Legal* Method. London: Sweet & Maxwell.

Palmer, Francis, and Morse, Geoffrey. 1982. *Palmer's Company Law 23rd ed*. United Kingdom: Stevens. (Specialist Editor)

Farrar, John H., Russell, Mark W., and Hampton, Lindsay F. 1985. *Company Law and Securities Regulation in New Zealand*. Wellington: Butterworths.

Palmer, Francis, and Morse, Geoffrey. 1987. *Palmer's Company Law 24th ed*. United Kingdom: Stevens. (Specialist Editor)

Hahlo, H. R., and Farrar, John H. 1987. *Hahlo's Cases and Materials on Company Law 3rd ed*. London: Sweet & Maxwell.

Farrar, John H., and Scragg, Richard J. 1987. *Chattel Security: Revision and Update*. Wellington: The Society.

Farrar, John H. 1987.*Contemporary Issues in Company Law*. Auckland: Commerce Clearing House. (Editor and contributor)

Farrar, John H., and Dugdale, Anthony M. 1990. *An Introduction to Legal Method* 3rd edition. London: Sweet & Maxwell.

Farrar, John H., and Borrowddale, Andrew. 1992. *Commercial Law in New Zealand 2nd edition.* Wellington: Butterworths. (Author of Chapters 1, 11–21, 36, 39, 40, 42–51).

Farrar, John H. 1993. *Takeovers, Institutional Investors and the Modernization of Corporate Laws O.U.P.* Auckland: Oxford University Press. (Editor and contributor of Chapters 1, 11 and 12).

Farrar, John H., et al. 1998. *Farrar's Company Law 4th ed.* London: Butterworths.

Farrar, John H. 2001. *Corporate Governance in Australia and New Zealand.* Melbourne: Oxford University Press.

Farrar, John H., and Bosh, H. 2003. *Guidelines on Corporate Governance for Small and Medium Sized Enterprise.* Hong Kong: The Hong Kong Institute of Directors, Hong Kong.

Farrar, John H. 2003. *Comparative Corporate Governance.* Gold Coast: Bond University. (Editor and contributor)

Farrar, John H. 2005. *Corporate Governance: Theories, Principles and Practice 2nd edition.* South Melbourne: Oxford University Press.

Farrar, John H. 2008. *Corporate Governance: Theories, Principles and Practice 3rd edition.* South Melbourne: Oxford University Press.

Farrar, John H, and Taylor, Lynne. 2008. *Company and Securities Law in New Zealand.* Wellington: Thomson Brookers.

Farrar, John H. 2010. *Legal Reasoning.* Pyrmont: Thomson Reuter.

Farrar, John H., and Watson, Susan. 2011 *Contemporary Issues in Corporate Governance.* Christchurch, Centre for Commercial and Corporate Law University of Canterbury.

Ariff, Mohamad, Farrar, John, and Khalid, Ahmed M. 2012. *Regulatory Failure and the Global Financial Crisis.* Cheltenham, Edward Elgar.

Farrar, John H., Watson, Susan and Taylor, Lynne. 2013. *Company and Securities Law in New Zealand.* Wellington: Brookers.

Farrar, John H., and Mayes, David Christopher. 2013. *Globalisation, the Crisis and the State.* Cheltenham: Edward Elgar.

Watson, Susan, et al. 2018. *Corporate Law in New Zealand.* Wellington: Thomson Reuters.

Farrar, John H, Lo, Vai Io, and Bee Chen, Goh. 2019. *Scholarship Practice and Education in Comparative Law—A Festschrift in Honour of Mary Hiscock.* Singapore, Berlin: Springer.(Co-Author of chapters titled: Introduction: Comparative Dimensions of Law in Context; and Financial Stability After the Global Financial Crisis: Globalisation, Nationalism and the Potential Demise of a Rules-Based Order)

Chapters in Books

Farrar, John H. 1987. Ownership and Control of the Public Listed Company—Revising or Rejecting the Concept of Control. In *Company Law in Change*, ed. B.G. Pettet, 39–67. London: Stevens.

Farrar, John H., and McLay, Geoffrey. 1992. The Interface of Floating Charges, Romalpa Clauses and Credit Factoring. In *Dimensions in Business Finance* Law, ed. John Prebble, 65–92. Wellington: Butterworths.

Farrar, John H. 1994. The Responsibility of Directors and Shareholders for a Company's Debts Under New Zealand Law. In *Current Developments in International and Comparative Corporate Insolvency Law*, ed. Jacob S. Ziegel, 521–546. New York: Clarendon Press and United Kingdom: Oxford University Press.

Farrar, John H. 1995. CER and Harmonization of Laws between Australia and New Zealand. In *Essays on the Constitution*, ed. Phillip A. Joseph. Wellington: Brooker's.

Farrar, John H., and Darroch, A. 1995. Insolvency and Corporate Groups—the Problem of Consolidation. In *Corporate Insolvency* Law, eds. Jim Corkery and John Lessing. Gold Coast: Bond University.

Farrar, John H. 1996. Voluntary Administration in Australia and the United Kingdom—A Comparative Study. In *Essays on Corporate Restructuring and Insolvency*, ed. Charles Rickett, 69–90. Wellington: Brookers.

Farrar, John H. 1998. The Duty of Care of Company Directors in Australia and New Zealand. In *The Realm of Company Law—A Collection of Papers in Honour of Professor Leonard Sealy*, ed. Barry A. K. Rider, 37–52. London, Kluwer Law.

Farrar, John H. 2002. The New Financial Architecture and Effective Corporate Governance. In *Key Developments in Corporate Law and Trusts Law—Essays in Honour of Professor Harold Ford*, ed. Ian M. Ramsay. Sydney: Lexis Nexis Butterworths.

Farrar, John H. 2008. Codification of Commercial Law. In *Law, Liberty, Legislation*, eds. Finn and Todd. Wellington: Lexis Nexis.

Farrar, John H. 2012. The Governance and Regulation of Complex Conglomerates. In *The Sage Handbook of Corporate Governance*,eds. Thomas Clarke and Douglas M. Branson, 520–530. London: Sage Publications Ltd.

Farrar, John H. 2012. Improving the Governance of Financial Institutions *Regulatory Failure and The Global financial Crisis*, eds. Mohamed Ariff, John H. Farrar, and Ahmed M. Khalil, 127–138. Cheltenham: Edward Elgar.

Farrar, John H., and Mayes, Daniel. 2013. Globalising the Modern State. In *Globalisation, the Crisis and the State*, ed. John H. Farrar. Cheltenham: Edward Elgar.

Farrar, John H., and Ariff, Mohamed. 2013. The Governance and Regulation of Sovereign Wealth Funds and Foreign Exchange Reserves in a Post GFC World. In *Globalisation, the Crisis and the State*, ed. John H. Farrar. Cheltenham: Edward Elgar.

Farrar, John H., and Ariff, Mohamed. 2014. BRICS: Experiments within State Capitalism and Institutional Investment. In *The Rise of BRICS: Changing Paradigms for The Global Financial Political Economy*, eds. Vai Lo and M Hiscock, 142–161. Cheltenham: Edward Elgar.

Farrar, John H. 2015. Hard Choices! Defining Australia's National Interest in the Asian Century. In *Australia's Trade, Investment and Security in the Asian Century*, eds. John H. Farrar, Mary Hiscock and Vai Io Lo, 3–23. Singapore: World Scientific Publishing Company.

Farrar, John H. 2018. The Future of Australian Legal Education: A Comparative View. In *The Future of Australian Legal Education*, ds. Kevin Lindgren, Francois Kunc, and Michael Coper, 143–155. Sydney: Thomson Reuters.

Farrar, John H. and Louise Parsons, Chapter 6 "Financial Stability after the Global Financial Crisis: Globalisation, Nationalism and the Potential Demise of a Rules based Order." in Farrar, John H, Lo, Vai Io, and Bee Chen, Goh. 2019. *Scholarship Practice and Education in Comparative Law—A Festschrift in Honour of Mary Hiscock*. Singapore, Berlin: Springer.

Farrar, John H. 2020. The Duties of Controlling Shareholders: Complex Relationships, Legal Confusion and New Approaches. In *Governance and Law Contemporary Views*, ed. Heath S. Grow, and Anona Armstrong, 44–55. Victoria University.

Reports

Farrar, John H. 1992. *Modernizing Australian Corporations Law*. Report for the Business Council of Australia and Australian Institute of Company Directors. Business Council Bulletin.

Farrar, John H. 1993. *Legal Impediments to Increased Institutional Investor Involvement in Corporate Governance*. Report for Australian Investment.

Hoare, David, Lavarch, Michael, and the Australian Attorney-General's Department. 1994. *Super Voting Shares*. Report by Commonwealth Attorney General's Expert Panel of Inquiry into Desirability of Super Voting Shares for Listed Companies (Australia). (Member and Co-author).

Tribute

Dominic Esposito[1]

It is a great pleasure to honor Prof. John Farrar in his academic and related personal competencies and in his role in the legal academic community.

I do this as a former student and long-standing friend, having maintained a relationship with him since 1978.

I received inspiration and care from John at Canterbury University, as a first-year law student and later in the subject company law (both as lecturer and tutor), which resulted in me completing a law degree and then conducting legal practice for thirty-six years in Melbourne. An enduring result.

I struggled with the usual first-year student trepidation about a legal career pathway, and John was instrumental to me maintaining interest and completing the legal journey.

Mentoring and care are pivotal to vocational development, which John generously afforded to me.

I initially attended university to pursue an agricultural science degree, populating my studies with science papers and one course in law taken by John.

I was inspired by John as he represented competency and excellence in the law and was educated and academically formed in Great Britain, the fountain of the common law.

Part of the curriculum for first-year students was a necessary and enlightening read of John's book, Legal Reasoning.

I recall some of the learnings within the book even now.

John spoke with authority and care about the profession, induction within the profession, the academic aspect of the law and what a student needed to do to be part of the discipline.

John was unparalleled in his kindness, care and understanding, in assisting me in adopting new skills and personally vetting my work on several occasions, where I was learning the ropes with new material and disciplines.

---

[1] Dominic Esposito, Dominic Esposito Solicitors, Royal Blue Terrace, 235 Rathdowne Street, Carlton VIC 3053 esposito@esposito.com.au.

John shared with me and the other students his experiences in Britain in private practice, academia and as the author of legal writing.

Separate from the special relationship established at Canterbury University, I reconnected with John when he was teaching at Melbourne University, many years later.

I took note of a post-graduate company law course that he was presenting together with his colleague Prof. Douglas Branson from the USA.

After leaving Melbourne, John continued teaching the post-graduate course at Melbourne over the succeeding years, and I took the opportunity to spend time with John and his colleagues and was able to have a pseudo-engagement with post-graduate learning and teaching, elegantly delivered by him.

Contents

Contributors

Authors

Bruce Baer Arnold
Narelle Bedford
Wendy Elizabeth Bonython
Laurence Boulle
Douglas M. Branson
Ian Edwards
Umair Ghori
Mary Hiscock
Louise Parsons
Vai Io Lo
Michael Lupton
Michelle Markham
Judge Peter Spiller
Casey Watters

Student Editors

Aaron Hollis
Madeline Ransley
Tarisa Yasin

Chapter 1
Human and Economic Perspectives of Globalisation: An Introduction

Umair Ghori, Mary Hiscock, Louise Parsons, and Casey Watters

Abstract In examining the ever-evolving phenomenon of globalisation, and its human and economic impacts, the contributors to this book draw on their own diverse perspectives from different legal systems and present a range of related yet different topics. It highlights how advancements in trade, technology, and corporate governance have transformed economies worldwide. To this end, the chapter emphasizes that globalisation extends beyond corporate law and banking, impacting social issues and human discourse. In exploring these themes, the authors also pay tribute to Prof John Farrar, with whom they have had a close connection, and honour the many areas of law to which he has contributed throughout his career in academia. In the first part, the authors consider the human and social impact of globalisation, through examination of topics including immigration, First Nations people, ageing, and the regulation of medicine and therapeutic goods and pharmaceutical products. In the second part, the authors reflect on the economic aspects of globalisation and debate nuances of corporate law, including the concept of a corporation's social licence to operate, and international perspectives on cross-border insolvency. The discussions also include an analysis of the impact of global crises on central banks, and improvements in tax treaty-related disputes between jurisdictions. The last chapter examines the scope of corporate responsibility to a range of new stakeholders, reflecting changed relationships between hard and soft law and morality. Together, the chapters capture the multifaceted struggle of the law to adapt to the ever-changing social, business, and economic landscape carved by globalisation.

U. Ghori (✉) · M. Hiscock · L. Parsons · C. Watters
Faculty of Law, Bond University, Gold Coast, Australia
e-mail: ughori@bond.edu.au

M. Hiscock
e-mail: mhiscock@bond.edu.au

L. Parsons
e-mail: lparsons@bond.edu.au

C. Watters
e-mail: cwatters@bond.edu.au

U. Ghori et al. (eds.), *Globalisation in Transition*,
https://doi.org/10.1007/978-981-99-2439-4_1

Globalisation is constantly evolving. Periodically, the trends in globalisation shift. Several economies around the world have been shaped by trends flowing from globalisation. In trade, for example, advancements in transport, storage and processing have seen several economies transition from an agricultural base to manufacturing. The information technology revolution has altered marketing, commerce and consumerism. The governance of domestic corporations and their integration with foreign entities have completely transformed regulatory paradigms.

The consequences of globalisation have gone further than areas of corporate law and banking, and include social issues. These not only impact the flow of goods and services but also the human discourse. The cross-diffusion of ideas and the connectivity of society enabled through globalisation has affected (for better or worse) local cultures, customs and even the esoteric practices of nation-states.

This book brings together diverse ideas on selected facets of globalisation. The scholars contributing to the project examine the phenomenon of globalisation through varied lenses: from macro to micro. They came originally from many different legal systems but now are connected through John Farrar and Bond University Faculty of Law.

The book does not attempt to provide answers to the challenges of globalisation. Instead, it discusses selected, aspects of globalisation that derive from and are connected to the authors' own research. The thematic diversity of the book is a true strength and should draw a broad range of readers. While the book is primarily written from a legal angle, its content overlaps into broader specialised policy areas, with contributions ranging from taxation to ageing, from insolvency to social licences and from refugees to the treatment of first nations people. In short, there is something for everyone in this book.

Due to technological advancements and relative peace since WWII, globalisation is often viewed as the inevitable convergence of economic standards and social norms. Whether this vision is utopian or dystopian is a matter of perspective and has resulted in some rejecting the traditional view of globalisation, being that of convergence, in favour of one of cooperation. One of the defining characteristics of the last century is the struggle to bring the world together while embracing social and economic distinctiveness. As a tribute to the life's work of an outstanding legal scholar, Professor John Farrar, this book explores legal responses to the social and economic impacts of globalisation. After personal acknowledgments from colleagues highlighting the significance of his scholarship,[1] the book is divided into three parts after this introduction. The first part addresses the social impact of globalisation, focusing on immigration and the impact on First Nations peoples. Changes in the regulation of medicine and technologies related to ageing are also addressed in this part. In part two, the book addresses the transitioning corporate law landscape and notions of fairness and good faith in the law. The final part is the conclusions, reflections, and synthesis of the editors.

---

[1] Douglas M. Branson 'John Farrar: Leading Experts and Scholar in Company Law and Corporate Governance' (Chap. 2); Dominic Esposito 'A Tribute to John Farrar'; Laurence Boulle and Ian Edwards 'John Farrar and His /juːˈbɪkwɪti/ in Legal Education' (Chap. 8).

1.1 Human Perspectives

The book acknowledges that the foremost impact of globalisation has been on people. Accordingly, the book includes two unique contributions that consider the human impact of globalisation from opposing spectra. Judge Spiller's important contribution focuses on New Zealand as a haven for refugees and asylum-seekers.[2] He provides insights into the difficult process of decision-making that carries profound human impact. This process represents a delicate balancing act between competing considerations such as protection of borders, interests of family unity, the best interests of children and the sanctity of human life. Building on Judge Spiller's contribution, Bedford offers an insight into principles of human pluralism and the need for cross-cultural sensitivity.[3] Bedford compares the experience of First Nations people from both Australia and New Zealand and connects that to Professor Farrar's work in the area.

An often-overlooked aspect of globalisation, but perhaps less so in the COVID-19 pandemic, is its impact on medicine and therapeutic goods harmonization. Bonython and Arnold's contribution lifts the veil over the heavily regulated pharmaceutical sectors.[4] They explores the conflicting dynamics between global-consumer welfare and the erosion of public interests due to neoliberalism that has permeated an increasingly globalised marketplace.

Continuing the thread of human perspectives on globalisation, Lo's contribution explores the role of law in the promotion of synergistic developments of ageing and globalisation.[5] The chapter by Lupton considers issues around ageing and the objectives of anti-ageing treatment.[6]

1.2 Economic Perspectives

In part two of the book, the authors debate the nuances of corporate law, highlighting the changing business environment in response to globalisation. Ghori's contribution is more focussed in that it looks at a particular aspect of corporate governance that intersects with the concept of a corporation's 'social licence to operate' (SLO) and the need for compliance with the regulatory environment.[7] Ghori uses a case study of the Australian live export sector and posits that SLO-based regulation of Australian companies engaging in live exports exhibits a dual-layered regulatory environment.

[2] Judge Peter Spiller 'Globalisation in the Immigration and Refugee Context' (Chap. 3).

[3] Narelle Bedford 'Comparative First Nations Treat Experiences Across the Tasman' (Chap. 6).

[4] Wendy Bonython and Bruce Arnold 'Transitioning up to Best Practice, or Down to the Bare Minimum? Global Harmonisation of Regulation of Therapeutic Goods' (Chap. 5).

[5] Vai I Lo 'The Criss-Cross of Ageing and Globalisation' (Chap. 6).

[6] Michael Lupton 'A Peek Behind the Curtain of Anti-Aging Science' (Chap. 7).

[7] Umair Ghori 'Calculated Compliance in a Globalised World: The response to Social Licence compulsions by the Australian Live Export Sector' (Chap. 9).

The dual-layered environment carries additional compliance costs and an increased cost of doing business.

From compliance to the end-of-company-life issues, Watters provides an international perspective on the issue of cross-border insolvency.[8] Watters' important contribution looks at developments in establishing court-to-court communication protocols to facilitate cross-border insolvency. The recent developments are particularly timely because of increased insolvencies following the slowdown of economic activities due to the COVID-19 pandemic. The contribution by Parsons enlarges the scope of the debate by looking at the regulatory mandates of central banks in times of crisis.[9] The chapter by Parsons examines the governance of central banks considering their evolving mandates in times of global crises.

A well-rounded coverage of international taxation law is provided by Markham.[10] The 15 Final Actions recently implemented exemplify globalisation in transition, as they reflect the realisation that international tax solutions now require dialogue on a global basis. Markham focuses on the sophisticated nature of tax disciplines across the world and explores improvement in tax treaty-related disputes between jurisdictions and the need to achieve global law uniformity. Markham analyses the outcomes in terms of efficiency and effectiveness in improving international dispute resolution mechanisms on a global basis.

Hiscock reviews the traditional indifference of the common law to morality as opposed to legality in commercial transactions and corporate governance.[11] The development of wider obligations on corporations in recent years has extended the range of values and interests that the company has to manage. There is increased scrutiny of the behaviour of corporations by a larger cast of stakeholders, calling for proactivity by boards as well as ticking boxes of statutory obligations.

The book seeks to capture the multifaceted struggle of the law to adapt to the ever-changing social, business, and economic landscape carved by globalisation. From protecting the rights of indigenous peoples, to recognising the touchpoints between and harmonisation of separate national legal systems, to adjudicating cross-border commercial disputes, the impact of the law increasingly reaches beyond national border.

---

[8] Casey Watters 'Developing Protocols for Court-to-Court Communication in Insolvency Proceedings: A Limited Framework for Cooperation' (Chap. 11).

[9] Louise Parsons 'Central Banks in Crisis Times: Mandates in Crisis?' (Chap. 12).

[10] Michelle Markham 'Towards More Effective and Inclusive Globalisation Strategies in International Tax: The Use of Peer Reviews in Evaluating Tax Treaty Dispute Resolution Mechanisms' (Chap. 10).

[11] Mary Hiscock 'Moral Virtue and Corporate Law' (Chap. 13).

Chapter 2
John Farrar: Leading Expert and Scholar in Company Law and Corporate Governance

Douglas M. Branson

Abstract I have known John for 32 years, more or less. He is an expert about many matters, including fine Australian and New Zealand wines (particularly the latter). Professionally, though, he possesses an international reputation in company law, and is known and highly regarded in the U.K., Hong Kong, Malaysia, Singapore, and the U.S., among others, as well as in Australia and New Zealand (Farrar and Hannigan in Farrar's Company Law. Butterworths, London, 1998). With John, for fourteen years, I co-taught the Master of Laws course "Duties of Directors and Corporate Governance" at the University of Melbourne Law School, a course in which Professor Farrar pulled the laboring oar. This essay centers on what, in the first instance, John taught me, and in the second instance, the ways in which John helped expand my incipient understanding. John is a leading attorney and scholar in the field of corporate governance, as author of *Corporate Governance: Theories, Principles, and Evidence* evidences (Farrar in Principles of corporate governance: theories, principles, and practice. Oxford University Press, Melbourne, 2005). "Corporate Governance," John notes in his introduction, though, "is far too important a subject to be left to lawyers" (*Principles of Corporate Governance*, xxvi.). It also is much more than law, composed as is of law, legal concepts, "hard soft law" (ASIC and ASX regulations, for example), and soft soft law, extending outward to business ethics and moral precepts.

2.1 The Changing Face of Corporate Governance

Not too long ago, say the 1950s, U.S. corporations had larger boards of directors, with *Fortune 500* boards' size averaging 11–12 directors but ranging up to 18 or 21. General Motors, for instance, had a board of 18 or so individuals. In Australia, boards have mainly been smaller with ranging between five to eight directors.

D. M. Branson (✉)
University of Pittsburgh, Pittsburgh, USA
e-mail: branson@pitt.edu

U. Ghori et al. (eds.), *Globalisation in Transition*,
https://doi.org/10.1007/978-981-99-2439-4_2

The principal board committee was the executive committee, charged with exercising the full board's power between meetings. In the era before Skype, Facetime, Zoom, speaker phones, and conference telephone calls, a directors' executive committee frequently was thought "necessary." Insiders, that is, non-independents such as the President (CEO today),[1] Executive Vice-President (COO in today's parlance), one other corporate manager, and a generally available and often pliable independent director, constituted the committee.

So, the picture that emerges from the 1950s and 1960s, at least in the U.S., is a large board rendered impotent by its size alone ("I am only one of 15. What difference can I make?"). Into the vacuum so created comes an insider-dominated executive committee, read the CFO or the CFO and a sidekick, which either makes important decisions on its own or offers up "recommendations" that the full board invariably follows. The executive committee device often could be a means whereby an end run was made around the full board of directors, not merely once or twice but on a frequent basis.

Whatever the picture, in the U.S. or in Australia and New Zealand, the inference that arises was that few, if any, corporate officers, directors, or influencers were serious about governance. Good governance existed only here and there, as an aberration.[2]

I do not know what caused change: Margaret Thatcher, Ronald Regan, or a reaction to the law and economics movement of the 1980s. The latter was a minimalist jurisprudence holding that market forces (in product markets, the market for managers, and the market for corporate control) govern better and faster than laws or lawsuits ever could. Accordingly, the function a corporate statute could serve was to describe an off-the-rack contract approximating that to which the players would have bargained, absent transaction costs. Governance was rendered of little or no importance.

Whatever the cause, perhaps in reaction, a good governance movement or emphasis sprung forward in the nineties. It has not only been with us ever since but has gathered importance. Boards are smaller. In the U.S., the number of *Fortune 500* directors had shrunken from close to 6000 to less than 5200.[3] Executive committees have disappeared. In its place are a smaller number of working committees of directors (usually between five and seven) who deal, hands-on, with finance, safety, governance, nominations, accounting and auditing, and other matters. A typical medium or large size corporation's board will meet eight or ten times a year, with telephonic or zoom meetings in-between when the need arises (probably with many more of the latter in these times of the COVID-19 pandemic).

The median, mean and mode of board committees has risen to a number between six and seven, with anything below five an outlier. The legacy committees carrying

---

[1] Under a company law schematic, substitute "managing director," although the trend everywhere seems to be to adoption of the CEO (Chief Executive Officer) title.

[2] The large board-executive committee model is frequently encountered in the not-for-profit sphere.

[3] Branson (2007). See page 88 (5821 *Fortune 500* company directors in 2001) and page 97 (5161 directors in 2007).

over from the early days of the good governance movement are finance, safety (especially in extractive industries), investment (when liquid assets are plentiful), and charitable, or social, responsibility. The compensation committee, now since 2010 effectively required of U.S. public corporations, must consist of outside or independent directors.[4] The governance committee concerns itself with committee charters, election processes, meeting arrangements, and so on.

Particularly important is the audit committee. In the early years of their prevalence, audit committees met twice a year. The committee would conduct an entry meeting with the outside accountants who were to conduct the annual audit, pointing the latter to issues believed to be problematic and asking for an evaluation of internal accounting staff or methods of operation. After the audit, the committee would meet again with the auditors, asking four or five principal questions:

- Did everyone in-house cooperate with you?
- Have the financial statements been prepared in accordance with Generally Accepted Accounting Principles (GAAP)?
- GAAP aside, do the financial statements present a fair and accurate view of the company's assets, liabilities, and financial results for the most recent accounting period?
- Are there any accounting issues or changes in method or principle of which we should be aware?

That was it. By contrast, today audit committees meet between seven to nine times per year. It must be comprised of independent directors, at least one of whom must be a "financial expert," defined as person who has hands-on experience auditing public companies. Audit committees have become the principal receptacle for whistleblower complaints. The audit committee leads the investigation of corporate wrongdoing, or allegations of wrongdoing. The committee conducts teach-ins about internal accounting controls and changes in accounting rules and principles. The audit committee has become the Christmas tree or Chanukah bush upon which legislators and corporate boards alike hang each new responsibility.

The message underlying these developments is a new-found reliance on structure and process. In that vein, good governance results, in turn increasing the chances for better outcomes. According to Professor Farrar, "[b]usinesses are becoming more professional ... [p]art of a trend toward greater accountability."[5] The upshot of all these developments has been structure and process.

---

[4] Dodd-Frank. The U.S. federal scheme is pursuant to a disclosure mandate. So, the statute itself requires companies to disclose if they have a compensation committee and, if not, why not. Few, if any, registrants follow the latter course. Thus, the disclosure framework translates into a de facto substantive requirement. All, or almost all, public companies have a compensation committee.

[5] Farrar (2005), 127. Professor Farrar adds, "more is being expected, perhaps to an unrealistic degree and in a bureaucratic manner."

2.2 Sound Processes: The Business Judgement Rule

No better example of the emphasis on process exists than the renewed, and many times, "clincher," known as the business judgment rule. Australia has adopted a statutory business judgment rule,[6] although in the U.S. the rule remains the product of judge-made law. A few of the U.S.'s fifty plus incorporating jurisdictions such as Nevada have enacted statutory versions but, by and large, the rule is common law product.[7] New Zealand has not codified a version of the rule.

The first feature of the rule to note, though, is that it is not a rule at all. It is not mandatory, and other defenses to allegations of officer or director wrongdoing may exist (market terms, fairness are examples). After the fact, the rule provides a safe harbor, or strong presumption, that in acting directors or officers complied with their fiduciary duty of care.[8]

Before the fact, the rule provides a practice guide, or checklist, for decision-making by a collegial body and its advisors. The policy basis is that compliance with the rule will elevate the quality of decision-making, leading to better if not the best substantive outcome. The Australian statute reads as follows:

> A director or officer of a corporation who makes a business decision is taken to meet the requirements of [fiduciary duty], and their equivalent duties at common law and in equity, in respect of the judgement if they:
>
> (a) *make the judgement in good faith for a proper purpose, and*
> (b) *does not have a material personal interest in the subject matter of the judgement; and*
> (c) *inform themselves about the subject matter of the judgement to the extent they reasonably believe to be appropriate; and*
> (d) *rationally believe that the judgement is in the best interests of the corporation.*[9]

The Australian rule is similar to that existent in U.S. jurisdictions with some minor differences and one major difference.[10] The latter is the insertion of "for a proper purpose language." The U.S. rule shields from scrutiny the board's adoption of extreme takeover defenses, defenses bordering on the conclusive or draconian nullifying shareholder opportunity to consider the third-party bid.[11] Australian

---

[6] *Corporations Act 2001* (Cth) s180(2). *See generally* Farrar (2017).

[7] Nev. Rev. Stat. §78.138(7)(a-b) (directors or officers not liable unless that have engaged in "intentional misconduct, fraud, or a knowing violation of law"). See also *Wynn Resorts v. Eighth Judicial District*, 399 P.3rd 34, 354 (Nev. 2017). Nevada is the Delaware of the West, a fact known in the western U.S., but little noted in the remainder of the states.

[8] Branson (2002). See also page 645 (discussion of differences between safe harbor and presumption).

[9] *Corporations Act 2001* (Cth) s180(2).

[10] American Law Institute, Corporate Governance Project §4.01(c)(1994). *Cf. Warshaw v. Calhoun*, 221 A.2d 487 (Del. 1966)(business judgement rule as a presumption). *See also Aronson v. Lewis*, 473 A.2d 805 (Del. 1984) (same).

[11] The Delaware Supreme Court has decreed that the business judgment rule is available to shield from judicial scrutiny directors' adoption of most, but not all, takeover defenses. *See Unocal Corp. v.*

draftspersons thought the U.S. rule offered protection beyond the pale. As a result, the drafters added the "for a proper purpose" language.

This is not an essay about the ins and outs of the business judgement rule. It is an essay about process. So, a few process observations:

- The rule that is not a rule protects judgements, so the directors have to have made a decision or judgement, including a decision to not make a decision.
- Along those lines, directors might ask themselves if they merely are rubber-stamping a decision made by others, such as a powerful CEO or an influential investment banker. If so, they may not come within any safe harbor.
- The rule does not shield a director from a duty of loyalty violation such as self-dealing; directors who have an arguable conflict of interest should leave the room while the remaining directors discuss the matter, at least after the absenting director has disclosed their possible conflict and its ramifications. The meeting record should reflect that the foregoing took place.
- How much information is enough information is itself a matter of business judgement (inform themselves "to the extent that they reasonably believe to be appropriate"). If the rule required a reasonable amount of information, an objective rather than quasi-subjective standard, trials and other extended proceedings would be necessary, vitiating an ancillary purpose of the rule, namely, the conservation of judicial resources.
- The requirement is "rationally" believe, not reasonably believe, the decision is the company's best interest. If the requirement were to be "reasonably believes," again, judges would have to hold full-blown trials or extensive inquiries. One subsidiary purpose of the rule is conservation of judicial resources, allowing courts to resolve cases on a summary basis. Another is that business persons acting in good faith, not judges, govern incorporated entities.

John Farrar was a leader in Australia's adoption of a business judgment rule as well as a leading expert on the rule itself.

Mesa Petroleum Co., 493 A.2d 946 (Del. 1985) (business judgment rule applies with the add-on that the defense adopted must be proportionate to the threat posed); *Revlon, Inc. v. Macandrews & Forbes Holdings, Inc.*, 506 A.2d 173 (Del. 1986)(action phase business judgment rule: when directors have decided, or circumstances dictate, that the company will be sold, the board ceases to be a defender of the corporate bastion and must seek the best prices for shareholders). These and other Delaware cases have become and represent the U.S.'s national standards. Nothing, though, under any U.S. law protects directors' adoption of a takeover defense that s "draconian" or "preclusive."

2.3 Risk Management

Twenty-five or thirty years ago if one thought of risk management, they pictured the manager in charge of the corporation's insurance scheme. They concerned themselves with insuring the company's facilities, and obtaining employees' unemployment insurance coverage, insurance against suits for defective products, or allegations of nuisance, and director and officer insurance. The risk management portfolio encompassed a bounded sphere of matters.

A quarter century later, risk management has become open-ended, an unbounded sphere (if there is such a thing). Risk managers, their staff, and board risk management committees oversee an inventory of risks the company faces across the entire spectrum of its ownership and operations.[12] The risk manager and staff evaluate the risk, estimate the range of damage or liability should the risk eventuate, do a probability analysis of various outcomes, and implement or suggest solutions aimed at ameliorating the risk they have identified. Recommendations may include insurance, self-insurance, diversification of investments, hedging transactions (in the case of commodities or other fungible items) to lessen risks market gyrations may pose.

An early "wakeup" decision was by an intermediate appellate court in the U.S. state of Indiana, not known as a hotbed of business jurisprudence. In its silos, a smallish Indiana grain elevator stored large stocks of farmers' wheat and corn, holding the stocks for higher, more opportune market prices. What, though, would happen if the open market price of grain fell rather than increased? The elevator and the farmers could lose significant amounts—which was precisely what occurred. Prudent risk management by the elevator's managers would have involved selling futures contracts allowing the elevator to sell some or all of the grain at a price below the then market but limiting the size of future losses to a manageable amount. The Indiana court held that by failing to engage in or discuss risk management (hedging) the grain elevator's board of directors violated their fiduciary duty of care.[13]

So, hedging, once thought to be the province of the "big boys and girls," is a risk management tool that would affect any company that produces a large quantity of a fungible commodity as well as a company that purchases and consumes or resells the same. As a seller, a natural gas company in Victoria, anticipating a colder winter, might purchase option contracts to purchase natural gas in Queensland as a safeguard against the eventuality that the colder winter might exhaust its usual supplies.

Although many other alarms went off since the Indiana decision, twenty-eight years later another wake-up call spread out over three continents (Asia, North America, and Europe), attracting much attention, and sounding alarms concerning faults in risk management. Several financial institutions made extraordinary loans to a hedge fund and another corporation, Greensill Capital, Inc. The latter was founded

---

[12] Farrar, Corporate Governance, 377: "Modern financial management is aimed at protecting the company against risk in the areas of interest rates, credit, currency, and liquidity. [T]he modern concept of risk management extends beyond financial management risks to such matters as health and safety, public liability, trade practices, property and environmental protection ...."

[13] *Brane v. Roth*, 590 N.E.2d 587 (Ind. App. 1993).

by an Australian, Lex Greensill, to make and securitize supply chain financing. The former, the Archegos hedge fund, became hopelessly insolvent with over USD 10 billion US owed to the banks.[14] In making loans, and buying Greensill's securitised loans, the banks, it seems, had run roughshod over their diversification guidelines. Further, they had conducted little or no due diligence about the borrowers. Had they done so, the bank staff would have learned how leveraged the borrowers had been, borrowing an amount many multiples of their equity capital. United Bank of Switzerland (UBS) described the debacle as a failure of risk management: "the bank [is] reviewing its risk management systems." At UBS, the situation had resulted "because the bank didn't have the full picture on [Archegos]'s investments" across the board.[15]

At Japan's Nomura, senior management "shuffled several executives who oversee the bank's risk management."[16] The bank replaced its risk manager as well as hiving off risk management for American operations to a separate risk manager and staff.[17]

Credit Suisse, headquartered in Switzerland but prominent in the U.S., received the most attention. Its losses exceeded USD 5.5 billion US. The Credit Suisse board brought in a new chief executive officer (CEO). "[H]e identified three priorities: risk management, strategy, and culture. Risk was his immediate priority."[18] The board also replaced the chief of the board's risk management committee who also stood down as a director, opting not to seek re-election. "We need to foster a culture that reinforces the importance of risk management," the new CEO told the annual Credit Suisse shareholders meeting.[19] One immediate step was to bifurcate risk management from compliance. Previously, the two overlapping areas of responsibility had resided in a single executive, staff, and department.

Ramifications of the Archegos debacle were wider than merely at the three prominent companies involved. Bank after bank and financial institution after financial institution pontificated about the importance of risk management. They also intimated that in the future they would set higher standards for loans to hedge funds, private equity firms, and other sorts of financial engineers.[20]

Risk management is about process and structure in corporate governance. Perhaps the most important take is that governance is not static. It evolves and emphasis escalates as secular trends influence what good governance consists of. Risk management is an example. In his corporate governance treatise, Professor Farrar reproduces

---

[14] Patrick and Webb (2021).

[15] Archegos Hit Tops $10 Billion, 2.

[16] Both in the U.S. and internationally, many financial firms such as Normura and UBS became banks during the 2008–09 worldwide financial crisis. Qualifying with U.S. regulators as banks, the financial institutions were able to gain access to the U.S.'s Federal Reserve "discount window." In that manner, they were able to obtain large loans at low, low interest rates, enabling them to amass capital sufficient to navigate the 2008–2009 crisis.

[17] Ibid.

[18] Toplensky (2021)

[19] Patrick (2021).

[20] *See generally* Chung et al. (2021).

segments of the ASX recommendation on risk management.[21] He notes that the growing emphasis on risk management has come to affect the audit of company accounts: "[A] development is the shift in perspective among some of the major accounting firms to a strategic risk perspective to auditing."[22]

2.4 Corporate Governance for Small and Medium Size Enterprises (SMEs)

Professor Farrar then is a leading scholar and advocate in the field of corporate governance and risk management. Another and much-neglected area in which John Farrar is a leader in governance for private and small publicly held companies. Those entities may face cost constraints as well as philosophical objections to the governance apparatus recommended for large, publicly held entities. But they may need certain of them.

In corporate governance symposia I have attended or at which I have spoken, questions from the audience include, "How much attention should my client (say a proprietary company) pay to these developments?," or "As a client company grows when should I as the attorney recommend implementation of certain of these devices or practices?" I always answer that a company may become a public company in senses other than shareholding, such as product markets, turnover, value of assets, or size of staff. When that occurs, the power or powers that be in the company must begin thought about good governance. If the product market and the turnover grow beyond local or regional markets, or the staff grows beyond one or two dozen employees, thought about these issues and the future becomes necessary.

I once consulted on a case involving a family company with three shareholders (sons of the founder) but with almost USD 2 billion in annual turnover, forty-seven acres of valuable real estate in St. Louis, Missouri, and a 3000-employee staff. Happily, the company and its attorneys were several steps ahead of me. The Board of five had two independent directors, one of whom was a financial expert. The expert chaired an audit committee that met frequently. The board regularly reviewed the risk manager and discussed risk management.

In those instances, my reactions, though, were seat-of-the-pants responses. With far more thought and expertise, in 2003 and into this unexplored and murky field came Professor Farrar and Melbourne senior attorney Henry Bosch. Together, the two gentlemen crafted and published *Corporate Governance Guidelines for SMEs in Hong Kong*, published by the Hong Kong Institute of Directors.[23] It remains a leading work, surprisingly one of the few comprehensive treatments in existence.

---

[21] ASX Recommendation 6.1 reproduced in Farrar (2017), 378–79.

[22] Farrar (2017), 380.

[23] Farrar and Bosch (2003).

In his corporate governance treatise, Professor Farrar points out that "Family owned business [FOBs] accounts for 83% of all business and employs approximately 50% of the private sector workforce in Australia."

- Within that group, "Fifty per cent of Australian FOBs generated sales in the USD 5 million to USD 20 million region."
- "[The] most common size was fifty employees with the largest firm reporting 4600 staff."
- "A majority of firms (71%) … had offices/factories in more than one location, and in some cases these additional sites were overseas."[24]

By means of those and similar recitations, Professor Farrar makes evident the scope of the subject in Australia and New Zealand as well.

I do not intend to reproduce, let alone analyse, Messrs Farrar and Bosch's insights and recommendations. A sampler might include:

- In family-owned companies, the importance of a succession plan, as well as an up-to-date business plan, financial statements, and possibly a governance plan, is imperative.
- Anticipating sibling rivalry as a founding member or members retire and the next, and usually more populous, generation succeeds to control of the company.
- Provision or at least thought about provisions for payment of estate taxes upon each founder's demise.
- Maintaining numerical control or working control in smaller companies in which maintenance of control is especially important and where over-sized proportions of personal wealth are often tied up in the company. Shareholder voting agreements and provisions for family councils may aid in the achievement of the goals sought.
- Addition of at least one outside board member who may act as *Arbitrator, Gap filler, Resource, Father confessor, Devil's advocate, Catalyst and agent of change, Image builder, Corporate networking agent.*[25]

2.5 A Final Tribute to Professor Farrar

John Farrar is a companion, friend, and teacher to me as well as to students, a leading attorney (corporate law, corporate governance, solvency law, and more), law professor, dean of three law schools (sequentially rather than at once), a vice-chancellor, and a scholar and author of international repute. I first met John when I was a visiting professor at Victoria University in Wellington, New Zealand, where we hit it off at once. So, it is fitting perhaps that I use a bit of slang I first heard in New Zealand but may be current in Australia as well: "He's good value, that one is." But John is, and will continue to be, much more than good value. He is a great, great

[24] Farrar (2017), 403–404.

[25] Ibid., 408–410 (emphasis in original).

contributor to life as well as to the law. I wish him and Lynne well and hope to see them again soon.

References

Branson, Douglas M. 2002. Indiana Supreme Court Lecture: The Rule That Isn't a Rule – The Business Judgment Rule. Valparaiso University Law Review 36(3): 631
Branson, Douglas M. 2007. *No Seat at the Table: How Governance and Law Keep Women Out of the Boardroom*. New York: New York University Press.
Juliet Chung et al., "Bans Tighten Up After Archegos," Wall Street Journal, May 6, 2021, A-6.
Farrar, John H., and Bosch, Henry. 2003 *Guidelines on Corporate Governance for SMEs in Hong Kong*. Hong Kong Institute of Directors.
Farrar J. H., and Hannigan, Brenda. 1998. *Farrar's Company Law*, 4th ed. London: Butterworths.
Farrar, John. 2005. *Principles of Corporate Governance: Theories, Principles, and Practice*, 2nd ed. Melbourne: Oxford University Press.
Farrar, John H. 2017. *Corporate Governance*. Chatswood: LexisNexis Butterworths, 139–45.
Patrick, Margot, "New Credit Suisse Head Resets Agenda," Wall Street Journal, May 1, 2021, B-12.
Patrick, Margot & Quentin Webb, "Archegos Hit Tops $10 Billion After Losses at UBS, Nomura," Wall Street Journal, April 28, 2021, A-1.
Toplensky, Rachel, "Credit Suisse Brings in a Fixer," Wall Street Journal, May 1, 2021, B-14.

Part I
Globalisation in Transition: Human Perspectives

Chapter 3
Globalisation in the Immigration Context

Judge Peter Spiller

Abstract One of the significant features of globalisation is the migration and movement of people. My chapter reflects on this aspect of globalisation in light of my seven-year experience as Chair of the New Zealand Immigration and Protection Tribunal. The chapter highlights the "push and pull" theory that has been widely used in research on the global migration of people. As revealed in my Tribunal, the factors that have pushed people to move away from their homeland have included inadequate, constraining living conditions, and in some cases intolerable and life-threatening circumstances. In particular, people have been driven away by the ruthless exercise of power and control by repressive regimes, which stifle individual liberties for religious, political and/or racial motives. The factors that have pulled people to New Zealand have included an attractive way of life, new opportunities, relatively accommodating immigration policies, the accessibility of international travel, and the enterprising spirit of would-be immigrants. The challenge of a host country's immigration system is to respond appropriately to the humanitarian circumstances of those who seek to begin a new life, while observing the need to uphold the integrity of the host country's immigration system and competing demands of the national interest.

3.1 Introduction and Background

In April 2000, the International Monetary Fund (IMF) identified, as one of the features of globalisation, the migration and movement of people.[1] Both John Farrar and I have been part of the migration phenomenon, John having emigrated from the United Kingdom and I from South Africa. It is, therefore, apt that I should contribute this chapter on globalisation in the immigration context.

[1] International Monetary Fund Staff. 2000. Globalisation: Threat or Opportunity? https://www.imf.org/external/np/exr/ib/2000/041200to.htm.

J. P. Spiller (✉)
Faculty of Law, University of Waikato, Hamilton, New Zealand
e-mail: judge.spiller@justice.govt.nz

U. Ghori et al. (eds.), *Globalisation in Transition*,
https://doi.org/10.1007/978-981-99-2439-4_3

I have recently concluded seven years as Chair of the New Zealand Immigration and Protection Tribunal (the Tribunal). This Tribunal hears appeals from people who have unsuccessfully sought residency status or refugee or protected person status in New Zealand, or who face deportation liability.[2] During my tenure as Chair of the Tribunal, I decided around 1400 appeals. This chapter presents the prevalent reasons that have driven the appellants, who appeared before me, to migrate from their home country to New Zealand.

3.2 Persons Wishing to Establish a New Life

The predominant motivation of appellants in the Tribunal, in leaving their home country to come to New Zealand, is the quest for a better quality of life than they had experienced before. New Zealand's standard of living (like Australia's) is amongst the highest in the world, in terms of the public and private services available and the environment on offer.[3]

By 2014, when I took office in the Tribunal, there was in place a relatively benign immigration policy framework, designed to recruit immigrants to meet the economic and labour market requirements of New Zealand. There was said to be a "multi-party acceptance that immigration is part of the New Zealand story in the early twenty-first century".[4] The result was that, during the ensuing years in which I served in the Tribunal, there were record levels of immigration to New Zealand.[5] Whereas in New Zealand, as recently as 2012, there was a net migration loss of over 170,000 people, during the years 2014–2020, there was an average net migration gain of nearly 670,000 people per year.[6]

By virtue of New Zealand's position in the South Pacific, a large number of appellants continued to arrive from the Pacific Islands. New Zealand has recognised a historical relationship with the Pacific through the Samoan Quota and the Pacific Access Category programme (for citizens of Kiribati, Tuvalu, Tonga or Fiji), that

---

[2] New Zealand accepts a quota of refugees per year (currently 1500), and also conducts a Refugee Quota (Family Reunification) Programme (see *AR (Afghanistan)* [2016] NZIPT 600148). Outside of this quota, people may claim refugee or protected person status to the Refugee Status Unit (RSU) of the Ministry of Business, Innovation and Employment (MBIE). Those whose claims are denied may appeal to the Tribunal. Persons who seek residence status apply to Immigration New Zealand (INZ), which is also part of MBIE, and those whose applications are declined may appeal to the Tribunal. Persons may face liability for deportation if they do not hold a valid visa to be in New Zealand, or have been issued with a Deportation Liability Notice, and they too have an appeal to the Tribunal.

[3] OECD Better Life Index: New Zealand. N.d. https://www.oecdbetterlifeindex.org/countries/new-zealand/. New Zealand is seen to rank above the average in health status, income and wealth, environmental quality, personal security, civic engagement, housing, subjective well-being, education and skills, jobs and earnings, and social connections.

[4] Spoonley (2014).

[5] Pool and Jackson (2018).

[6] Statistics New Zealand. N.d. International Migration. www.stats.govt.nz.

have allowed about 1750 people to be granted residence in New Zealand annually.[7] Other people from these countries have arrived in New Zealand, as adults or as children of migrants, on temporary visas and then stayed on.[8] Their stories tell of the desire to enjoy better living conditions. A Kiribati man wrote of coastal erosion, unsafe drinking water, inadequate economic opportunities and overpopulation in his country.[9] A Tuvaluan woman and her daughter wished to leave their remote outer island, where they had a small piece of land and a very basic shelter, and struggled to support themselves on a diet of subsistence vegetables.[10] Migrants from South Pacific countries also looked for better educational and employment opportunities in New Zealand.[11] A Tongan woman, who had earlier completed her high school education in New Zealand, wished to return to study towards a degree to become a teaching nun or a social worker.[12]

People in the heavily-populated countries of south Asia, particularly India, have also been increasingly drawn to the comparative advantages that New Zealand has been seen to offer.[13] Those from non-English speaking countries such as Vietnam, South Korea and China, have come to New Zealand to study English.[14] An Indonesian Islamic religious teacher and his wife came for better job opportunities[15]; and a South Korean woman came to New Zealand to create a better environment as she and her children had suffered from negative perceptions following her divorce.[16] Other migrants have come from a wide variety of countries. They have included the United Kingdom, the traditional source of migrants to New Zealand.[17] Some have

[7] New Zealand Ministry of Business, Innovation and Employment. 2019. Evaluation of the Samoan Quota and Pacific Access Category Settlement Information Pilot – Final Report. https://www.mbie.govt.nz; *Petero* [2017] NZIPT 502960 (Tuvalu); *VQ (Partnership)* [2018] NZIPT 204729 (Samoa).

[8] Samoa: *Perulale* [2015] NZIPT 501795; *Selesele* [2015] NZIPT 501892; *Elia Sagala* [2015] NZIPT 501976–977. Tuvalu: *Fatonuga* [2015] NZIPT 502069–070; *Sio* [2020] NZIPT 504864. Tonga: Tu'akoi [2015] NZIPT 502008; *Manoa* [2017] NZIPT 502982–983; *Pomana* [2019] NZIPT 504372; *KD (Partnership)* [2021] NZIPT 206170. Fiji: *Autar* [2015] NZIPT 502102; *Nadan* [2015] NZIPT 502158; *Devi* [2015] NZIPT 501709; *Goundar* [2015] NZIPT 502211; *Avez* [2015] NZIPT 502277.

[9] *Ioran* [2020] NZIPT 504842.

[10] *Fatonuga* [2015] NZIPT 502069–070.

[11] *Laufou* [2015] NZIPT 501997 (Tuvalu).

[12] *Otutaha* [2015] NZIPT 501720.

[13] *BC (India)* [2015] NZIPT 501674–675; *Bhatti* [2017] NZIPT 503713; *KZ (India)* [2021] NZIPT 505253–254; See also Statistics New Zealand. 2019. New Zealand's population reflects growing diversity. https://www.stats.govt.nz/news/new-zealands-population-reflects-growingdiversity#:~:text=Results%20from%20the%202018%20Census,2018%20who%20were%20born%20overseas. The Punjab in India has, in recent years, provided many migrants to New Zealand.

[14] *Nguyen* [2014] NZIPT 501557 (Vietnam); *Lim* [2015] NZIPT 502187 (South Korea); *BC (India)* [2015] NZIPT 501674–675.

[15] *Soekirman/Risnawati* [2018] NZIPT 504220–221.

[16] *Kwon* [2015] NZIPT 502004.

[17] *Hodgson* [2018] NZIPT 503863.

been drawn by New Zealand immigration programmes such as the "Working Holiday Scheme", and then decided to remain in New Zealand.[18]

In due course, partners, children, parents and siblings have come to join family members who had settled permanently in New Zealand.[19] Thus, where a Fijian woman had moved to New Zealand with her children in search of a better life for her family, her husband spoke of his dream to be reunited with his family.[20] A Chilean man, who came from a poor family and had a hard life, was sponsored by his brother who had earlier come to New Zealand, and who thought it would be good for the appellant to start a new life and have the opportunity to do well.[21]

The increase in international travel (until the COVID-19 pandemic) provided greater opportunities for New Zealanders to meet overseas partners (sometimes of their own culture), during visits, thus prompting the wish of couples to live together in New Zealand.[22] Long-term relationships between New Zealanders and overseas partners, and resultant migration, have also resulted from the use of social media and online dating sites.[23] A man in the Philippines, whose wife had died aged 35 years, leaving three young children, and medical bills which forced him to sell his well-established transport business, began communicating via social media with a Philippines-born New Zealand resident. This communication led to him and his children coming to New Zealand to start a new life and to allow him to re-establish himself financially.[24]

3.2.1 Case Study[25]

GY was born in 1987 in a small rural village in Punjab, India. She grew up in a culturally traditional family of five people, consisting of her parents, two brothers and a sister. Her parents and brothers still live in the same village, and her sister

---

[18] *Vannozzi* [2015] NZIPT 502288 (Italy); *McCashin* [2016] NZIPT 502541 (United Kingdom); *AG (Chile)* [2018] NZIPT 600456; *YL (Partnership)* [2019] NZIPT 205193 (USA); *AB (Sweden)* [2021] NZIPT 505236.

[19] *Bumagat* [2015] NZIPT 502034 (Philippines); *Erasmus* [2015] NZIPT 502043 (South Africa); *Samuel* [2015] NZIPT 502062 (Zimbabwe); *Vakalala* [2015] NZIPT 502116 (Fiji); *Kumar* [2015] NZIPT 502262 (India); *Tesimale* [2017] NZIPT 503020 (Tuvalu); *Kama* [2017] NZIPT 503042, 503044 (Tonga); *VQ (Partnership)* [2018] NZIPT 204729 (Samoa); *XJ (Partnership)* [2018] NZIPT 204892 (Afghanistan).

[20] *Sikivou* [2014] NZIPT 501583.

[21] *AG (Chile)* [2018] NZIPT 600456.

[22] *Tse* [2014] NZIPT 501606 (China); *Horvatova* [2015] NZIPT 502024 (Czech); *Clark* [2015] NZIPT 502252 (Philippines); *Kumar* [2015] NZIPT 502262 (India); *Satheesan* [2019] NZIPT 504247 (Sri Lanka); *XJ (Partnership)* [2018] NZIPT 204892 (Afghanistan); *Foe* [2021] NZIPT 505157 (Samoa).

[23] *YL (Partnership)* [2019] NZIPT 205193 (USA).

[24] *JR (Partnership)* [2021] NZIPT 206119 (Philippines).

[25] *GY (Partnership)* [2020] NZIPT 205911.

moved to her husband's house after getting married. GY proved to be a person of considerable academic ability, and completed a Bachelor of Science degree, a Master of Science degree and a Bachelor of Education degree.

In November 2013, GY was engaged to her husband through a culturally arranged marriage, and they were married 10 days later with Sikh traditions and rituals. Her husband was born in India but had lived in New Zealand since 1996. He married a New Zealand citizen in 1999, and obtained New Zealand residence through this marriage, which ended in 2002. The following year he married an Indian citizen. She obtained New Zealand residence on the basis of their relationship, but this also subsequently ended.

After GY's marriage to her husband in November 2013, he returned to New Zealand, and GY remained living with her family in India. However, she had to confront the reality that, in her religion and culture, it was not socially acceptable for a married woman to live separately from her husband. In March 2015, she left India and joined her husband in New Zealand. Here she recommenced studies and completed a Diploma in Business Management. She and her husband then established a café business together and bought a house, and she gave birth to two daughters, who were New Zealand citizens.

GY applied for New Zealand residence on the basis of her marriage to her husband. However, GY's application was declined by Immigration New Zealand because her husband was, in terms of New Zealand residence instructions, not eligible to support her application. This was in view of the fact that, in relation to his two previous wives, he had been a partner in more than one successful application for residence. GY appealed to the Tribunal. The law dictated that the Tribunal had to confirm Immigration New Zealand's decision as being correct. However, the Tribunal found that GY's had special circumstances such as to warrant a recommendation to the Associate Minister of Immigration for consideration of an exception to residence instructions.[26] The Associate Minister decided to grant a resident visa to GY as an exception to instructions.

3.3 Persons Escaping Persecution in Their Home Country

New Zealand, like Australia, is a signatory to the 1951 Refugee Convention.[27] This Convention forms the basis for the Tribunal's decisions that are made in relation to those claiming refugee status.[28] Article 1A(2) of the Refugee Convention provides that a refugee is a person who:

---

[26] *Immigration Act 2009* (New Zealand), s 188(1)(f).

[27] The Convention Relating to the Status of Refugees, Geneva. 1951. In force 22 April 1954. Australia acceded on that date, and New Zealand on 30 June 1960.

[28] *Immigration Act 2009* (New Zealand), s 129(1) provides that a person must be recognised as a refugee in accordance with this Act if he or she is a refugee within the meaning of the Refugee Convention. Note, appellants may also appeal on the basis that they are protected persons under the 1984 Convention Against Torture (s 130) and the 1966 International Covenant on Civil and

> owing to well-founded fear of being persecuted for reasons of race, religion, nationality, membership of a particular social group or political opinion, is outside the country of his nationality and is unable or, owing to such fear, is unwilling to avail himself of the protection of that country; or who, not having a nationality and being outside the country of his former habitual residence, is unable or, owing to such fear, is unwilling to return to it.

The approach followed by the Tribunal, in deciding on refugee status, is that "being persecuted" requires serious harm arising from the sustained or systemic violation of internationally recognised human rights, demonstrative of a failure of state protection.[29] A well-founded fear of being persecuted is established when there is a real, as opposed to a remote or speculative, chance of persecution occurring.[30]

My experience is that the pervading feature of persecution, driving people from their homeland, is the ruthless exercise of power and control by repressive regimes, which stifle individual liberties for religious, political and/or racial motives. In particular, religious persecution features strongly. Prominent amongst those who successfully claim religious persecution are those who come from Islamic states, and whose fear of persecution arises out of conversion to Christianity, being of a non-Muslim religion, being of a minority variant of Islam, or being non-religious.[31] There are also fears of religious persecution in countries (such as India and Sri Lanka) which, while nominally tolerant of religious diversity, are not seen to afford adequate protection against extremist groups from the dominant religion.[32]

At times, religious persecution also has political dimensions. One example of this is the sustained persecution of the Falun Gong movement in Communist China. Falun Gong is a form of spiritual practice that involves meditation, energy exercises, and a set of moral principles that guide adherents' daily lives. Since the 1990s, Falun Gong's popularity, its proclaimed independence from the state, and its moral and spiritual content, have been seen by the Chinese Communist authorities to be at odds with the ruling Party's Marxist–Leninist atheist ideology.[33] At times, religion also joins with racial features to give rise to persecution, as has been evident in the treatment of the Shia Hazara people by the Taliban in Afghanistan.[34]

Political Rights ("the ICCPR") (s 131). However, such appeals are only rarely granted and were not the basis of any of my decisions.

[29] *DS (Iran)* [2016] NZIPT 800788, [114]–[130], [177]–[183].

[30] *Refugee Appeal No 76044* (2008), [57], following the approach in *Chan v Minister for Immigration and Ethnic Affairs* (1989) 169 CLR 379.

[31] *DB (Iran)* [2014] NZIPT 800605; *CL (Pakistan)* [2017] NZIPT 801042; *BM (Bangladesh)* [2017] NZIPT 801057; *EI (Iran)* [2018] NZIPT 801344–345; *BE (Iraq)* [2018] NZIPT 801416; *EP (Iran)* [2018] NZIPT 801734.

[32] *FR (Sri Lanka)* [2018] NZIPT 801462; *KY (India)* [2021] NZIPT 505235, 505237.

[33] *DL (China)* [2018] NZIPT 801254; *EL (China)* [2018] NZIPT 801419; *EN (China)* [2018] NZIPT 801464; *GB (China)* [2018] NZIPT 801745. Another example of persecution for combined religious and political reasons is that of the Gülen movement, which is a sub-sect of Sunni Islam and designated as a terrorist organization by Turkey and certain other countries (*BK (Turkey)* [2018] NZIPT 504058).

[34] *AR (Afghanistan)* [2016] NZIPT 600148; *BQ (Afghanistan)* [2018] NZIPT 801246A; *BG (Afghanistan)* [2018] NZIPT 801324.

3.3.1 Case Study[35]

EI lived in Tehran, Iran, from her birth in 1980 until her departure in 2017. She was raised in a secular family and was not religious. She did not believe in compulsory religious rules, such as the wearing of the hijab for women. She had freedom only within her family, and later with her husband, and she censored herself when in public. She believed that people like herself had no place in Iranian society.

In December 2009, EI was involved in an anti-regime demonstration. She was forcibly detained at the demonstration, and, in the ensuing month, she was tied, strip-searched, blindfolded, interrogated, and her health suffered. At the end of her detention, she was required to promise that she would submit to any orders made against her, would honour the regime, and would not repeat her actions. She was released on bail, was not allowed to leave Tehran for one year, had to report to the authorities within two hours if they wanted to see her, and was prohibited from publishing any complaints or attending demonstrations against the regime. Her telephone was monitored, and her accounts were blocked for a year. Two months after her release, she was expelled from the university where she had been studying.

Thereafter EI kept mainly to her home and had to pretend to practise Islam. In February 2013, she was harassed by a paramilitary officer because of her mode of dress. In July 2017, her father-in-law and brother-in-law, who were strictly Muslim, forcibly removed her elder son. They told her that she was not allowed to see him again, because of her political and non-religious views. They also threatened that they would take her younger son if she complained, and reminded her that she had been released from detention with conditions, and could be reported to the authorities. Two months later she left Iran with her younger son. They arrived in New Zealand, where her sister lived, and claimed refugee status. Her claim was dismissed by the Refugee Status Unit, and she then appealed to the Tribunal.

At the Tribunal hearing, recent country information on Iran confirmed that it was a theocratic republic dominated by Shia Muslim clergy. Laws required Muslim citizens to conform to the state's interpretation of Sharia law and prohibited them from changing or renouncing their religious beliefs. Atheists were at risk of persecution, including arrest, imprisonment, and possible execution.[36] Women remained subject to entrenched discrimination in law and practice, including in family and criminal law.[37] Compulsory veiling allowed police and paramilitary forces to harass and detain women. The rights of children in terms of the United Nations Convention on the Rights of the Child were limited by the Government's right not to apply the provisions of the Convention that were "incompatible with Islamic laws".[38] Within this context, and in light of EI's experiences, she was found to have a well-founded

---

[35] *EI (Iran)* [2018] NZIPT 801344–345.

[36] U.S. Department of State. 2017. Country Reports on Human Rights Practices 2016: Iran; Human Rights Watch. 2016. World Report 2016: Iran.

[37] Amnesty International. 2018. State of the World's Human Rights 2017/18: Iran.

[38] Persia Educational Foundation. 2017. A Legal Study on Children's Rights and Iran's Laws.

fear of persecution arising out of her political and religious views, and was recognised as a refugee.

3.4 Persons Migrating for Humanitarian Reasons

Since 1991, there has been provision in New Zealand for appeal against deportation liability on the grounds that the appellant has exceptional circumstances of a humanitarian nature that would make it unjust or unduly harsh to be deported from New Zealand, and it would not be contrary to the public interest to allow the appellant to remain in New Zealand.[39]

A notable innovation of the Immigration Act 2009 (which established the present Tribunal) is that those who appeal on the basis of being refugees can, as a back-up if the refugee appeal fails, also appeal on the basis that they have exceptional humanitarian circumstances that would make it.[40] These humanitarian appeals repeatedly bring to light harassment and discrimination in the appellant's home country which, while not at the level of persecution, give rise to exceptional humanitarian circumstances. Cases range across a wide spectrum, including ongoing discrimination endured by Alevi Kurds in Turkey,[41] repeated insulting and intrusive behaviour inflicted on an elderly Muslim couple in India by extremists of the ruling Hindu party,[42] and significant difficulties experienced by a gay couple of lower socio-economic status in South Africa.[43] A recurrent feature of these cases was that the persons concerned lacked meaningful family or other support in their home country, and so faced an ongoing threatened and anxious existence alone.[44]

In both refugee-related humanitarian appeals and those not associated with refugee appeals, difficulties in the appellants' home circumstances are sometimes exacerbated by particular traumatic experiences, such as the death of a family member, giving rise to the appellants' vulnerable psychological state.[45] Some appellants,

39 This jurisdiction was vested in the Removal Review Authority by the *Immigration Amendment Act 1991* (New Zealand), s 31. There had hitherto been an appeal by such persons to the Minister of Immigration on humanitarian grounds. The jurisdiction was vested in the Immigration and Protection Tribunal by the *Immigration Act 2009* (New Zealand), s 207(1).

40 An obvious example is the child of parents who have been granted refugee status, on account of persecution in their home country, but where the persecution is not seen to extend to the child. See *BO (Turkey)* [2019] NZIPT 504448; *EO (China)* [2019] NZIPT 504506.

41 *BV (Turkey)* [2021] NZIPT 505191–192.

42 *KY (India)* [2021] NZIPT 505235, 505237.

43 *BY (South Africa)* [2017] NZIPT 503405, 503410.

44 See also *BM (South Africa)* [2016] NZIPT 502734; *BK (Turkey)* [2018] NZIPT 504058; *BT (Afghanistan)* [2019] NZIPT 504462.

45 *CU (Bangladesh)* [2019] NZIPT 504173–175.

particularly women, leave their home country to escape domestic violence of a physical and/or sexual nature.[46] A Tuvaluan girl, aged 14 years, had for two years been subjected to sexual abuse by her stepfather, leaving her without "peace in her body and soul", and causing her to see life as a "chain of failure and shame with no happiness in it".[47]

A recurrent situation is that of the aged, and often frail, widowed parent of immigrants who have settled in New Zealand, and the parent has limited or no family members or support systems left in their home country.[48] A typical example was that of a 79-year-old South African female suffering from senile dementia, all of whose children resided lawfully in New Zealand and she had no family or other support in South Africa. Her children asked that she be allowed to stay with them and her grandchildren in the last phase of her life.[49]

A multitude of other circumstances, arising out of the distinct personal histories of appellants, present themselves to be exceptional, and so qualify for relief.[50] For example, a Tuvaluan female presented with a skin condition known as albinism (lack of pigment), rendering her susceptible to intense sunlight and to vision impairment. She came from an outer island where there was only one nurse, and transport took a day by boat to the doctor on the main island and, from there, a four-day trip to the nearest hospital in Fiji.[51]

3.4.1 Case Study[52]

Silia and her son Amanaki were born and lived in Tonga. Around late September 2015, Amanaki (then 18) developed kidney problems in Tonga. There was evident deterioration of his kidney functions, and he was told that no treatment for this deterioration was available in Tonga. He and Silia therefore decided that he should be medically examined in New Zealand and receive treatment there.

---

[46] *Matati*A [2014] NZIPT 501542 (Kiribati); *Watkins* [2014] NZIPT 501572 (the Philippines); *DR (India)* [2017] NZIPT 502981.

[47] *AG (Tuvalu)* [2016] NZIPT 502616.

[48] New Zealand immigration policy previously allowed immigrants whose adult children already had residence or citizenship, to join them, but the policy was suspended in 2016.

[49] *Van Wyk* [2016] NZIPT 502738. See also *Kiran* [2015] NZIPT 501673 (Fiji); *Rednakov* [2015] NZIPT 501959 (Russia); *Murdoch* [2015] NZIPT 502269 (Kiribati); *Latu* [2016] NZIPT 502564 (Tonga); *Kaur* [2017] NZIPT 503139 (India); *Han* [2017] NZIPT 503196 (Cambodia); *Pulusi* [2017] NZIPT 503477 (Tuvalu); *Chiroscа* [2018] NZIPT 503881 (Moldova).

[50] *BT (Afghanistan)* [2019] NZIPT 504462, where the appellant would be required to return to a country where he had not lived except for eight nights of his life, where his only family members were distant relations with whom he had had no contact and who lived in a dangerous part of the country, where he had no support networks or connections, where he could expect little if any government support, and where there were serious security concerns.

[51] *Faatonunga* [2015] NZIPT 502066.

[52] *Taimi* [2016] NZIPT 502605–606.

On 26 October 2015, Silia applied for visitor visas for herself and Amanaki, to come to New Zealand. The purpose of the visit was stated to be to attend a relative's graduation. In answer to the question "Do you or any person included in this application have any medical condition that requires, or may require, one of the following during your stay in New Zealand?" (the options being renal dialysis, hospital care and residential care), Silia ticked the "no" rather than the "yes" box. The estimated date of arrival in New Zealand was noted by her as 28 October 2015 and the estimated date of departure from New Zealand was noted as 4 November 2015. A supporting letter from a Tongan Member of Parliament affirmed that Silia and Amanaki would not become a public charge while in New Zealand and that they would depart prior to the expiration of their authorised stay. The principal of Amanaki's school confirmed that he would resume school as a student when he was back in Tonga.

Silia and Amanaki came to New Zealand on 29 October 2015. Their visitor visas were valid for two months. On 31 October 2015, Amanaki was admitted to the renal services unit of a New Zealand hospital because of complications relating to acute deterioration of kidney disease. He was diagnosed with end-stage and irreversible renal failure and commenced renal replacement therapy. In November 2015, Silia and Amanaki applied for further visitor visas. Their applications were declined, and they became unlawfully in New Zealand on 23 December 2015. They appealed to the Tribunal on humanitarian grounds.

The Tribunal accepted that Amanaki's humanitarian circumstances were exceptional, in light of the fact that he had end-stage renal failure which required ongoing dialysis treatment in New Zealand, and that he would die in Tonga without the treatment because it was not available there.[53] The Tribunal dismissed the appeal in that it did not meet the public interest test. This was in view of the significant burden which Amanaki placed on the New Zealand health system, and the need to uphold the integrity of the immigration system which had been defrauded. However, in view of Amanaki's grave predicament, the Tribunal granted Amanaki and Silia 12-month visas to allow time for Amanaki to explore whatever health options were available to him.

3.5 Conclusion

The "push and pull" theory has been widely used in research on the global migration of people.[54] In my experience in the New Zealand Immigration and Protection Tribunal, the factors that have pushed people to move away from their homeland

---

[53] Tonga Broadcasting Commission. 2016. It will take years for Tonga to prepare for the dialysis treatment of its people. http://www.tonga-broadcasting.net/?p=2578. The lack of renal services in Tonga has remained an ongoing problem, see Moala (2021).

[54] The theory was introduced by Ernst Ravenstein in his work on migration. See Ravenstein (1885).

have included inadequate, constraining living conditions, and in some cases intolerable and life-threatening circumstances. The factors that have pulled people to New Zealand have included an attractive way of life, new opportunities, relatively accommodating immigration policies, the accessibility of international travel, and an underlying enterprising spirit of would-be immigrants.

As an immigrant myself, who is descended from immigrants, these factors strike a chord. I know that my Lithuanian ancestors were pushed to leave their homeland under Tsarist repression, and that my French Huguenot ancestors suffered religious persecution. For my other ancestors, their emigration appeared to be primarily driven by the pull of a developing country which offered more than they had. In my own case, I was pushed to leave an oppressive and unfair apartheid regime in South Africa, and pulled towards New Zealand's relatively egalitarian, prosperous and peaceful society, which offered me good employment and opportunities for my family. Some of my children have continued the migration path. My son, in settling in the United Kingdom, has retraced the steps which his English great-grandfather took a century before. As is illustrated in the lives of John Farrar, my own family, and the people I served in the Immigration and Protection Tribunal, the migration and movement of people has remained a central feature of the globalisation phenomenon.

References

Moala, Kalafi. 2021. The urgent need continues for dialysis treatment in Tonga to save lives. https://fangongomediawatch.com/local/the-urgent-need-for-dialysis-treatment-in-tonga-to-save-lives/.

Pool, I., and Jackson, N. 2018. Population Change: Migration. TeAra: The Encyclopedia of New Zealand. www.teara.govt.nz.

Ravenstein, Ernst. 1885. The laws of migration. *Journal of Royal Statistical Society of London* 48: 167–235.

Spoonley, P. 2014. Rising Asian immigration highlights New Zealand's changing demographics. The Conversation. https://theconversation.com/rising-asian-immigration-highlights-new-zealands-changing-demographics23002#:~:text=In%20terms%20of%20New%20Zealand,295%2C900%20for%20Pacific%20Island%20populations.

Chapter 4
Comparative First Nations Treaty Experiences Across the Tasman

Narelle Bedford

Abstract This analysis offers a comparative perspective on First Nations treaty experiences between Aotearoa/New Zealand and Australia. Despite obvious historical differences, comparative analysis remains useful, as all relationships between First Nations peoples and settlers/colonisers are in a constant condition of evolution. It is an essential function of modern society to continue improving and progressing these relationships and the status of First Nations peoples. International law, through the United Nations Declaration on the Rights of Indigenous Peoples (UNDRIP), provides insights on issues such as self-determination. In Australia, the Uluru Statement From the Heart seeks a constitutionally- enshrined Voice to Parliament; a *Makarrata* process of agreement making between First Nations and governments; and a process of comprehensive truth-telling. The opportunity presented by the Uluru Statement is unique and would have many benefits, including a lasting positive impact on national pride and nation-building. As seen in Aotearoa/New Zealand, having a treaty does not guarantee perfect relationships. The best way forward is through legal pluralism, which refers to the co-existence of more than one legal system within a nation. In respect of First Nations peoples, it means the recognition that there are other ways that social order can be maintained beyond the dominant settler/coloniser legal system.

This chapter is inspired by my mother Jackie Bedford, a proud and dedicated Yuin woman.

N. Bedford (✉)
Faculty of Law, Bond University, Gold Coast, Australia
e-mail: nbedford@bond.edu.au

U. Ghori et al. (eds.), *Globalisation in Transition*,
https://doi.org/10.1007/978-981-99-2439-4_4

4.1 Tribute

Professor John Farrar is renowned for his scholarly contributions on legal theory,[1] and law reform,[2] and is well regarded as a leading authority on private law issues generally. This contribution chooses to focus attention on his impact in the field of public law. Professor Farrar's interest in legal theory is expansive, as within it he holds a long-standing legal philosophy interest in conceptions of the 'State'.[3] Professor Farrar contrasted the traditional understanding of the State to the contemporary model developed in public international law. His perspectives on Statehood extended beyond theoretical musings to encompass the implications that western notions of Statehood have had for First Nations peoples. Indeed, the depth of his cross cultural understanding was recorded in 2011 as follows:

> A consequence of this is that we seek to impose Western concepts on Māori which do not fit.[4]

Thus, his scholarship accepted the principles of legal pluralism and displayed an awareness of the need for cross cultural sensitivity. His comment above highlighted his awareness of positionality and the insights gained through evaluating concepts from various differing perspectives.

Professor Farrar's scholarly attention encompasses a personal interest in Aboriginal and Torres Strait Islander peoples in Australia and the Uluru Statement—with its invitation to the Australian people centred on Voice, *Makarrata* (Treaty) and Truth.[5] Professor Farrar's interests reflect his life shared between Aotearoa/New Zealand and Australia, mirrored in his ongoing honorary academic appointments on both sides of the 'ditch'. It is, therefore, fitting that this analysis on comparative First Nations treaty experiences in Aotearoa/New Zealand and Australia be made in honour of Professor Farrar's scholarship and interests.

4.2 Introduction

This analysis offers a comparative perspective on First Nations treaty experiences between Aotearoa/New Zealand and Australia, arguing that despite very evident historical differences between the two nations, comparative analysis remains useful as all relationships between First Nations peoples and settlers/colonisers are in a constant condition of evolution, if not always positive progress. It is argued that the

---

[1] Farrar (2010), Farrar and Dugdale (1990).

[2] Farrar (1976), Farrar (1974). Law Reform in New Zealand—The State of Play. *Canterbury Law Review* 1: 104; Farrar (1987).

[3] Farrar (2011).

[4] Ibid.

[5] Uluru Statement from the Heart (National Constitutional Convention, 26 May 2017) (*'Uluru Statement'*).

formal, legal status of these relationships form an important, and indeed core, pillar of modern public law in each country. A state of perfect nirvana has not been reached, and progress obliges constant re-evaluations.

To commence this analysis, the global context is explained through an examination of the UNDRIP. The second part of this analysis begins with Farrar's scholarship on early conceptions of the State in Aotearoa/New Zealand and the limitations inherent in the concept of the State. It considers more recent scholarship and necessarily investigates recent developments concerning the te Tiriti o Waitangi/Treaty of Waitangi. The third part of the analysis is concerned with Australian public law and the recent innovation of the Uluru Statement. The Uluru Statement is striking in that it originated organically and democratically from First Nations peoples themselves and was issued as an invitation to the Australian people rather than as a binary dialogue with the government. That it remains unimplemented is regrettable. The fourth part of the analysis offers arguments in favour of comparitivism. It suggests that legal pluralism is the best option for positive future developments in relationships with First Nations peoples and for nation building. The final part of the analysis concludes that while relationships with First Nations peoples will present challenges, it is an essential function of modern society to continue improving and progressing these relationships and the status of First Nations peoples. In this area, law reform will continue to be crucial, whether this occurs through the adoption of treaty documents, Constitutional recognition (which is possible in either a written or unwritten Constitutional system) or jurisprudential advances.

4.3 United Nations Declaration on the Rights of Indigenous Peoples

At the outset, it is relevant to record the interrelatedness of several key concepts discussed in this analysis. The concept of the State/Statehood is closely linked to sovereignty, the latter being a complex idea capable of an array of meanings depending on the context. Sovereignty at its most general level covers the power and authority to govern. It can refer to external or internal control, it can be experienced on a collective or personal level,[6] and it can be tied to a place or location.[7] Equally interrelated to sovereignty in a First Nations context is self-determination.[8] In a First Nations context, self-determination refers to the ability to have control and power over decisions that impact on the person concerned or a group of people. Thus it can operate on a personal or collective level. In this analysis, the collective form of self-determination is relevant.

UNDRIP is especially relevant as it formalises the important priorities for First Nations people on a global scale. It discloses at the macro-level how international law

[6] For discussions of personal sovereignty see Behrendt (2003), Watego (2021).

[7] Williams and Hobbs (2020), 140 ('*Williams & Hobbs*').

[8] Ibid., 146.

views First Nations peoples generally and it evidences the priority areas identified by First Nations peoples throughout the world in their on-going relationships with settlers/colonisers. UNDRIP reflects the world-wide agreement that was able to be reached on those priority areas, indicating a level of universal consensus on those priority areas and the key concepts contained in them. The history of Aotearoa/New Zealand and Australia's participation in UNDRIP provides an insight into the evolution that is possible in the position of States as time elapses and the domestic political environment in individual countries inevitably changes.

UNDRIP was adopted by the United Nations General Assembly in 2007, with Australia and Aotearoa/New Zealand being two of only four nations that officially objected to it.[9] Later, those recalcitrant positions were reversed, and both nations subsequently ratified UNDRIP.[10] This historical setting is significant, as UNDRIP particularly emphasises self-determination for First Nations peoples. Therefore, the principle of self-determination should take on an enhanced relevance in Australia and Aotearoa/New Zealand. Self-determination is a concept that is inherently important to First Nations peoples (and other minorities), as it has 'little work to do for non-indigenous populations, whose rights are presupposed'.[11]

Self-determination is the entire focus of Article 3 of UNDRIP, while the concept of sovereignty is not mentioned at all. Self-determination is used in an expansive sense in UNDRIP:

> Indigenous peoples have the right to self-determination. By virtue of that right they freely determine their political status and freely pursue their economic, social and cultural development.[12]

Article 4 explains that a right to self-determination means 'the right to autonomy or self-government in matters relating to … internal and local affairs, as well as ways and means for financing … autonomous functions'. Legal concepts such as Statehood, sovereignty and self-determination are all engaged when considering relationships between First Nations peoples and settler/coloniser populations. All of these concepts resonate in both domestic legal systems and international law. Treaties provide one vehicle for furthering progress towards achieving sovereignty and self-determination, and it is therefore where the next two parts of this analysis turn.

[9] The other two objector nations were Canada and the USA.

[10] See Davis (2012a, 2012b), Maguire (2014).

[11] Larkin and Galloway (2018) ('*Larkin & Galloway*').

[12] UN General Assembly, *United Nations Declaration on the Rights of Indigenous Peoples: Resolution /Adopted by the General Assembly*, 2 October 2007, A/RES/61/295, Art 3.

4.4 Early Conceptions of State in Aotearoa/New Zealand and the Te Tiriti o Waitangi/Treaty of Waitangi

Farrar recorded that the early history of Aotearoa/New Zealand was 'very complex' and that there was a 'natural tendency to focus on the Treaty of Waitangi', which he noted had a 'special role'.[13] He claims that the te Tiriti o Waitangi/Treaty of Waitangi remained a powerful force in Aotearoa/New Zealand politics and inter-ethnic relationships.[14] Turning to the examination of the concept of Statehood, Farrar traversed the historical development of domestic understandings of the State, contrasting this with the accepted public international law's definition of the State. He concluded that there was a 'poor fit' between the two. Reflecting his passion for law reform, he advocated that 'it is necessary to evolve theory' and not be 'bogged down in some archaic legalism'.[15]

The traditional conception of the State did not align with the structure and culture of First Nations peoples and specifically Māori, and Farrar was brutal in his assessment, asserting that 'to impose upon them the confused Western concepts was an act of ethnocentrism'—even if it was well-intended.[16] Acknowledging the immense impact of colonisation, Farrar recognised 'it seems incredible that a European Parliament and legal system was imposed on a predominantly Māori New Zealand'.[17]

According to Farrar, the understanding of modern notions of the State would continue to undergo change, as Statehood was not a static concept.[18] His concluding plea has withstood the test of time and remains as insightful and inspirational as it was when he issued it in 2010:

> ...we have evolved as a hybrid community which is now fast becoming multicultural. It is important that we recognise this history and treat each other with respect.[19]

More recently, as Farrar had, Burrows continued this tradition of devoting scholarly attention to relations between First Nations peoples and the State.[20] Burrows noted that the te Tiriti o Waitangi/Treaty of Waitangi incorporated concepts related to sovereignty and expressly recognised fundamental Māori concepts such as kawanatanga (meaning governorship), taonga (meaning culture) and rangatiratanga (meaning self-determination).[21] This complexity surrounding First Nations sovereignty has seen an evolving understanding, as Aotearoa/New Zealand itself developed as a nation. Indeed by 2014, the te Rōpū Whakamana i te Tiriti o Waitangi/

[13] Farrar (2011), 51 & 52.
[14] Ibid., 54.
[15] Ibid., 52.
[16] Ibid., 53.
[17] Ibid., 59.
[18] Ibid., 64.
[19] Ibid., 65.
[20] Burrows (2006).
[21] Ibid., 190.

Waitangi Tribunal considered the meaning of sovereignty,[22] and officially recorded that Māori had not ceded sovereignty by virtue of signing the te Tiriti o Waitangi/ Treaty of Waitangi.[23] It concluded as follows:

> Rather, they agreed to share power and authority with the Governor. They agreed to a relationship: one in which they ... were to be equal – equal while having different roles and different spheres of influence. In essence, rangatira (Māori Chiefdom) retained their authority over their hapū (the basic political unit of clans/descent groups within Māori society) and territories, while {the Crown} was given authority to control Pākehā (non-Māori).[24]

Agreeing with the sentiment expressed by Farrar about the centrality of the te Tiriti o Waitangi/Treaty of Waitangi, Burrows noted it has served as a 'common reference point in New Zealand's ongoing creation', and its positive potential endured despite treaty breaches by the Crown.[25] Without in any way dismissing or minimising that brutal history, Burrows exhorted:

> Honouring treaties is about taking responsibility for our history and constructing the rule of law from that experience based on the best available (and most persuasive) sources.[26]

Burrows focused particularly on the optimistic impact that treaties could have on nation building and future relations. Burrows argued that treaties between First Nations peoples and the Crown, if interpreted in their best light, could build a country on principles of cooperation and consent.[27] Burrows contended that treaties should be regarded as law and interpreted in light of contemporary legal principles which respect Indigenous rights as part of the rule of law.[28] He asserted that treaties provided a platform for ideas surrounding national 'formation and reformation', and that treaties with First Nations peoples could strengthen and enrich nations.[29]

I agree with Burrow's position and amplify his points about the positive, nation-building capability inherent in a treaty, as the arguments advanced by Burrows can apply with equal force to the proposals contained in the Uluru Statement and its call for a *Makarrata* (a Yolngu word literally meaning the coming together after a struggle, which is also widely understood to refer to a treaty). Mary Graham, a Kombumerri and Wakka Wakka woman, explained that the culture of First Nations people in Australia is fundamentally characterised by relationality.[30] Thus, constructively responding to the invitation issued for a *Makarrata* would be one mechanism of demonstrating a long-term intention to foster better relations between First Nations peoples and all other Australians.

---

[22] te Rōpū Whakamana i te Tiriti o Waitangi/Waitangi Tribunal, Waitangi Tribunal Report 2014 (WAI 1040, 2014) 9.

[23] Ibid., xxii.

[24] Ibid.

[25] Ibid., 190–191.

[26] Ibid., 191.

[27] Ibid., 199.

[28] Ibid., 202.

[29] Ibid., 194.

[30] Graham (2014). See also Tynan (2021).

4.5 Australian Public Law and the Uluru Statement

In this third part of the analysis, a conscious decision has been made to cite and rely on the body of existing scholarship undertaken by prominent First Nations academics (Davis, Watson and Larkin). Collectively, their impact can be exhibited through the significant body of research they have generated, which grappled with relations between First Nations peoples and settler/colonial States.

Australia does not have a document equivalent to the te Tiriti o Waitangi/Treaty of Waitangi. In respect of formal treaty documents between First Nations peoples and settler/colonisers, Australia stands far apart from the historical experience in Aotearoa/New Zealand. Notwithstanding this key difference, the challenges and opportunities in the ongoing relationship between First Nations peoples and settler/coloniser populations continue to be fundamentally important in each State which had pre-existing First Nations peoples inhabiting and caring for the land and wildlife.

The Uluru Statement From the Heart was issued in 2017 as the culmination of an extensive consultation process amongst First Nations peoples throughout Australia.[31] The Uluru Statement is striking in that it originated organically and democratically from First Nations peoples themselves and was issued as an invitation to the Australian people, rather than as a binary dialogue initiated by the government and its experts.[32] It is comprehensive in its scope and admits the reality that a treaty is not of itself sufficient to achieve the 'better future' it envisions. The Uluru Statement seeks a Constitutionally enshrined Voice to Parliament; a *Makarrata* process of agreement making between First Nations and governments, and for a process of comprehensive truth-telling.

The Uluru Statement argues for a Voice to Parliament as opposed to a voice to government. The former is achieved by Constitutional change, so that it is entrenched and has a wide scope of impact in that it directly advises the Parliament, which necessarily includes not only the government but also opposition, other parties and independents on matters impacting First Nations peoples. However, it is not a third chamber as disingenuously claimed by some conservative politicians, as it has not been designed in any way to possess powers to create and pass legislation.[33] By contrast, a voice to government would be created by legislation and would introduce a filter as advice would pass first through the government and then at their discretion onto the public service and/or Parliament.

The expressly advocated position in the Uluru Statement for a constitutionally enshrined Voice to Parliament has been derived from the experience of the legislative creation and then legislative abolition of an earlier body—the Aboriginal and Torres Strait Islander Commission, formerly known as ATSIC.[34] ATSIC was a voice to government which was constituted by elected representatives of First Nations voters,

---

[31] Davis and Williams (2021).

[32] Appleby and McKinnon (2017), Fredericks and Bradfield (2021).

[33] Davis (2018).

[34] *Aboriginal and Torres Strait Islander Commission Act 1989* (Cth), repealed by the *Aboriginal and Torres Strait Islander Commission Amendment Act 2004* (Cth).

but this democratic authority was not sufficient to preserve its status and functioning once the government decided to repeal the legislation which created it.[35]

The truth-telling that the Uluru Statement advocates for is likewise wide-ranging and covers all aspects of the historical and current relationship between First Nations people and non-indigenous people.[36] The parties envisioned within its scope are governments at all levels (federal, state/territory and local), as well as government institutions including the police, all public servants, and non-State institutions such as religious and other non-government organisations and individuals. In terms of the issues which would be covered, truth-telling would encompass, but not be limited to, the Stolen Generations, the Stolen Wages and other past historical injustices such as massacres and land dispossession.[37] The benefits from truth-telling could potentially include changes to the nation's education curriculum, and the creation of a record which recorded the 'contested nature and experience of Australia's history'.[38]

Therefore, in its scope of vision, the Uluru Statement encapsulates one of the conclusions reached by Williams and Hobbs that 'treaties are only ever one part of the picture'.[39] While the Uluru Statement does not expressly refer to a treaty, it is implicit in the notion of agreements between First Nations peoples and governments. It is carefully designed and the sequencing of its three major reforms is very deliberate. It seeks first the Constitutionally embedded structural change of a Voice to Parliament, then a *Makarrata*, and then finally truth-telling, in that order.

That the Uluru Statement remains unimplemented is regrettable, but it is never too late for Australia to do so. This analysis argues that based on the experience of Māori people in Aotearoa/New Zealand, the opportunity presented by the Uluru Statement is unique and would have a lasting impact in terms of national pride and nation-building.

Viewed in the context of the legacy of Farrar's scholarship, it is remarkable that the Uluru Statement refers to the concept of sovereignty.[40] It asserts that 'our Aboriginal and Torres Strait Islander tribes were the first sovereign Nations of the Australian continent and its adjacent islands, and possessed it under our own laws and customs' and then explains that sovereignty:

> … is a spiritual notion: the ancestral tie between the land, or 'mother nature', and the Aboriginal and Torres Strait Islander peoples who were born therefrom, remain attached thereto, and must one day return thither to be united with our ancestors. This link is the basis of the ownership of the soil, or better, of sovereignty.[41]

The positive link between sovereignty for First Nations peoples and the State in terms of fostering an improved sense of nationhood and positive nation building was articulated in the Uluru Statement.

[35] See Behrendt (2005), Morris (2004), Jonas and Dick (2004).

[36] Appleby and Davis (2018).

[37] Ibid., 502.

[38] Ibid., 509.

[39] Williams and Hobbs (2020), 205.

[40] Lee et al. (2020).

[41] Uluru Statement from the Heart (National Constitutional Convention, 26 May 2017.

> With substantive constitutional change and structural reform, we believe this ancient sovereignty can shine through as a fuller expression of Australia's nationhood.[42]

Davis, who is a Cobble Cobble woman, has been concerned, as Farrar has been, with the different conceptions of what Statehood or sovereignty might mean in a context structured by the co-existence of First Nations peoples and settler/colonisers.[43] She argued that recognition of First Nations peoples in the Australian *Constitution* would not foreclose sovereignty for Aboriginal and Torres Strait Islander peoples, as the definition of sovereignty was capable of different meanings.[44] The most relevant of which, paralleling Farrar's scholarship, was a definition of sovereignty centred on self-determination.[45] Davis affirmed that:

> Aboriginal people have never consented nor ceded. Sovereignty did not pass from Aboriginal people to the settlers.[46]

Watson, a Tanganekald, Meintangk Boandik woman, concurred with Davis, as she asserted that Aboriginal and Torres Strait Islander peoples were once sovereign and still are.[47] Watson was concerned, as was Farrar, with the limitations of the colonial foundations of the concept of the State.[48] Watson, however, argued that it was not reform of Euro-centric law that should be a priority, but rather the re-emergence and valuing of the ancient laws.[49] She advocated for a change in perspective and for repositioning the standpoint to centre First Nations culture and knowledges.[50] For her, sovereignty meant being in a relationship with, belonging and being responsible for the lands of the ancestors and preserving relationality with 'all life forms'.[51]

More recently, Larkin, a Bundjalung and Kungarykany woman, and Galloway have conducted research and undertaken critical thinking following the issuance of the Uluru Statement From the Heart and the invitation contained in it to the people of Australia.[52] They argued that the Uluru Statement should be regarded as forming an important part of Australian public law pluralism.[53] They claimed it presented an Indigenous-led legal, political, and cultural solution for bringing together Indigenous and non-Indigenous Australians within the Australian system of governance. However, the transformation of Australian governance would depend on a shift in mentality and for any associated claims made by the dominant elite to be

---

42 Ibid.

43 Davis (2012a, 2012b).

44 Ibid.

45 Ibid., 13.

46 Ibid., 14.

47 Watson (2012).

48 Ibid.

49 Watson (2017).

50 Ibid., 216.

51 Watson (2011). Cited in Williams and Hobbs (2020), pg 142.

52 Larkin and Galloway (2018).

53 Ibid., 336. See also Larkin and Galloway (2021).

reality checked and tested.[54] The imperative for this change is stark. They explained that:

> As long as Australia maintains institutional structures designed to exclude the voices of Indigenous communities, we will remain ill-equipped to support communities to solve the complex problems they face.[55]

Once again, the theme of respect as identified in Farrar's scholarship emerged, as Larkin and Galloway argued that.

> [w]here Indigenous Australians themselves author proposals to move the nation forward, it behoves us to pay attention, and respect the legitimacy of appeals for self-determination.[56]

The Uluru Statement endures as an invitation that has not yet officially commenced towards implementation. It is comprehensive in its scope and offers the potential for positive outcomes at both a practical and inspirational level.[57] The experience of Aotearoa/New Zealand provides many insights. Therefore, the next part of this chapter focuses on comparative perspectives and, in particular, the link between the adoption of a treaty and the acceptance of legal pluralism to benefit States.

4.6 Comparative Perspectives, Treaties and Legal Pluralism

In this part of the analysis, observations based on comparative perspectives are made, and what emerges is the modern acceptance that legal pluralism has many positive benefits for nations. Legal pluralism refers to the co-existence of more than one legal system within a nation. In respect of First Nations peoples, legal pluralism means the recognition that there are other ways that social order is maintained beyond the dominant settler/coloniser legal system.

In their book 'Treaty', Williams and Hobbs issued a warning that although Aotearoa/New Zealand had a treaty.

> to define the relationship between Indigenous peoples and the settler state … legislation, court decisions and government action have later whittled away the position Indigenous peoples originally secured by agreement with the colonising State.[58]

Notwithstanding this universal and disappointing experience,[59] they contended that 'treaty-making has returned as a means of defining the place of Indigenous groups in

[54] Ibid., 344.

[55] Ibid.

[56] Ibid., 344–345.

[57] See Rubenstein (2018).

[58] Williams and Hobbs (2020), 163.

[59] They cite Canada and the U.S. as sharing a similar history of formal agreements/documents between First Nations peoples and settler populations.

the modern state'.[60] The main benefits which are able to be gained through comparative analysis, they claimed, was to avoid the pitfalls, learn from others, and replicate the beneficial features.[61] Specifically, on Aotearoa/New Zealand, they stated that the te Tiriti o Waitangi/Treaty of Waitangi 'provides a useful comparison when developing ideas about how a treaty can impact on practical policy outcomes'.[62] They acknowledged the pervasive reality that despite the existence of treaties, socio-economic problems have endured for First Nations peoples and that their rights and interests have not been fully protected,[63] but overall they concluded:

> Treaties can have a profound impact. They can introduce notions of rights and sovereignty into the dialogue between Indigenous and non-indigenous people in a way that can affect the outcomes of that discussion.[64]

Another dimension to the benefits of a treaty is the accountability aspect it introduces through the recognition of occupation prior to settlement and the enduring culture of First Nations peoples. There is also the added impact of holding future governments to account for the recognition, promises and commitments made in a treaty. Having a treaty does not guarantee perfect relationships with governments,[65] but it does provide a documentary basis to structure the relationship and deal with any future disputes. Williams and Hobbs noted that 'the idea of treaty-making continues to shape contemporary relationships.'[66] This is because a treaty can be regarded as part of the broader public law underpinning any society and can stand as a testament to the intentions and commitment of the government.

Importantly, it has been feasible for Māori to assert their sovereignty alongside the traditional sovereignty of the Aotearoa/New Zealand government. Williams and Hobbs raised the practical possibility of the co-existence of shared sovereignty within a State.[67] Importantly, they concluded, acceptance of the sovereignty of Māori people in Aotearoa/New Zealand need not and had not undermined or diluted the existing laws of the colonisers. The te Tiriti o Waitangi/Treaty of Waitangi has endured as an authoritative document that was negotiated 'in the exercise of their {Māori} sovereignty'.[68] It is an exemplar of what is possible for First Nations people in Australia should the invitation for a *Makarrata* be realised and acted upon. Indeed, the wording of the Uluru Statement itself explicitly affirms the reality of shared sovereignty in its explanation that sovereignty.

> has never been ceded or extinguished and co-exists with the sovereignty of the Crown.[69]

---

[60] Williams and Hobbs (2020), 163.

[61] Ibid.

[62] Ibid., 202.

[63] Ibid., 203.

[64] Ibid.

[65] Ibid., 204.

[66] Ibid.

[67] Ibid. See also Hobbs and Benjamin (2022).

[68] Ibid.

[69] Uluru Statement from the Heart (National Constitutional Convention, 26 May 2017).

Farrar's concerns about the ethnocentrism that can arise in applying traditional legal concepts to First Nations peoples must be continually interrogated and guarded against. However, if First Nations peoples develop their own understanding of concepts such as sovereignty as being inherent to them and not dependent on the conferral, recognition or acceptance by settler/colonisers, then any ethnocentrism concerns will be ameliorated.

Moving outside the realm of academia, the journalist Laura Tingle asserted that despite the differences between Aotearoa/New Zealand and Australia in terms of First Nations history and experiences, comparisons do still have utility.[70] Similar to Burrows' confidence, Tingle claimed.

> [w]hat New Zealand gives us is a slightly different prism through which to observe the positive value these things {treaties} can bring to a country without undoing it.[71]

The Uluru Statement calls for the establishment of a *Makarrata* Commission to 'supervise a process of agreement-making between governments and First Nations and truth-telling about our history'.[72] The different prism that Tingle noted is extant in Aotearoa/New Zealand is further evident in the te Rōpū Whakamana i te Tiriti o Waitangi/Waitangi Tribunal, which in many senses is analogous to the *Makarrata* Commission. Tingle charted the evolution of the te Rōpū Whakamana i te Tiriti o Waitangi/Waitangi Tribunal from 'a basic land rights court' to it becoming a path to 'truth and reconciliation for the country'.[73] She cited with approval the opinion that reports issued by the body had begun

> to sketch a historical backdrop which had largely been hidden from the eyes of ordinary New Zealanders [as] case by case there was an examination of injustices that had never been resolved...nor openly admitted.[74]

Tingle reached three conclusions about the cultural and political nature of Aotearoa/ New Zealand and noted how they resonated with the contents of the Uluru Statement.[75] The first was the power of structures (such as the te Rōpū Whakamana i te Tiriti o Waitangi/Waitangi Tribunal), which need not threaten the dominant community. The second was the benefits obtained from celebrating the intrinsic value of First Nations culture. The third was the power of truth-telling 'for a country'. Aotearoa/ New Zealand offered.

> the benefit of seeing them from a different perspective, one where everything you have heard is impossible has already happened, and proved completely possible.[76]

The former chair of the te Rōpū Whakamana i te Tiriti o Waitangi/Waitangi Tribunal, Justice Joe Williams, has publicly argued that Aotearoa/New Zealand should aim for

---

[70] Tingle (2020).

[71] Ibid., 16.

[72] Uluru Statement from the Heart (National Constitutional Convention, 26 May 2017).

[73] Ibid., 31.

[74] Ibid.

[75] Ibid., 37–38.

[76] Ibid., 38.

the development of a *Lex Aotearoa* which would be an alignment between the Măori legal tradition and that of settler/coloniser laws so that a fully bicultural justice system would emerge to the benefit of all.[77] Indeed in this vein, the six law schools in Aotearoa/New Zealand have all committed to teaching the existence of a bijural, bicultural and bilingual legal system in Aotearoa/New Zealand.[78] This universal position on the law curriculum was achieved based on research conducted by the *te Kaupeka Tăti Ture* (Faculty of Law) at te Whare Wănanga o Otăgo (Otago University) and justified on the grounds that

> [t]here can be no systemic change to how we understand law in a contemporary Aotearoa/New Zealand if we do not teach it differently in our law schools.[79]

These calls for reform in the law curriculum have been echoed in Australia, with the Council of Australian Law Deans (CALD) publicly recognising past injustices perpetrated by the Australian legal system and the role of law schools in resolving that and being an active part of the solution;

> CALD urges all Australian law schools to work in partnership with First Nations peoples to give priority to the creation of culturally competent and culturally safe courses and programs. In so doing, CALD acknowledges the part that Australian legal education has played in supporting, either tacitly or openly, the law's systemic discrimination and structural bias against First Nations peoples. At the same time, CALD affirms the positive contribution Australian law schools can, should and will make, in full partnership with First Nations peoples, in exposing, critiquing and remedying all forms of institutionalised injustice.[80]

These developments collectively demonstrate that it is entirely possible to proceed with respect for all cultures as called for by Farrar. They also stand as a testament to the practical implementation of legal pluralism and the benefits it can bring on a larger scale. Specifically, the recognition of First Nations peoples' culture and laws need not diminish the settler/coloniser legal system.

4.7 Conclusion

As Farrar recognised, treaties between First Nations peoples and settler/coloniser populations present a positive opportunity for legal pluralism, even though historical conceptions of the State do not have a cultural basis in traditional First Nations understanding. Questions and issues in what Farrar termed 'inter-ethnic relationships' remain a core feature in the future development of domestic public law and international public law and moral as well as ethical evolution within States.

Despite very evident historical differences between Aotearoa/New Zealand and Australia, comparative analysis remains useful as the relationship between First

[77] McCrone (2021).

[78] Bedford et al. (2021).

[79] Ibid., 397.

[80] Council of Australian Law Deans (2020).

Nations peoples and settlers/colonisers is in a constant condition of evolution, if not always enjoying positive progress. The formal, legal status of these relationships form an important, and indeed core, pillar of modern public law in each country.

Legal pluralism is the best option for positive future developments in relationships with First Nations peoples and nation building. While relationships with First Nations peoples will present challenges, it is an essential function of modern society to continue to improve and progress these relationships and the status of First Nations peoples. In this area, law reform will continue to be crucial, whether this occurs through one of the many avenues of law reform such as the adoption of a treaty, Constitutional recognition (which is possible in either a written or unwritten Constitutional system) or jurisprudential advances.

This is not to say that any nation has developed a perfect system or that any First Nations peoples no longer experience structural disadvantages or inequalities. Rather what is argued is that comparative perspectives can help each nation to better evolve and develop its sense of Statehood in a fuller, inclusive and more positive manner if the principles of legal pluralism are accepted and implemented. Farrar's call for the recognition of history and the essential need for respect in the treatment of First Nations peoples retains its clarity and remains critical in the modern Australian context. The Uluru Statement with its call for a *Makarrata* is an invitation to imagine a better Australia, and it suggests reforms that have the potential to "transcend past injustices in providing a new way forward based on the principles of mutual recognition and respect."[81]

References

Appleby, Gabrielle, and Megan Davis. 2018. The Uluru Statement and the Promises of Truth. *Australian Historical Studies* 49(4): 501–509

Appleby, Gabrielle and Gemma McKinnon. 2017. The Uluru Statement. *Law Society of NSW Journal* 37: 36

Bedford, Narelle, McAvoy, Tony and Stevenson-Graf, Lindsey. 2021. First Nations Peoples, Climate Change, Human Rights and Legal Rights. *University of Queensland Law Journal* 40(3); 371–402, 397

Behrendt, Larissa. 2003. *Achieving Social Justice*. Federation Press, pgs 100–101

Behrendt, Larissa. 2005. The Abolition of ATSIC – Implications for Democracy. Democratic Audit of Australia https://apo.org.au/node/2807

Burrows, John. 2006. Ground-rules: Indigenous Treaties in Canada and New Zealand. New Zealand Universities Law Review 22(2): 188

Council of Australian Law Deans. 2020. CALD Statement on Australian Law's Systemic Discrimination and Structural Bias Against First Nations Peoples. https://cald.asn.au/blog/2020/12/03/cald-statement-on-australian-laws-systemic-discrimination-and-structural-bias-against-first-nations-peoples/.

Davis, Megan. 2012a. To Bind or Not to Bind: UNDRIP Five Years On. *Australian International Law Journal* 19: 17

[81] Williams and Hobbs (2020), 206.

Davis, Megan. 2012b. Constitutional Recognition Does Not Foreclose on Aboriginal Sovereignty. *Indigenous Law Bulletin* 8(1); 12–14
Davis, Megan. 2018. The Long Road to Uluru, Walking Together: Truth Before Justice. *Griffith Review* 60: 13
Davis, Megan, and Williams, George. 2021. *Everything You Need to Know About the Uluru Statement from the Heart*. Sydney: UNSW Press
Farrar, John. 1976. Law Reform Now - a Comparative View. International and Comparative Law Quarterly 25: 214
Farrar, John. 1987. Law Reform in New Zealand. Oxford Journal of Legal Studies 7: 151
Farrar, John. 2011. Early conceptions of the state in New Zealand. *Yearbook of New Zealand Jurisprudence* 13/14: 51–65
Farrar, John & Dugdale, A. M. 1990. *An Introduction to Legal Method*. Sweet & Maxwell
Farrar, John. 1974. *Law Reform and the Law Commission: Modern Legal Studies*. Sweet & Maxwell; Farrar, John. 1980
Farrar, John. 2010. *Legal Reasoning 3rd edition*. Thomson Reuters
Fredericks, Bronwyn and Bradfield, Abraham. 2021. More Than a Thought Bubble: The Uluru Statement From the Heart and Indigenous Voice to Parliament. *M/C Journal* 24(1)
Graham, Mary. 2014. Aboriginal Nations of Relationality and Positionalism: A Reply to Weber. *Global Discourse* 4(1): 17–22
Hobbs, Harry, and Jones, Benjamin T. 2022. Egalitarian Nationhoods: A Political Theory in Defence of the Voice to Parliament in the Uluru Statement from the Heart. Australian Journal of Political Science 57(2); 129–144
Jonas, William and, Dick, Darren. 2004. The Abolition of ATSIC: Silencing Indigenous Voices. Dialogue 3(2): 4
Larkin, Dani, and Kate Galloway. 2018. Uluru Statement from the Heart: Australian Public Law Pluralism 30(2) *Bond Law Review* 30(2): 335
Larkin, Dani and Galloway, Kate. 2021. Uluru Statement from the Heart: Australian Public Law Pluralism. *Australian Law Librarian* 29; 151–160
Lee, Richardson, and Helen Ross. 2020. The Uluru Statement from the Heart: Investigating Indigenous Australian Sovereignty. *Australian Journal of Indigenous Issues* 23 (1–2); 18
Maguire, Amy. 2014. The UDRIP and Self-Determination in Australia: Using a Human Rights Approach to Promote Accountability. *New Zealand Yearbook of International Law* 12: 105
McCrone, John. 2021. New Zealand Challenged by Māori Academics to Decolonise its Legal Training. Stuff.co.nz. https://www.stuff.co.nz/pou-tiaki/123424061/new-zealand-challenged-by-mori-academics-to-decolonise-its-legal-training.
Morris, Barry. 2004. Abolishing ATSIC in the Enabling State. Australia Journal of Anthropology 15(3): 324-328
Rubenstein, Kim. 2018. Power, Control and Citizenship: The Uluru Statement From the Heart as Active Citizenship. Bond Law Review 30(1): 19
Tingle, Laura. 2020. The High Road: What Australia Can Learn From New Zealand. Quarterly Essay 80; 1-112
Tynan, Lauren. 2021. What is Relationality? Indigenous Knowledges, Practices and Responsibilities with Kin. *Cultural Geographies* 28(4): 597, 603
Watego, Chelsea. 2021. *Another Day in the Colony*. University of Queensland Press
Watson, Irene. 2011. The 2007 Declaration on the Rights of Indigenous People: Indigenous Survival – Where to From Here. Griffith Law Review 20; 507, 509
Watson, Irene. 2012. The Future Is Our Past: We Once Were Sovereign and We Still Are. *Indigenous Law Bulletin* 8(3); 12–15
Watson, Irene. 2017. What is the Mainstream? The Laws of First Nations Peoples. In *New Directions for Law in Australia: Essays in Contemporary Law Reform*, ed. Ron Levy et al, 213–220. ANU Press
Williams, George, and Hobbs, Harry. 2020. *Treaty 2nd edition*. Federation Press

Chapter 5
Transitioning Up to Best Practice, or Down to the Bare Minimum? Global Harmonisation of Regulation of Therapeutic Goods

Wendy Elizabeth Bonython and Bruce Baer Arnold

Abstract The COVID-19 pandemic has highlighted legal and ethical tensions within global markets for medical devices and pharmaceuticals. The global medical market is highly profitable, socially important, and tightly but inconsistently regulated. That regulation is ostensibly predicated on reducing risks to consumers by excluding unsafe therapeutic goods. Historically, market regulation has occurred nationally, with limited cross-recognition of approvals from other jurisdictions, reflecting the gravity of the state's role in protecting its citizens and fostering local manufacturing. It is a persuasive rationale for the existence of the State. Globalisation of medical markets has prompted increased efforts at international harmonisation of those markets in line with neoliberal understandings of economies and the state. Standardisation of regulatory requirements across jurisdictions lowers compliance costs through reduced duplication of effort, incentivising investment in further research and development. However, there are risks associated with moving towards a globally harmonised regulatory framework, particularly if the threshold for an emerging single market is biased towards corporate stakeholders and provides inadequate protection to consumers from harms posed by therapeutic goods. This chapter examines whether protecting consumer safety remains the objective of a globally harmonised regulatory standard, or whether hegemonic market values have eroded the public harm minimisation foundations on which drug and device regulation are built.

5.1 Introduction

Globalisation, governance, and regulatory failure are key themes evident within John Farrar's body of scholarship, including regulatory and governance responses to the

---

W. E. Bonython (✉)
Faculty of Law, Bond University, Gold Coast, Australia
e-mail: wbonytho@bond.edu.au

B. B. Arnold
Faculty of Business, Government and Law, University of Canberra, Canberra, Australia
e-mail: Bruce.arnold@canberra.edu.au

U. Ghori et al. (eds.), *Globalisation in Transition*,
https://doi.org/10.1007/978-981-99-2439-4_5

Global Financial Crisis.[1] The current COVID-19 pandemic presents an array of challenges to existing models of governance and regulation in another globalised market environment, that of the market(s) for therapeutic goods. Indeed, a conclusion that may be drawn from this chapter is that, from a globalised regulation perspective, COVID-19 may be this sector's own GFC.

Writing about regional and global harmonisation of drugs in 2000, Braithwaite and Drahos questioned whether harmonisation and mutual recognition contribute to deregulation (a race to the bottom) or world's best practice (a race to the top)?[2] Some 22 years later, amid a global pandemic—the outcomes of which are increasingly dependent on geopolitics—it seems timely to revisit that question.[3]

This chapter considers the nature of the global market—or markets—for pharmaceuticals and medical devices (therapeutic goods) in an environment of polymorphic regulation that involves multiple regulatory actors within, rather than merely across, jurisdictions and questions about how to evaluate the effectiveness of harmonisation in terms of national interest, corporate benefit and public health.[4] It identifies divergent priorities and rhetoric of stakeholders regarding regulation of therapeutic goods markets, including those responsible for developing and producing goods, those responsible for regulating their access to the market, those who pay for them within that market, and those who ultimately use or consume them. In many situations, the same actors may fulfil more than one of those roles; in others, there may be no consensus of interest between stakeholders with the same or conflicting functions.

The chapter centres on intellectual property harmonisation arrangements (notably regarding patents) often perceived as a key barrier preventing therapeutic goods from reaching those most in need. That perception is reflected in the current global preoccupation with the role of TRIPs waivers in facilitating access to coronavirus vaccines.[5] Despite this perception, TRIPS waivers alone will not remove all regulatory barriers preventing global distribution of covid vaccines and other goods. Instead, each jurisdiction has its own (potentially harmonised but nonetheless distinct) therapeutic goods safety and quality regimes to ensure those products are safe and effective, both overall and on an individual batch basis.

One expectation for the World Trade Organisation (WTO) was that regulation would allow information, like capital, to flow freely.[6] That has not been the case regarding COVID-19 procurement. It is beyond this chapter's scope to delve deeply into a key aspect of economic regulation—pricing, not least because of confidentiality

[1] Farrar (2010), Farrar and Parsons (2012, 2013), Farrar (2019), 11, Farrar and Mayes (2013), Ariff et al. (2012).

[2] Braithwaite, and Drahos (2000), 388. See also Drahos (2004), Yu (2013); Dutfield, and Suthersanen (2005).

[3] Fidler (2020), Miller (2021), Kickbusch and Anna (2021).

[4] Levi-Faur (2013).

[5] Wijesinghe et al. (2022), Gostin (2021). See more broadly Mitchell et al. (2010).

[6] Drahos (1995), Drahos and John (2004), Maisonrouge (1981).

and diverse pricing regulation models within jurisdictions under normal circumstances, let alone during the pandemic.[7] Necessarily it will only briefly address pricing regulation, noting that harmonisation of pricing mechanisms and data sharing is an underdeveloped aspect of regulatory harmonisation.

Using COVID-19 vaccines and COVID-19-relevant medical devices such as diagnostic kits, ventilators, and personal protective equipment—i.e., therapeutic goods with potential strong protection under intellectual property law—as a case study, the chapter revisits Braithwaite and Drahos's question to consider how effectively pre-pandemic harmonisation efforts have withstood the rigours of the pandemic. It also considers whether harmonisation reforms have achieved the diverse objectives that provided their legitimacy, finding that whether harmonisation is 'a race to the top, or a race to the bottom' depends on the objectives of the perceiver. The experiences of TRIPS and harmonisation of safety frameworks may be informative to members of the international community who are currently considering the need for a human rights-based 'Pandemic Treaty'[8] whose purpose may include avoiding some of these obstacles to vaccine production and distribution encountered during this pandemic.[9]

5.2 The COVID-19 Lens

Despite global access to COVID-19 vaccines being identified as essential to ending the current pandemic,[10] both the Global North and Global South have experienced difficulty in accessing diagnostic and therapeutic goods,[11] challenging globalisation models of borderless markets with ongoing economic expansion and readily-available goods in exchange for free flowing capital and protection of expertise.[12] Data from February 2022 shows that vaccination rates are far lower in many low income and lower-middle income countries (LIC/LMIC) than elsewhere, a matter of inadequate supply from patent holders rather than inadequate infrastructure or vaccine hesitancy in the South where most of the LICs/LMICs are located.[13]

The COVAX initiative—a technology accelerator established for the purpose of ensuring equitable global access to vaccines was established early in the pandemic, before any vaccines had been developed.[14] The COVAX model operates by compiling a portfolio of candidate vaccines, and permitting countries to either commit to purchasing doses, or purchase an option to purchase doses, of a particular vaccine

[7] Evaluation of those models is hindered by the opacity of many of the deals between rights holders and national governments. See for example Sciacchitano and Armando (2021).

[8] Moon and Kickbusch (2021), Labonté et al. (2021).

[9] Mirchandani (2020).

[10] World Health Organisation (2021). See also Wouters et al. (2021), Phelan et al. (2020).

[11] McMahon (2021), Stephenson (2021).

[12] For a perspective see Mirowski (2013).

[13] Ritchie et al. (2020).

[14] Eccleston-Turner and Upton (2021), Stein (2021).

via an up-front partial payment prior to candidate vaccines receiving regulatory approval for use. The funds raised were allocated to manufacturers to offset costs of scaling up production in anticipation of receiving regulatory approval, rather than waiting for confirmation of approval before investing in scale-up infrastructure. Intended to be 'the world's primary distributor of COVID-19 vaccines',[15] including through the COVAX Advanced Market Commitment program, whose purpose was to independently fund and support access of LIC/LMIC to vaccines,[16] "rich nations largely sidestepped COVAX, hoarding doses for their own populations and cutting deals directly with low- and middle-income countries",[17] undermining the effectiveness of COVAX, and derailing the WHO's *Strategy to Achieve Global COVID-19 Vaccination by Mid-2022*.[18]

Alongside the blunted efficacy of the COVAX initiative, the prolonged deliberations at the WTO regarding a proposal by South Africa and India to utilise the TRIPS waivers for COVID-19 related pharmaceuticals and devices[19] raise significant questions about effective global regulation of essential medicines and devices, including efforts to harmonise intellectual property protections through TRIPS, and harmonisation of pharmaceutical and medical device safety regulation.[20]

Collectively, the COVAX initiative and the TRIPS waiver address the three key regulatory aspects of therapeutic goods in a globalised environment: intellectual property, safety, and pricing.

5.3 One Market, or Many?

The 'regulatory space'[21] for pharmaceutical and medical devices is complex. Its scope may encompass intellectual property protection, clinical trials governance, quality assurance and control, pricing, authorised supply and distribution chains, advertising and tort law.[22] Within any single national jurisdiction, those activities may be distributed individually or collectively across a range of regulatory actors,

---

[15] Achieving 70% COVID-19 Immunization Coverage by Mid-2022: Statement of the Independent Allocation of Vaccines Group (IAVG) of COVAX. 2021. https://www.who.int/news/item/23-12-2021-achieving-70-covid-19-immunization-coverage-by-mid-2022.

[16] Berkley (2020).

[17] Ibid.

[18] See n 10 above.

[19] The Waiver from Certain Provisions of the TRIPS Agreement for the Prevention, Containment and Treatment of COVID-19: Communication from India and South Africa. 2020. WTO DOC. IP/C/W/669. file:///C:/Users/taris/Downloads/W669.pdf.

[20] Zaman (2022).

[21] Term coined by Hancher and Moran in their seminal 'Mapping the regulatory Space'. Although whether pharmaceutical and medical device regulation, occupy a single 'space' encompassing multiple issues, or multiple spaces each containing single issues, is unclear from the literature, which seems to use both models. See Hancher and Michael (1998), Braithwaite et al. (2007).

[22] Black (2001), Kingsford Smith (2002), Koop and Lodge (2017).

whose objectives in undertaking regulation may not always be clear and on occasion are in conflict.[23]

Lack of clarity around the objectives of regulation performed by regulatory actors hampers attempts to evaluate the effectiveness of regulation in achieving goals that legitimate the implementation or reform of regulation. When reforms relate to efforts to achieve global harmonisation of regulation, the need for clarity of purpose as a requirement for evaluation of effectiveness becomes even more critical. It prompts discussion about global harmonisation as making a world safe for consumers or investors,[24] a manifestation of hegemonic values,[25] the efficacy of 'red tape' reduction as the best/only solution,[26] and cooperation by regulatory agencies.[27]

There is no over-arching and enforceable global 'right to safe and effective' therapeutic goods that overrides intellectual property or other regulatory frameworks.[28] The aspirational Right to Health[29] in international law encompasses a right to medicines and medical devices which support both individual and public health. Access alone is not enough: those goods must also be safe and effective,[30] to minimise avoidable harms to consumers and to foster trust in fact-based medicine.[31] Implicitly, there is a requirement that they also be affordable, something potentially at odds with the monopoly rights granted under patent law and strengthened through 'TRIPS Plus' trade agreements.[32] Access to adequate healthcare has been identified in the Sustainable Development goals[33] and is a key aspect of international law and policy and philanthropic efforts around the world.[34] However, pharmaceuticals and medical devices are big business: recent estimations value the global pharmaceutical market at USD 1.27 trillion in 2020,[35] and the medical technology market, including implantable medical devices and diagnostic and surgical equipment, at USD 500

---

[23] Levi-Faur (2013).

[24] Wells and Ahmed (2007), Levi-Faur (2009), Maynard and Bloor (2015).

[25] Gamble (2014), Hartwick and Peet (2003), Slaughter (2009).

[26] Gunningham (2015).

[27] Slaughter (2000).

[28] The differentiation between 'safe' and 'effective' is pertinent given that therapeutic goods regulators such as Australia's Therapeutic Goods Administration (TGA), counterpart of the U.S. Food & Drugs Administration, focuses on the exclusion of harmful goods rather than promoting those that are effective. Regulation in Australia accordingly enables the marketing of homeopathic and other products that at best serve as placebos.

[29] See Tobin (2012), Backman et al. (2008).

[30] Vogel (1998). The paradigmatic safety event is Thalidomide, discussed in Carpenter (2014). See also Sonia and Chakraborty (2019).

[31] Vergara et al. (2021), Ozawa and Stack (2013).

[32] Sell (2007), Yu (2021), El Said (2022).

[33] Kruk et al. (2018).

[34] llingworth (2020), McBride et al. (2019). See also Rimmer (2021).

[35] Statista. Pharmaceutical Products and Markets. https://www.statista.com/markets/412/topic/456/pharmaceutical-products-market/

billion.[36] The cost of developing new drugs and medical devices is high[37]; there are significant regulatory barriers that manufacturers and distributors must clear before they can release their products onto the market. The costs of producing devices and pharmaceuticals, once approved, may also be high, particularly for emerging categories of drugs.[38] Patent law as a regulatory mechanism disregards research and production costs, and is agnostic regarding pricing: high prices of patent protected medicines may permit developers to recoup R&D and patent costs, causing the patent system to act as a further economic barrier to access.[39]

Globally, one significant challenge posed by the market is the uneven distribution of pharmaceutical and medical device manufacturers and their consumers. Many of the large manufacturers (and more of the dominant patent holders) are in just three jurisdictions—the U.S., the E.U., and Japan—with the trade strategies of those jurisdictions seeking to preserve national competitive advantage.[40] Consumers—either the State, through nationalised pharmaceutical and medical device purchasing schemes, NGOs, or individual citizen consumers—are distributed around the world. This is significant considering the representation of stakeholder interests in harmonisation efforts, a point returned to below.

Secondly, these markets do not operate according to free market principles assumed by some theorists. As ongoing debate about drug costs in the U.S. highlights, many countries negotiate jurisdiction-specific pricing agreements to subsidise drug and device costs, making them affordable—in some cases free. There is little transparency around the agreed pricing, with negotiations and outcomes cloaked in confidentiality, a matter of the regulated exercising power in an investor-driven view of corporate responsibility. Some insight into the negotiations has emerged regarding vaccine supply deals negotiated during the pandemic.[41] The pandemic has also illustrated the tensions that arise when public funding is provided to develop a particular product, yet a commercial manufacturer seeks to claim significant intellectual property protection, with a view to sequestering profits derived from the technology.[42]

It is often claimed that regulatory intervention is necessary to address structural market weaknesses or defects than cannot be managed by free market economics.

---

[36] Statista, Medical technology industry- Statistics and Facts. https://www.statista.com/topics/1702/medical-technology-industry/#dossierSummary__chapter3

[37] Morgan et al. (2011), Avorn (2015), DiMasi and Grabowski (2021), Light and Warburton (2011).

[38] See for example Zolgensma, a gene-based drug used to treat spinal muscular atrophy, which cost USD 2,124 million per patient when approved by the FDA: Stein, Rob. 2019 'At $2.1 Million, New Gene Therapy Is the Most Expensive Drug Ever. NPR. https://www.npr.org/sections/health-shots/2019/05/24/725404168/at-2-125-million-new-gene-therapy-is-the-most-expensive-drug-ever: See also DiMasi et al. (2003), Eisenberg (2003).

[39] World Health Organisation (2017).

[40] Rimmer (2020), Kelsey (2019a, b).

[41] Sciacchitano and Bartolazzi (2021).

[42] Paradise (2020), Kapczynski (2021), Padmanabhan (2021).

Breyer, outlining common justifications for regulation, noted that evaluation of regulation requires consideration of the objectives it seeks to achieve.[43] Those justifications include controlling (natural) monopolies; compensating for externalities; excessive profits; information asymmetries or inadequacies; excessive competition, unequal bargaining power, moral hazard, paternalism, and scarcity.

Monopolies within pharmaceutical markets are not natural, instead protected—if not created—by intellectual property, contract, and confidentiality laws that properties knowledge. Pharmaceutical companies have been accused historically of seeking profits through abuse of market power.[44] Recent controversies over the different costs of Pfizer vaccines offered to different countries during the pandemic exemplify rent-seeking behaviour and the inadequacy of the foundational TRIPS agreement.[45]

Information asymmetries or inadequacies are characteristic of high technology markets. Asymmetry is axiomatic in patent-based pharmaceutical and medical device markets, given consumers—the patient—typically have the weakest knowledge base and agency regarding their drug regime or device functionality *ex ante*.[46] The information asymmetry necessarily puts the consumers/patients in a weak bargaining position compared to the drug or device manufacturer/supplier, a vulnerability further compounded by the essential nature of medicines and medical devices, and the small scale on which the consumers/patients are seeking to purchase them.

Large scale Government/NGO purchasers negotiating bulk purchase prices directly with manufacturers to subsidise products for end consumers may still be vulnerable, notwithstanding protection afforded by scale, due to lack of competition. Government entities are particularly susceptible to political pressures, including trade-offs for defence or other support or sanctions (evident in the U.S. 'watch listing') and because constituents may have strong views regarding affordability and accessibility of healthcare. Responding to those sensitivities, rights holders and industry associations are adept at lobbying government for concessions in many, if not all, developed economies, reinforcing a hegemonic view of corporate interest in high technology as a matter of national interest.[47] Moral hazard—arising when somebody other than the end consumer pays for the product—is another justification for regulation in these markets given pharmaceutical and medical device subsidisation schemes operating in most countries.

The existence and potential abuse of these justifications mean regulation of some sort is required within pharmaceutical and medical device markets at the national level. Those justifications do not, however, necessarily identify what type of regulation should be implemented or prima facie demonstrate a need for, or even benefit of, global harmonisation. So how do we decide what type of regulation should be

---

43 Breyer (1998).

44 Dutfield (2021).

45 See e.g., Rizvi (2021), Stevis-Gridneff et al. (2021).

46 As distinct from having the best insight into the way their illness or condition, and any treatments, affect them individually.

47 Drahos and Braithwaite (2004), Alford (1996). See also Laffont and Tirole (1991).

imposed? This depends in large part on what objectives the regulation is supposed to achieve.

In a complex stakeholder environment, such as pharmaceutical and medical device markets, stakeholders have different expectations about priorities and what purpose regulation serves. Some commercial stakeholders seek protection of monopoly control of products, reflecting investment in the research, development, and trust by consumers. Others seek reforms enabling generic versions of products developed by others, thereby capitalising on markets constrained by lack of supply, and avoiding development costs. Consumers and health practitioners may consider a regulator's priority to be public health or alternatively individual patient access to novel emerging medicines rather than industry support, reflecting interests in safety, effectiveness, and access to those medicines and devices. Governments, in contrast, may be preoccupied with unstated policy offsets[48] or pricing considerations, particularly in countries where the state exercises economies of scale to harness bargaining power, and/or subsidises the cost to consumer medical devices and pharmaceuticals under universal medical schemes. Different aspects of regulation—for example, intellectual property, safety, and pricing—may be wholly or partly distributed between multiple regulatory actors, resulting in overlap and arbitrage. Regulators may themselves lack clarity surrounding their primary objectives, particularly if their funding is dependent on certain stakeholders. The absence of clear objectives compromises evaluation of the effectiveness of regulatory reforms in this space.

Since the late 1980s, the international community has pursued parallel harmonisation agendas of relevance to pharmaceutical and medical device markets, driven by both neoliberal understandings of the State and a deepening of global trade frameworks around the WTO rather than a consumer-oriented global health agreement. Trade negotiations from 1986 led to the investor-oriented TRIPS agreement. In 1991, the U.S., as the dominant generator of health goods innovation, joined the European Community and Japan for trilateral discussions on pharmaceutical standards at the International Conference on Harmonisation.

5.4 Harmonisation of Patent Protection—Why?

An ostensible objective of economic globalisation is the removal of barriers restricting the flow of goods, services, and technologies between countries. It is somewhat counterintuitive that reforms to raise or implement minimum standards for intellectual property have formed a critical part of this agenda, with tensions between the WTO and the World Intellectual Property Organisation (WIPO) regarding the Trade Related Aspects of Intellectual Property Agreement (TRIPS) and 'TRIPS

---

[48] Governments have typically not expressly referred to defence alignments or the importance of avoiding trade sanctions against politically powerful sectors such as farming as being determinative of policy that reflects the interest of hegemonic partners in making a 'world safe for Big Pharma'. See however Kelsey (2019a, b), 11.

Plus' bi/multilateral Free Trade Agreements that serve to erode concessions by the global North under the Doha Agreement.[49]

TRIPS, rather than creating a single global system of regulation for intellectual property or a regulatory framework specifically addressing issues regarding the efficacy and safety of therapeutic goods, instead outlines a harmonised minimum standard of intellectual property protections to which all members of the WTO must adhere. Individual member states are permitted to impose higher levels of intellectual property protection; adherence is the price states pay for full participation in the global economy.[50]

A rationale for imposing minimum standards is the protection and incentivisation of investment in research and development, by affording those who invest in those activities an exclusive opportunity to capitalise on any resultant market.[51] Rights holders, in common with other high technology industries, rely on industrial property to offset the costs of product development and on support by the hegemonic states for an international regulatory framework—centred on but exclusive to patents—that fosters their activity.[52]

Sell, in examining the background to TRIPS, identified twelve senior executives from a range of U.S. corporations—notably Merck, Johnson & Johnson, and Pfizer—who, collectivised as the informal or ad hoc U.S. Intellectual Property Committee (IPC) in advising trade delegates to the TRIPS negotiations, essentially determined the trade-focused interpretation of intellectual property that the U.S. adopted.[53] According to Sell, the IPC 'made IP rules that now bind most of the globe',[54] based on 'a far from consensual' but now hegemonic concept of intellectual property which 'privileges protection over diffusion' and 'closely mirrors the expressed wishes of the twelve CEO's who spearheaded this effort'.[55] Sell attributes IPC's influence over U.S. trade policy, manifested in TRIPS as a global regulatory framework, to its model of IP protection as a solution to a perceived decline in U.S. trade, very attractive to a country losing competitive advantages as other nations adapted U.S. industrial know-how, including through production of counterfeit products.[56] In addition to exercising domestic political influence, Sell notes that the IPC actively recruited support from international counterparts, notably in Europe and Japan, who shared a neoliberal understanding of the State and in turn lobbied their domestic trade representatives.[57]

[49] Weissman (2004).

[50] Drahos et al. (2004), Baird (2013).

[51] Sundaram (2015), Cockburn and Long (2015).

[52] The framework thus features mechanisms such as Investor State Dispute Settlement provisions in free trade agreements that inhibit national initiatives that might disadvantage foreign investors through intervention based on public health, environmental or cultural protection. See Samples, Tim (2019), Hawkins and Holden (2016), Soudias (2021).

[53] Sell (2003).

[54] Ibid., 2.

[55] Sell (2011), 91.

[56] Ibid., 98.

[57] Ibid., 101.

TRIPS has been criticised for its privileging of the North (and capital) at the expense of the less developed world. Under the original agreement, disadvantaged countries were required to scale up their intellectual property protections to meet the interests of corporations in developed countries, with few assurances of improved access to, and affordability of, goods/services. Access to essential medicines, an aspect of any right to health, salient for the HIV epidemic in Africa, Southeast Asia and other LIC/LMIC regions, provided a flashpoint for concerns about global equity.[58]

The TRIPS Agreement was promoted as balancing economic and humanitarian interests by permitting certain exceptions to TRIPS provisions for 'inventions whose commercial exploitation need to be prevented to protect human, animal or plant life or health'[59]; 'diagnostic, therapeutic and surgical methods for treating human or animals'[60]; and 'certain plant and animal innovations'.[61] Governments, under TRIPS, are permitted to refuse patent protection to innovations falling within one or more of those categories. Additionally, compulsory licensing—use of the industrial property without the patent holder's agreement—notionally also provides for access to goods in circumstances of necessity, such as a national emergency, in domestic markets. However, it assumes a country has pre-existing indigenous manufacturing capacity, not the case in much of the Global South, or more generally in the context of emerging medical technologies, such as RNA vaccine production.

The subsequent *Declaration on the TRIPS Agreement and Public Health* (Doha) sought to address inadequacies by stating that TRIPS does not operate to prevent member states from implementing public health measures. Doha contains provisions directly addressing pharmaceutical and medical device patent protections, most importantly permitting countries with manufacturing capacity to export generic medicines under compulsory licencing arrangements to countries lacking the requisite capacity.[62]

Perhaps unsurprisingly, parts of the pharmaceutical sector opposed Doha. According to 't Hoen, corporations initially argued against Doha on the grounds that 'patents are not a problem' and 'weakening patent protection would have devastating effects on the R&D capabilities of the research-based industry'.[63] The International Federation of Pharmaceutical Manufacturers described compulsory licensing as 'a threat to good public health by denying patients around the world the future benefits of R&D capabilities of the research-based industry from which new therapies

[58] See e.g., Yamane, Hiroko. *Interpreting TRIPS: Globalisation of Intellectual Property Rights and Access to Medicines* (Hart, 2011), Ellen 't Hoen, 'TRIPS, Pharmaceutical Patents, and Access to Essential Medicines: A Long Way from Seattle to Doha' (2002) 3 *Chicago Journal of International Law* 27, 43, Sundaram, (2015) note 50.

[59] Agreement on Trade-Related Aspects of Intellectual Property Rights, Apr. 15, 1994, Marrakesh Agreement Establishing the World Trade Organization, Annex 1C, 1869 U.N.T.S. 299, 33 I.L.M. 1197 (1994) (Hereon 'TRIPS') Article 27.2.

[60] TRIPS Article 27.3a.

[61] TRIPS Article 27.3b.

[62] Abbott (2002), Murthy (2001), Sun (2004).

[63] 't Hoen (2002).

come'.[64] Generic drug manufacturers in the North and South welcomed opportunities presented by the compulsory licensing provisions but noted concerns that outside Doha some states might apply diplomatic pressure in unilateral negotiations to prevent weaker states from exercising those provisions.[65] History has demonstrated that these concerns were substantive: the Medicines Law and Policy database indicates compulsory licensing provisions have been used only 125 times, primarily for treatment of HIV/AIDS, mainly in LIC/LMIC, with occasional use of the compulsory licensing provisions by developed countries. [66] Even in the face of limited access to medicines, countries remain reluctant to use TRIPS flexibilities and compulsory licensing provisions.

During COVID-19, compulsory licensing provisions have been either executed or threatened by several developed countries—including the U.S. and E.U. members—to address the affordability of putative therapeutics, including Remdesivir, a five-day course of which was priced at USD 2340 per patient but estimated to cost the manufacturer between USD 5—USD 10/patient to produce.[67] Describing TRIPS as:

> the outcome of a nondemocratic process driven by a club of U.S. corporations. TRIPS has not been debated and negotiated as a global public good. On the contrary, it has been strongly pushed by the U.S.. In particular, it is the outcome of the pressures made by a handful of U.S. corporations which have successfully asked their government to act on their behalf[68]

Archibugi and Filippetti concluded:

> TRIPS may serve the interests of western corporations but not necessarily of western economies. There is no evidence that TRIPS has been advantageous for American citizens at large. On the contrary, it seems that TRIPS has been important to allow TNCs to expand their innovative activities globally, relying on stronger IP regimes abroad.[69]

Further analysis, drawing for example on work by Mirowski and Plehwe, or Levi-Faur, might recognise TRIPS as a manifestation of a 'neoliberal' understanding common to policymakers, journalists, and corporations across the globe over the past 40 years. Some governments, responsible for tacitly outsourcing their international trade law-making policy in a 'Faustian bargain',[70] may finally be coming to realise that outcomes delivered by TRIPS were not in their—or their populations'—interests.[71]

---

[64] Ibid.

[65] Ibid.

[66] Medicines Law and Policy Database TRIPS Flexibilities. http://tripsflexibilities.medicineslawandpolicy.org.

[67] Urias and Ramani (2020).

[68] Archibugi and Filippetti (2010).

[69] Ibid., 146.

[70] Ibid., 138.

[71] Ibid., 143.

5.5 Harmonisation of Safety Standards—Why?

If protection of intellectual property for the benefit of multinationals—albeit sold as the potential benefits to future consumers from yet-to-be discovered treatments through incentivising R&D—was the objective of harmonisation of intellectual property regulation, what was the objective underpinning harmonisation of drug and medical device safety regulations?

Therapeutic goods regulators are gatekeepers. Unconcerned with patent protection, their role is to apply prescribed standards to a particular product (drug or device), to determine whether the benefits to patients claimed by the product sponsor (usually the patent holder or agent) outweigh any risks posed by using that product for the specified purpose. The regulator makes its assessment based on the sponsor's data, including confidential clinical trials data. If the regulator determines that the benefits do outweigh the risks, then the product will be approved to enter the market. If it fails to meet the specified benefit/risk ratio threshold, then market access will be withheld.

Market approval regulation typically occurs at the national level. A sponsor may be concurrently seeking regulatory approval to enter multiple markets, each with their own set of standards and requirements to persuade the regulator that the drug satisfies national benefit/risk requirements. Standardisation of regulatory requirements, through global and regional harmonisation efforts, is therefore, highly attractive to manufacturers and sponsors. Through standardisation of application processes and data requirements, for example, sponsors can minimise duplication of effort required to satisfy different regulatory standards across different jurisdictions. Regulators benefit from harmonisation too: increased standardisation and information sharing between regulators, encouraged by harmonisation initiatives, enables regulators to operate more effectively in the face of increasing resource constraints and increasing technical complexity of the products falling within their regulatory scope. Harmonisation does not create a single global market for goods: individual national regulators retain sovereignty to make their own determinations about whether to permit market access to any drug/device.[72]

In a recent report considering global regulation of medicines commissioned by the Food and Drug Authority (FDA), the U.S. therapeutic goods regulator, the National Academy of Sciences concluded that

> [p]rotecting and promoting public health in a time of globalisation and unprecedented advance in technologies in medicine – which are mirrored by the growing complexity of medicines and supply chains for their manufacture and production – is the single greatest challenge facing medicines regulatory authorities today. It is therefore imperative that regulatory authorities at all resource levels – well, moderately well, and lower – find ways to continue or expand on their ability and willingness to work together to maximise the use

[72] The ICH held its first meeting in 1990, attended by pharmaceutical regulators and industry stakeholders from the E.U., U.S., and Japan (https://www.ich.org/page/history). In 1992, medical device regulators and industry representatives from the U.S., E.U., Japan and Canada met to begin establishing the Global Harmonisation Task Force—subsequently redesignated the International Medical Device Regulators Forum—for the purpose of 'achieving harmonisation in medical device regulatory practices' (https://www.imdrf.org/ghtf/organisational-structure).

of their finite resource is so they can ensure the quality safety efficacy and availability of medicines for their jurisdictiosns in both emergency and non-emergency situations.[73]

Less clear is the link between harmonisation of regulatory standards, and benefits to public health and consumers. The International Council for Harmonisation (ICH), a forum presented as 'the global platform for harmonisation', uses the slogan 'Harmonisation for better health'.[74] Similarly, the literature is replete with claims that harmonisation benefits public and individual health. Additionally, many of the regulators involved identify public health as one of, if not their primary, objective. Yet evidence for claims that harmonisation necessarily benefits public health is lacking.

The benefits to public health used to legitimate harmonisation are both indirect and hypothetical. Empirical data does not support claims harmonisation is invariably good for public health, firstly because regulators operating under harmonised systems are faster and more effective at determining whether drugs are safe and should be granted market access, notwithstanding the increasing technical complexity of pharmaceutical products; and secondly that the money saved on duplication of effort by sponsors in complying with multiple divergent regulatory standards and processes will be redirected towards research and development, resulting in new, more effective drugs being made available to patients faster.

Abraham and others have demonstrated that neither of these claims are true. Returning to Braithwaite and Drahos's question about regulation, the first claim assumes that everyone, including countries with previously high regulatory standards, will either strengthen or at least maintain those standards—a 'race to the top' model of harmonisation. However, using empirical data, including post-market withdrawals over time, Abraham and others have demonstrated that this is not the case. In one example, their work shows that in the period coinciding with harmonisation, the U.S. regulator became less effective at preventing drugs subsequently demonstrated as unsafe from entering the market. Other research showed that despite enhanced information-sharing principles, regulators in some jurisdictions remained reluctant to withdraw products from the market in the face of adverse pharmacovigilance data from other jurisdictions.

Perhaps unsurprisingly, the interests of commercial stakeholders once again feature prominently. Recent work by Abraham and Davis studied the effect of reforms occurring at each of the U.K. and U.S. drug safety regulators over the period 1971–1992, and 1993–2004.[75] The latter half of the period under review overlaps with peak global harmonisation reform efforts; the U.K. regulator is closely involved with the European Medicines Agency which, along with the FDA, are two of the original six members of the ICH. Those agencies both inform and emulate ICH models of harmonisation, including through reforms considered in Abraham and Davis's study.

[73] National Academies of Sciences, Engineering, and Medicine (2020).

[74] International Council for Harmonisation 30th Anniversary Publication—ICH—the global platform for harmonisation. 2021. https://www.ich.org/publication/ich-30th-anniversary-publication-ich-global-platform-harmonisation. See also Röttger-Wirtz (2021), Turner (2019).

[75] Abraham and Davis (2020).

The study found that although the U.S. regulator was more effective than the U.K. regulator in the earlier period, the U.S. became more aligned with the U.K.'s standards in the second, and its effectiveness deteriorated. The authors noted 'the regulatory cultures … are likely to converge further due to alignment of their safety data requirements and regulatory standards under the International Conference on Harmonisation',[76] providing some evidence to support the argument that, at least for jurisdictions which were previously leaders in regulatory standard-setting, harmonisation may have been regulating down. That effect, for the consumers located within those jurisdictions, is not a public health benefit.

The second justification—that more drugs will be developed, faster—also does not appear to hold true. Evidence demonstrates a decline in the number of new drugs being developed and marketed, while the cost of developing those drugs is increasing.[77] Further, as the industry moves beyond small chemical compounds into developing more costly and complex biologicals—which themselves may tax the technical capacity of regulators—the costs of producing those biologicals once approved may be prohibitive to government purchasers and individual consumers alike.

Despite claiming international harmonisation promotes public health through

> prevention of unnecessary duplication of clinical trials and post-market clinical evaluations; development and manufacturing of new medicines; registration and supervision of new medicines; and reduction of unnecessary animal testing without compromising safety and effectiveness accomplished through technical guidelines implemented by the regulatory authorities

none of these directly or immediately benefit consumers. Animal testing and duplication of clinical trials may be relevant for the purposes of research ethics and production of pre-market data by manufacturers, however if the product fails to receive regulatory approval, it does not benefit patients in any way. Similarly, development and manufacturing of new medicines, and registration and supervision of new medicines are activities that were previously undertaken by industry and the regulator respectively: they are not 'new', and harmonisation in many places has neither strengthened controls, nor excluded more unsafe products. Similarly, expedition of approvals only benefits consumers if the products being approved are in fact safe and effective. The benefit to the public of reforming these activities through harmonisation is not immediately obvious.

A clear gap in the regulatory framework evident during COVID-19 is the incoherence of national regulatory approval for various vaccines. Lack of coherence in decision-making and communication has added to global anxieties about vaccine efficacy, safety, and accessibility. Examples include vaccines approved and administered in other jurisdictions not being recognised for the purpose of national public

[76] Ibid., 9.

[77] See n 33 above. See also Cohen (2005); Pammolli et al. (2011); Gaudilliere (2021).

health laws,[78] and the potential for manufacturers to apply lower standards to export market vaccines than to domestic markets, an example of vaccine colonialism which has already been witnessed with vaccine donation.[79]

5.6 What Has Harmonisation Achieved? Regulating Up, or Down?

Despite extensive claims of public health benefits through harmonisation of both intellectual property and safety regulatory standards, harmonisation has, consistent with Stigler's much-cited observation, 'benefited the regulate'.[80] In each case, harmonisation proponents have relied on derivative and contingent hypothetical future public health benefits dependent on successful innovation by industry. The indirect and largely unrealised nature of these public health benefits is in sharp contrast to the immediate and direct benefits to industry.

COVID-19 has highlighted a deviation between the interests of state, and the interests of industry, that may not have been evident when harmonisation initiatives commenced. The pandemic has, understandably, refocussed the political agenda more towards questions of public health than of trade and industry. States have found themselves in weakened negotiation positions vis-a-vis manufacturers regarding devices and pharmaceuticals. The TRIPS framework has proven itself incapable of responding in a timely manner to global demand for pandemic-ending vaccines. Many months after the proposal by India and South Africa was presented, we still seem to be no closer to agreeing on a way forward past the intellectual property market barriers and that is before the question of domestic safety regulation and approvals for access to markets at the national level has occurred.[81]

Developed countries have been forced to use, or threaten to use, mechanisms primarily intended to benefit LIC/LMICs permitting them to unilaterally override intellectual property rights to corporations to overcome egregious rent-seeking by manufacturers. National regulators, some prompt in applying expedited approval processes for drugs in their own markets, have nonetheless proven unwilling to

---

[78] For example, in Australia some vaccines which have been approved by regulators in other countries are not approved for use in Australia and may not be recognised for the purposes of immigration: https://www.tga.gov.au/international-covid-19-vaccines-recognised-australia.

[79] For example, many donated doses of vaccine have had impracticably short shelf-lives: https://www.who.int/news/item/29-11-2021-joint-statement-on-dose-donations-of-covid-19-vaccines-to-african-countries.

[80] Stigler (1971).

[81] It is difficult to think of a circumstance more consistent with the requirements legitimating compulsory licencing than those presently faced. Notwithstanding that, in a recent submission PhRMA—one of the most powerful pharmaceutical manufacturing lobby groups—expressed its outrage that compulsory licensing and waivers were being sought and considered. See PhRMA. 2022. Special 201 Submission 2022. https://www.phrma.org/resource-center/Topics/Intellectual-Property/PhRMA-Special-301-Submission-2022.

recognise the approval processes of regulators in other jurisdictions. Their reasons for doing so may relate to concerns about technical capacity. However, their actions have not benefitted individual vaccine recipients. As an opportunity to provide a clear benefit to individual patients and consumers, harmonisation of limited recognition of regulatory approval in other jurisdictions for vaccines in emergency situations such as a global pandemic might be a good place to start.

So, how effective has harmonisation been? In large part, that question depends on the perspective of the viewer. For industry, whose interests have been privileged throughout the harmonisation processes, it may well be that harmonisation is working out exactly as planned. The industry has benefitted from protection of its commercial interests and profitability, consistent with the overt pro-industry approach taken in TRIPS, and the less obvious, but largely related, safety harmonisation agenda.

From the perspective of governments re-engaging with public health in a pandemic, however, the answer may be somewhat different. In allowing the establishment of global systems, which effectively subjugate public health interests to those of private industry, States—even those who host pharmaceutical multinationals—are increasingly finding themselves in positions of vulnerability vis-à-vis those corporations. If nothing else, the COVID-19 pandemic illustrates the need for the purposes and objectives of harmonisation to be recast from a broader, public health perspective, in its aftermath, and provides some salutary lessons for states considering their position on the mooted pandemic treaty.

References

Abbott, Frederick M. 2002. The Doha declaration on the TRIPS agreement and public health: lighting a dark corner at the WTO. *Journal of International Economic Law* 5(2): 469

Abraham, John, and Courtney Davis. 2020. International and Temporal Comparative Analysis of U.K. and U.S. Drug Safety Regulation in Changing Political Contexts. *Social science & medicine* 255:1-10 https://doi.org/10.1016/j.socscimed.2020.113005

Alford, William P. 1996. Making the World Safe for What: Intellectual Property Rights, Human Rights and Foreign Economic Policy in the Post-European Cold War World. *New York Journal of International Law & Policy* 29: 135

Archibugi, Daniele and Andrea Filippetti. 2010. The Globalisation of Intellectual Property Rights: Four Learned Lessons and Four Theses. *Global Policy* 1(2): 137, 143

Ariff, Mohamed, Farrar, John, and Khalid, Ahmed. 2012. *Regulatory failure and the global financial crisis: An Australian perspective.* Cheltenham: Edward Elgar Publishing

Avorn, Jerry. 2015. The $2.6 billion pill—methodologic and policy considerations. *New England Journal of Medicine* 372(20): 1877

Backman, Gunilla, Paul Hunt, Rajat Khosla, Camila Jaramillo-Strouss, Belachew Mekuria Fikre, Caroline Rumble, David Pevalin. 2008. Health systems and the right to health: an assessment of 194 countries. *The Lancet* 372(9655) : 2047

Baird, Sean. 2013. Magic and Hope: Relaxing TRIPS-Plus Provisions to Promote Access to Affordable Pharmaceuticals. *Boston College journal of law & social justice* 33(1): 107

Berkley, Seth. 2020. COVAX explained. https://www.gavi.org/vaccineswork/covax-explained

Black, Julia. 2001. Decentring regulation: Understanding the role of regulation and self-regulation in a 'post-regulatory' world. *Current legal problems* 54(1): 103

Braithwaite, John, and Drahos, Peter. 2000. *Global Business Regulation*. Cambridge, Melbourne: Cambridge University Press

Braithwaite, John, Cary Coglianese and David Levi-Faur. 2007. Can regulation and governance make a difference? *Regulation & Governance* 1(1): 1

Breyer, Stephen. 1998. Typical Justifications for regulation. In *A Reader on Regulation*, eds. Robert Baldwin, Colin Scott, Christopher Hood. Oxford University Press, pg 59

Daniel Carpenter, *Reputation and Power: Organizational Image and Pharmaceutical Regulation at the FDA* (Princeton University Press, 2014)

Cockburn, Iain & Genia Long. 2015. The importance of patents to innovation: updated cross-industry comparisons with biopharmaceuticals. *Expert Opinion on Therapeutic Patents* 25(7):739-742

Cohen, Fredric J. 2005. Macro trends in pharmaceutical innovation. *Nature Reviews Drug Discovery* 4(1): 78

DiMasi, Joseph, Ronald Hansen and Henry Grabowski. 2003. The Price of Innovation: New Estimates of Drug Development Costs. *Journal of Health Economics* 22: 151

DiMasi, Joseph A., and Henry G. Grabowski. 2021. R&D costs and returns to new drug development: a review of the evidence. In *The Oxford Handbook of the economics of the biopharmaceutical industry*, eds. Patricia M Danzon and Sean Nicolson. Oxford University Press, pg 21

Drahos, Peter. 1995. Global property rights in information: the story of TRIPS at the GATT. *Prometheus* 13(1): 6

Drahos, Peter. 2004. Intellectual property and pharmaceutical markets: a nodal governance approach. *Temple Law Review* 77(22): 401

Drahos, Peter and John Braithwaite. 2004. Hegemony based on knowledge: the role of intellectual property *Law in Context* 21(1): 204

Drahos, Peter, Buddhima Lokuge, Tom Faunce, Martyn Goddard, and David Henry. 2004. Pharmaceuticals, Intellectual Property and Free Trade: The Case of the U.S.-Australia Free Trade Agreement. *Prometheus* 22(3): 243–257

Dutfield, Graham, and Uma Suthersanen. 2005. 'Harmonisation or differentiation in intellectual property protection? The lessons of history. *Prometheus* 23(2): 131

Dutfield, Graham. 2021. *That High Design of Purest Gold*: A *Critical History of the Pharmaceutical Industry, 1880–2020. New Jersey: World Scientific;* Babar, Zaheer-Ud-Din ed. *Pharmaceutical prices in the 21st century*. Springer

Eccleston-Turner, Mark, and Harry Upton. 2021. International Collaboration to Ensure Equitable Access to Vaccines for COVID-19: The ACT-Accelerator and the COVAX Facility. *The Milbank Quarterly* 99(2): 426

El Said, Mohammed. 2022. The Impact of 'TRIPS-Plus' Rules on the Use of TRIPS Flexibilities: Dealing with the Implementation Challenges. In *Access to Medicines and Vaccines*, eds. Carlos M *Correa* and Reto M *Hilty. Spring Nature,* 297

Eisenberg, Rebecca. 2003. Patents, Product Exclusivity, and Information Dissemination: How Law Directs Biopharmaceutical R&D. *Fordham Law Review* 72: 477

Farrar, John. 2010. The global financial crisis and the governance of financial institutions. *Australian Journal of Corporate Law.* 24 (3): 227-243

Farrar, John. 2019. Billion Dollar Bonfires: A Comparative Study of Regulatory Failure in the Non-Bank Finance Sector in Australia and New Zealand. *New Zealand Business Law Quarterly*. 25(2): 213-223

Farrar, John and Mayes, David. 2013. *Globalisation, the global financial crisis and the State.* Cheltenham: Edward Elgar Publishing

Farrar, John, and Louise Parsons, 2012. Globalisation, the global financial crisis and the reinvention of the State. *Singapore Academy of Law* 24: 367-404

Farrar, John, and Louise Parsons. 2013. Globalisation, the GFC and Paradigm Shift. Banking & Financial Services Policy Report, 32(12): 14-21

Fidler, David P. 2020. The COVID-19 Pandemic, Geopolitics, and International Law. *Journal of International Humanitarian Legal Studies* 11(2): 237

Gamble, Andrew. 2014. Ideologies of governance. In *Handbook of the international political economy of governance*, eds. Anthony Payne and Nicola Phillips. Cheltenham: Edward Elgar, pg 13
Gaudilliere, Jean-Paul. 2021. Pharmaceutical innovation and its crisis: drug markets, screening, and the dialectics of value. *BioSocieties* 16(3): 411
Gostin, Lawrence O. 2021. 9 steps to end COVID-19 and prevent the next pandemic: essential outcomes from the World Health Assembly. *JAMA Health Forum* 2(6). https://doi.org/10.1001/jamahealthforum.2021.1852
Gunningham, Neil (2015). Two cheers for prescription? Lessons for the red tape reduction agenda. *University of New South Wales Law Journal* 38(3): 936
Hancher, Leigh and Michael Moran. 1998. Organizing Regulatory Space. In *A Reader on Regulation*, eds. Robert Baldwin, Colin Scott, and Christopher Hood. Oxford: Oxford University Press, 148
Hartwick, Elaine, and Richard Peet. 2003. Neoliberalism and nature: The case of the WTO. *The Annals of the American Academy of Political and Social Science* 590(1): 188
Hawkins, Benjamin and Chris Holden. 2016. A corporate veto on health policy? Global constitutionalism and investor–state dispute settlement. *Journal of Health Politics, Policy, and Law* 41(5): 969
Illingworth, Patricia. 2020. Giving Well: Philanthropy for Human Rights. In *Dimensions of Poverty: Measurement, Epistemic Injustices, Activism*, eds. Valentin Beck, Henning Hahn, Robert Lepenies. Cham: Spring Nature.
Amy Kapczynski. 2021. Realizing Public Rights Through Government Patent Use. *Journal of Law, Medicine & Ethics* 49(1): 34-38
Kelsey, Jane. 2019a. The Trans-Pacific Partnership Agreement and the Regional Comprehensive Economic Partnership: A Battleground for Competing Hegemons. In *Free Trade Agreements*. Singapore: Springer, pg 11
Kelsey, Jane. 2019b. The Trans-Pacific Partnership Agreement and the Regional Comprehensive Economic Partnership: A Battleground for Competing Hegemons. In *Free Trade Agreements*. Singapore: Springer
Kickbusch, Ilona and Anna Holzscheiter. 2021. Can geopolitics derail the pandemic treaty? *British Medical Journal* 375: 1-4. https://doi.org/10.1136/bmj-2021-069129.
Kingsford Smith, Dimity. 2002. What Is Regulation – A Reply to Julia Black. *Australasian Journal of Legal Philosophy* 27: 37
Koop, Christel, and Martin Lodge. 2017. What is regulation? An interdisciplinary concept analysis. *Regulation & Governance* 11(1): 95
Kruk, Margaret E., Anna D Gage, Catherine Arsenault, Keely Jordan, Hannah Leslie, Sanam Roder-DeWan, and Olusoji Adeyi. 2018. High-quality health systems in the Sustainable Development Goals era: time for a revolution. *The Lancet Global Health* 6(11): 1196.
Labonté, Ronald, Mary Wiktorowicz, Corinne Packer, Arne Ruckert, Kumanan Wilson, and Sam Halabi. 2021. A pandemic treaty, revised international health regulations, or both? *Globalisation and Health* 17(1): 1
Laffont, Jean-Jacques, and Jean Tirole. 1991. The Politics of Government Decision-making: A Theory of Regulatory Capture. *Quarterly Journal of Economics* 106(4): 1089
Levi-Faur, David. 2009. Regulatory capitalism and the reassertion of the public interest. *Policy and Society* 27(3): 181
Levi-Faur, David. 2013. The odyssey of the regulatory state: From a "thin" monomorphic concept to a "thick" and polymorphic concept. *Law & Policy* 35(1-2): 29
Light, Donald W. and Rebecca Warburton. 2011. Demythologizing the high costs of pharmaceutical research. *BioSocieties* 6(1): 34
Macleod Sonia, and Sweta Chakraborty. 2019. *Pharmaceutical and Medical Device Safety: A Study in Public and Private Regulation*. Oxford. Hart Publishing.
Maisonrouge, Jaques G. 1981. Regulation of international information flows. *The Information Society* 1(1): 17

Maynard, Alan, and Karen Bloor. 2015. Regulation of the Pharmaceutical Industry: Promoting Health or Protecting Wealth? *Journal of the Royal Society of Medicine* 108(6): 220–222
McBride, Bronwen, Sarah Hawkes and Kent Buse. 2019. Soft power and global health: the sustainable development goals (SDGs) era health agendas of the G7, G20 and BRICS. *BMC Public Health* 19(1): 815.
McMahon, Aisling. 2021. Global equitable access to vaccines, medicines and diagnostics for COVID-19: The role of patents as private governance. *Journal of Medical Ethics* 47(3): 142
Miller, Toby. 2021. *A COVID charter, a better world.* Rutgers University Press
National Academies of Sciences, Engineering, and Medicine. 2020. *Regulating Medicines in a Globalized World: The Need for Increased Reliance Among Regulators.* Washington, DC: The National Academies Press. https://doi.org/10.17226/25594
Mirchandani, Prakash. 2020. Health care supply chains: COVID-19 challenges and pressing actions. *Annals of Internal Medicine* 173(4): 300
Philip Mirowski. 2013. *Never let a serious crisis go to waste: How neoliberalism survived the financial meltdown.* London: Verso Books
Mitchell, Andrew D., and Voon, Tania. The TRIPS waiver as a recognition of public health concerns in the WTO. In *Incentives for Global Public Health: Patent Law and Access to Essential Medicines*, Pogge, Thomas., Rimmer, Matthew., and Rubenstein, Kim (Eds). Cambridge University Press, 56
Moon, Suerie, and Ilona Kickbusch. 2021. A pandemic treaty for a fragmented global polity. *The Lancet Public Health* 6(6): 335-336. https://doi.org/10.1016/S2468-2667(21)00103-1
Morgan, Steve, Paul Grootendorst, Joel Lexchin, Colleen Cunningham, and Devon Greyson. 2011. The cost of drug development: a systematic review. *Health policy* 100(1): 4
Murthy, Divya. 2001. The future of compulsory licensing: deciphering the Doha Declaration on the TRIPS Agreement and public health. *American International University Law Review* 17(6): 1299
Soudias, Dimitris (Plehwe, Dieter, Quinn Slobodian and Philip Mirowski (eds.)). 2021. Nine Lives of Neoliberalism. *Journal of Cultural Economy* 14(1): 117–121
Ozawa, Sachiko, and Meghan L Stack. 2013. Public trust and vaccine acceptance-international perspectives. *Human Vaccines & Immunotherapeutics* 9(8): 1774
Padmanabhan, Arjun. 2021. Coronavirus, Compulsory Licensing, and Collaboration: Analyzing the 2020 Global Vaccine Response with 20/20 Hindsight. *Texas Intellectual Property Law Journal* 30: 75-119
Pammolli, Fabio, Laura Magazzini and Massimo Riccaboni. 2011. The productivity crisis in pharmaceutical R&D. *Nature Reviews Drug discovery* 10(6): 428
Paradise, Jordan. 2020. COVID-IP: staring down the Bayh–Dole Act with 2020 vision. *Journal of Law and the Biosciences* 7(1): Issa073
Phelan, Alexandra L., Mark Eccleston-Turner, Michelle Rourke, Allan Maleche and Chenguang Wang. 2020. Legal agreements: barriers and enablers to global equitable COVID-19 vaccine access. *The Lancet* 396(10254): 800
Rimmer, Matthew. 2021. The People's Vaccine: Intellectual Property, Access to Essential Medicines, and the Coronavirus COVID-19. *Journal of Intellectual Property Studies* 1:1
Rimmer, Matthew. 2020. *The Trans-Pacific Partnership: Intellectual Property and Trade in the Pacific Rim.* Edward Elgar; Kelsey, Jane. 2019
Rizvi, Zain. 2021. Pfizer's Power. Public Citizen. https://www.citizen.org/article/pfizers-power
Ritchie, Hannah, Edouard Mathieu, Lucas Rodés-Guirao, Cameron Appel, Charlie Giattino, Esteban Ortiz-Ospina, Joe Hasell, Bobbie Macdonald, Diana Beltekian and Max Roser. 2020. Coronavirus Pandemic (COVID-19). OurWorldInData.org. https://ourworldindata.org/coronavirus
Röttger-Wirtz, Sabrina. 2021. *The Interplay of Global Standards and E.U. Pharmaceutical Regulation: The International Council for Harmonisation.* London: Hart Studies in Law and Health

Sciacchitano, Salvatore, and Armando Bartolazzi. 2021. Transparency in negotiation of European union with big pharma on COVID-19 vaccines. *Frontiers in Public Health* 9: 95
Sell, Susan K. 2003. *Private Power, Public Law: The Globalisation of Intellectual Property Rights*. Cambridge University Press
Sell, Susan K. 2007. TRIPS-plus free trade agreements and access to medicines. *Liverpool Law Review* 28(1): 41
Sell, Susan K. 2011. Structures, Agents and Institutions: Private Corporate Power and the Globalisation of Intellectual Property Rights. In *Non-State Actors and Authority in the Global System*, eds. Andreas Bieler, Richard Higgett and Geoffrey Underhill. London: Routledge
Slaughter, Anne-Marie. 2000. Governing the global economy through government networks. In *The role of law in international politics: essays in international relations and international law*, ed. Michael Byers. Oxford University Press, 181
Slaughter, Anne-Marie. 2009. *A New World Order*. Princeton University Press; Mirowski, Philip, and Dieter Plehwe eds. 2009. *The road from Mont Pèlerin: The making of the neoliberal thought collective*. Cambridge Massachusetts: Harvard University Press.
Stein, Felix. 2021. Risky business: COVAX and the financialization of global vaccine equity. *Globalisation and Health* 17(1): 1
Stephenson, Joan. 2021. Unequal access to COVID-19 vaccines leaves less-wealthy countries more vulnerable, poses threat to global immunity *JAMA Health Forum* 2(3)
Stevis-Gridneff, Matina, Margot Sanger-Katz, and Noah Weiland. 2021. A European Official Reveals a Secret: The U.S. Is Paying more for Coronavirus vaccines. The New York Times. https://www.nytimes.com/2020/12/18/upshot/coronavirus-vaccines-prices-europe-united-states.html
Stigler, George J. 1971. The Theory of Economic Regulation. *The Bell Journal of Economics* 2(1): 3–21
Sun, Haochen. 2004. The road to Doha and beyond: Some reflections on the TRIPS agreement and public health. *European journal of international law* 15(1): 123
Sundaram, Jae. 2015. Analysis of TRIPS Agreement and the justification of international IP rights protection in the WTO's multilateral trading system, with particular reference to pharmaceutical patents. *Information & Communications Technology Law* 24(2): 121-163
t Hoen, Ellen. 2002. TRIPS, Pharmaceutical Patents, and Access to Essential Medicines: A Long Way from Seattle to Doha. *Chicago Journal of International Law* 3: 27, 43
Tim R. 2019. Winning and losing in investor–state dispute settlement. *American Business Law Journal* 56(1): 115-175
Tobin, John. 2012. *The right to health in international law*. New York: Oxford University Press
Turner, J. Rick. 2019. The International Council for Harmonisation and a Case Study in Regulatory Science. *Therapeutic Innovation & Regulatory Science* 53(5): 561. https://doi.org/10.1177/2168479019869740
Urias, Eduardo and Shyama V. Ramani. 2020. Access to medicines after TRIPS: Is compulsory licensing an effective mechanism to lower drug prices? A review of the existing evidence. *Journal of International Business Policy* 3: 367
Vergara, Raymond John D., Philip Joseph D. Sarmiento, and James Darwin N. Lagman. 2021. Building public trust: a response to COVID-19 vaccine hesitancy predicament. *Journal of Public Health* 43(2): 291
Vogel, David. 1998. The globalisation of pharmaceutical regulation. *Governance* 11(1): 1
Weissman, Robert. 2004. A Long, Strange TRIPS: The Pharmaceutical Industry Drive to Harmonize Global Intellectual Property Rules, and the Remaining WTO Legal Alternatives Available to Third World Countries. *University of Pennsylvania journal of international economic law* 25(3): 1079–1132
Wells, Louis T., and Ahmed, Rafiq. 2007. *Making foreign investment safe: property rights and national sovereignty*. Oxford University Press
Wijesinghe, Sanath, Chaminya Adikari, and Ruwanthika Ariyaratna. 2022. The proposal for waiver of WTO's TRIPS Agreement to prevent, contain and treat COVID-19: investigating the benefits

and challenges for low-and middle-income countries. *Journal of Intellectual Property Law & Practice* 17(2): 179-192

World Health Organisation. 2017. Access to Medicines: making market forces serve the poor (10 year review). https://www.who.int/publications/10-year-review/chapter-medicines.pdf

World Health Organisation. 2021. Strategy to Achieve Global Covid-19 Vaccination by mid-2022. https://www.who.int/publications/m/item/strategy-to-achieve-global-covid-19-vaccination-by-mid-2022

Wouters, Olivier J., Kenneth C Shadlen, Maximilian Salcher-Konrad, Andrew J Pollard, Heidi J Larson, Yot Teerawattananon and Mark Jit. 2021. Challenges in ensuring global access to COVID-19 vaccines: production, affordability, allocation, and deployment. *The Lancet* 397(10278): 1023

Yu, Peter K. 2013. The objectives and principles of the TRIPS agreement. In *The Regulation of Services and Intellectual Property*, eds. Markus Krajewski and Bryan C Mercurio. Routledge

Yu, Peter K. 2021. Realigning TRIPS-plus negotiations with UN Sustainable Development Goals. In *Intellectual Property and Sustainable Markets*, eds. Ole-Andreas Rognstad and Inger B Ørstavik. Edward Elgar Publishing, 38

Zaman, Khorsed. 2022. The Waiver of Certain Intellectual Property Rights Provisions of the TRIPS for the Prevention, Containment and Treatment of COVID-19: A Review of the Proposal under WTO Jurisprudence. *European Journal of Risk Regulation* 13(2): 1–19. https://doi.org/10.1017/err.2021.60

Chapter 6
The Criss-Cross of Ageing and Globalisation

Vai Io Lo

Abstract Amid the trend of globalisation, the proportions of aged populations in various parts of the world are rising. Population ageing and globalisation are not two completely discrete phenomena. Instead, population ageing and globalisation are interconnected currents in contemporary times. This chapter examines the intersection of ageing and globalisation and explores the law and policy implications for the international community.

6.1 Introduction

'Globalisation' is an omnipresent but derivative word. Despite its extensive usage everywhere, the definition of 'globalisation' depends on the relevant context. That is to say, 'globalisation' can refer to a wide range of interactional activities or developments beyond the boundaries of nation-states, such as trade and foreign investment, migration and movement of people, flow of capital, and diffusion of knowledge and technology. Nonetheless, two essential attributes of globalisation are globality (the world as a whole)[1] and interconnectivity (related rather than isolated). For discussion purposes, 'globalisation' here refers to the interaction and the consequential interconnectedness of people, things, events, phenomena, and developments around the world. Amid globalisation, population ageing is one of the most significant trends of the twenty-first century.[2] A society is 'ageing' because the percentage of people aged

[1] See Robertson (1992).

[2] United Nations Population Fund ('UNFPA') and HelpAge International. 2012. Ageing in the Twentieth-First Century: A Celebration and A Challenge. 12.

V. I. Lo (✉)
Faculty of Law, Bond University, Gold Coast, Queensland, Australia
e-mail: vlo@bond.edu.au

U. Ghori et al. (eds.), *Globalisation in Transition*,
https://doi.org/10.1007/978-981-99-2439-4_6

60 and over in its total population is expanding vis-à-vis the younger generations.[3] 'Ageing' is more than a national issue—it is a phenomenon that is happening across the globe and generates common issues among different cultures, economies, polities, and societies. Population ageing and globalisation are not two completely discrete, parallel phenomena in contemporary times. Instead, ageing and globalisation intersect with each other. Although the economic and social impacts of globalisation on ageing can be ascertained more easily than it can be vice versa, population ageing also affects the scope, direction, and progress of globalisation. In other words, population ageing and globalisation can synergistically develop to effect reciprocal impact. This chapter, therefore, examines the intersection of ageing and globalisation and explores the law and policy implications for the international community.

6.2 Population Ageing Around the World

By 2050, one in five persons in the world will be aged 60 and over (a total of two billion older persons).[4] Thirty-three countries are expected to have ten million persons aged 60 and over, including five countries with more than 50 million older persons.[5] Besides, older persons will constitute more than 30% of the respective populations of 64 countries.[6] In fact, the number of centenarians is projected to increase from fewer than 316,600 in 2011 to 3.2 million in 2050.[7] Population ageing resulting from increased life expectancy[8] and declined fertility rate[9] is occurring in both developed and developing countries. In 2012, Europe in the developed world had the largest proportion of older persons,[10] whereas population ageing is progressing more quickly in developing countries.[11] Consequently, one question is whether the world is prepared and ready for this demographic shift.

[3] Although the retirement age varies from country to country and the aged population can be subdivided into such categories as 'youngest old' and 'oldest old'. The United Nations uses 60 years old as the threshold. Ibid., 20.

[4] UNFPA and HelpAge International. 2012. n 2, 12 and 19.

[5] Ibid., 19.

[6] Ibid., 23.

[7] Ibid., 26.

[8] In 2010–2015, life expectancy is 78 years in developed countries and 68 years in developing countries. By 2045–2050, life expectancy is expected to be 83 years in developed regions and 74 years in developing regions. Increased life expectancy stems mainly from improved nutrition, sanitation, health care, education, and economic well-being. Ibid., 12.

[9] The fertility rate dropped by half from five children per woman in 1950–1955 to 2.5 children per woman in 2010–2015. Ibid., 21.

[10] In 2012, 6% of the population in Africa was 60 years and over, compared with 10 percent in Latin America and the Caribbean, 11 percent in Asia, 15 percent in Oceania, 19 percent in Northern America, and 22 percent in Europe. Ibid., 22.

[11] At present, almost two in three persons aged 60 and over live in developing countries, but by 2050, almost four in five aged persons will live in developing countries. Ibid., 21.

As a rule, adults are divided into the groups of 'young', 'middle-aged', and 'old', based on chronological age. However, older persons do not constitute a homogeneous group because apart from personality and family and social backgrounds, experiences and vicissitudes across their lives have a cumulative impact on them. In general, older persons have a wealth of experience, so their wisdom is welcome in many situations. 'Youngest old' persons can take care of grandchildren and relatives who are sick or disabled. The pensions of some older persons can also be a source of income for low-income, three-generation families. Older persons have made various contributions that enable society to become what it is today. After retirement, older persons continue making contributions to society by playing the roles of mediators, educators, volunteers, guardians of culture, and political activists.[12] Certainly, increased longevity is one of the greatest achievements of humankind.[13] Nonetheless, the demographic shift resulting from population ageing has also generated cultural, social, and economic challenges, impinging on human rights and societal responsibility.

Although age does not define a person, ageism is prevalent in many societies. Ageism, a term coined by Robert N. Butler, is 'prejudice of one age group toward the other age groups'.[14] It is true that older generations also have prejudices toward younger generations, but in most cases, it is the younger persons who hold prejudices toward older persons. Prior to the twentieth century, old age was viewed either neutrally or predominately positively, because older persons played an important role in intergenerational homes and had the power to control the testamentary distribution of agrarian land.[15] However, at the turn of the twentieth century, there was an attitudinal shift to an increasingly negative view, because old age was gradually linked with physical and mental sickness, people were engrossed in efficiency engendered by industrialisation, and there was an increasing association between new technology and youth.[16] The negative view has resulted in misconceptions and stereotypes about persons who have attained advanced chronological age. For example, many people think that older persons cannot be productive due to cognitive and physical degeneration; older persons put a heavy strain on societal resources, despite the fact that many older persons are wealthy; and older persons are conservative, outdated, and burdensome. These kinds of misconceptions and stereotypes caused many younger persons to have dismissive attitudes toward the elderly. Even so, ageism is seldom confronted by social sanction.

With a negative view of ageing, many people forget that ageing is a natural stage in a person's life course. They dread becoming old and try to stay young by all possible means. For this reason, goods and services for maintaining youthfulness and cosmetic surgeries to remove discernible traces of ageing always have a steady stream of consumers. Even worse, many older persons believe that they are 'over

[12] Ibid., 35.

[13] Ibid., 12.

[14] Butler (1969), 243.

[15] Whitton (1997), 462.

[16] Ibid., 462–463.

the hill', so it is acceptable for younger generations to treat them differently or to ignore them. In fact, many older persons internalise ageism, probably as a result of cognitive dissonance, and conduct themselves in line with misconceptions and stereotypes about old age, which, in turn, has created a vicious cycle in promoting and nourishing ageism. The magnitude of ageism, whether it is overt or covert, varies from society to society. In any case, ageism has detrimental impacts on a society.

One harmful consequence of ageism is societal segregation, whether it is physical or mental, because of the 'us versus them' way of thinking. A segregated society resulting from misconceptions and stereotypes about a particular group will result in the exclusion of, and discrimination against, the target group. Regrettably, it is more often younger persons who exclude and discriminate against older persons than the other way around. Thus, if public policies and private decisions are made as a result of ageism, the livelihood and wellbeing of older persons will be negatively affected. For example, it is common knowledge that many people who have died of COVID-19 are elderly persons. This tragedy raises the question of how much weight is given by policymakers in various societies to protect the human rights of older persons in formulating and implementing countermeasures. Similarly, the fact that there is a shortage of healthcare professionals who are willing to specialise in gerontology and geriatrics[17] poses the question of whether ageism is an underlying factor despite the upward trend of population ageing worldwide. In this connection, it is notable that ageist biases among healthcare professionals can be found in clinical decision making or resource allocation. For example, some doctors believe that medical interventions for elderly persons are futile[18]; healthcare professionals prioritise young patients[19]; the treatment bias toward younger patients is strong in mental health services[20]; and older patients are often undertreated because signs of illnesses are misdiagnosed as part of normal ageing.[21] Apparently, the justification for the differential treatment of old and young patients is that the scarcity of health resources necessitates rationing.[22]

At the individual level, ageism results in the social exclusion of, and discrimination against, older persons in various circumstances. Simply stated, older persons are prevented from continuously and actively participating in society and from receiving the entitlements they should deserve. For example, an older person may be denied

[17] For example, one study found that there should be 0.4 full-time equivalent of geriatrician time per 10,000 persons in Australia. Commerford (2018); In 2016, there were 619 geriatricians employed in Australia, 95% of whom were clinicians, and there was an average of 2.4 clinicians per 100,000 population across Australia. Department of Health. 2017. Geriatric Medicine: 2106 Factsheet. https://hwd.health.gov.au/resources/publications/factsheet-mdcl-geriatric-2016.pdf. Accessed 4 March 2022; Similarly, the American Geriatrics Society reported that there was one geriatrician for every 2,600 persons aged 75 and over in the U.S. UNFPA. 2012. n 2, 73.

[18] Whitton (1997), 472.

[19] UNFPA and HelpAge International. 2012. n 2, 157.

[20] Whitton (1997), 472.

[21] The participants in a consultation project were told that their health issue was 'part of the old-age disease' that could not be treated. UNFPA and HelpAge International. 2019. n 2, 137.

[22] See Shortt (2001), 1.

the opportunity to acquire new vocational skills solely on the basis of their chronological age, or an older person may not be able to receive timely healthcare due to the scarcity of gerontological professionals. In a study conducted in multiple countries, some older persons who participated in consultations had lost their jobs due to mandatory retirement ages and had experienced age discrimination when they attempted to re-enter the job market.[23] Likewise, some older persons complained that age discrimination limited their access to credit facilities, so they found it difficult to set up a business.[24]

As a matter of fact, exclusion and discrimination often lead to apathy toward, as well as neglect and abuse of, older persons. That is, when younger persons are apathetic toward older persons, they pay little attention to the welfare of older persons, let alone the respect that older persons would like to receive. Elder abuse, whether it is physical violence, verbal denigration, sexual assault, emotional harm, or financial exploitation, is so common that the United Nations ('UN') officially recognised the World Elder Abuse Aware Day. In a study of elder abuse conducted in Europe, the World Health Organization estimated that millions of persons aged 60 and above suffered abuses every year, including physical abuse (4 million), sexual abuse (1 million), mental abuse (29 million), and financial abuse (6 million).[25] If older persons feel isolated and helpless due to social exclusion and neglect, they will lose a sense of belonging in the community. Coupled with other factors, such as poverty and poor health, older persons may end their lives earlier than expected. In fact, the suicide rates of older persons are not negligible.[26]

On the economic side, the priority concerns are whether societies have sufficient capacities to provide for the economic needs of older persons while maintaining intergenerational equity in terms of resource allocation, and whether older persons have affordable access to preventive, curative, and long term healthcare. Income security is of crucial importance to older persons. One recurrent question is whether the welfare state model, privatised/individualised retirement schemes, or both should be adopted to provide retirees with pensions. One study revealed that only one-third of countries had established comprehensive social protection schemes, which covered mainly persons in formal employment.[27] Besides, only one in five persons of today's older population has a pension.[28] Hence, older persons who do not have access to social insurance need to rely on personal savings or the support of family members or relatives. However, the structural change of many contemporary families, namely, from extended to nuclear families, has made it necessary for society to play a larger role

---

[23] UNFPA and HelpAge International. 2012. n 2, 59.

[24] Ibid.

[25] World Health Organization Regional Office for Europe. 2011. *European Report on Preventing Elder Maltreatment* 13.

[26] According to the American Association for Marriage and Family Therapy ('AAMFT'), older adults constitute 12% of the U.S. population but account for 18% of all suicide deaths. AAMFT. 2022. Suicide in the Elderly. https://www.aamft.org/AAMFT/Consumer_Updates/Suicide_in_the_Elderly.aspx. Accessed 13 March 2022.

[27] UNFPA and HelpAge International. 2012. n 2, 14.

[28] Ibid., 45.

in the care and support of older persons. In this regard, it is notable that older women are more vulnerable because although they tend to have stronger social networks than older men, they face cumulative effects of gender discrimination throughout their lives,[29] such as receiving smaller amounts of pensions. Thus, governments must establish institutional arrangements to provide basic social insurance for older persons, taking into consideration the needs of the disadvantaged.

Even if a social security system has been established, one controversial question is whether the contributions made by younger persons are sufficient to cover pensions distributed to the ever-expanding population of retirees. To prepare for the possible shortage of finances, some countries have raised the retirement age, reduced the amounts or types of benefits, increased contributions, or radically changed the system design.[30] Whether or not these initiatives are sound and effectual remains to be seen. Although some older persons have personal savings, the income security of most older persons hinges on the availability and sustainability of pensions, whether they are contributory or non-contributory schemes. Hence, many governments are under financial pressure to guarantee the livelihood of older persons.

Apart from the sustainability of a social security system, the availability of affordable healthcare is essential to the physical and emotional wellbeing of older persons. If the cost of healthcare is high, many older persons will not be able to access the necessary healthcare or may forego healthcare in order to maintain a comfortable living style. Similarly, older persons need suitable housing and convenient transportation to accommodate their needs so that they can continue to live independently. For these reasons, the necessary institutional arrangements and their concomitant costs, such as the availability of geriatric clinics, the training of gerontological professionals and community-based caregivers, the quantity and quality of long-term care facilities, and the provision of public and community-based transportation services, must be factored into the fiscal policy and financial budget of each society.

Accordingly, population ageing will be a pressing issue for many countries and for the whole world. The challenges arising from population ageing are multifaceted, including ageism, social segregation, age discrimination, elder abuse and neglect, the availability and sustainability of pension schemes, and the accessibility of healthcare, elder housing, and reliable transportation. At the national level, it is imperative for governments to formulate policies, rules, and measures to manage population ageing proactively and effectively, including such matters as the establishment of a social insurance system; training of family, community-based and professional caregivers; investment in geriatric and gerontological research; construction of facilities for rehabilitative and long-term care; and organisation of educational and cultural events to eliminate ageism. Internationally, one question is what the international community may do in terms of law and policy to address the challenges arising from population ageing amid the trend of globalisation.

[29] Ibid., 28.

[30] Ibid., 46.

6.3 Intersection of Ageing and Globalisation

Apparently, ageing and globalisation are two discrete developments. In reality, ageing and globalisation intersect with each other in various respects. In view of the cultural, social, and economic challenges posed by population ageing, the discussion below focuses on how globalisation plays a role in these challenges.

Nowadays, the flow of knowledge and information because of globalisation facilitates the rapid reach of cultural currents to many distant places in the world. The obsession with youthfulness in one society can spread quickly and unconsciously to other societies through the internet and social media. If movies, TV shows and commercials, popular songs, and even sporting events glorify youthfulness and depict older persons in fragile and abject conditions, ageism will be imparted to younger generations. It is noted that television, news, film, and advertising commonly feature stereotypes of ageing and older persons from the perspectives of decline and diminished value.[31] As discussed above, ageism further begets discrimination and social exclusion, which, in turn, results in the abuse and neglect of older persons who cannot live independently due to physical and cognitive impairments. With the diffusion of information technologies, ageism is no longer confined to a small number of countries. Instead, it has an increasingly global presence. Even so, globalisation can be a double-edged sword. This is because globalisation can also assist in the elimination of ageism through all sorts of communication via mass media.

Additionally, the movement of people across national borders has a definite impact on family as well as on older persons. Urbanisation and globalisation cause younger generations to go to the cities or move overseas to seek more desirable employment opportunities. Thus, older family members stay behind to take care of grandchildren and relatives who are either sick or cannot live independently without assistance. Consequently, there are many 'skipped-generation households'[32] in which grandparents raise small grandchildren while the parents work full-time in distant places. This is especially the case for developing countries because young adults go overseas to earn money to remit home so that the whole family can live in a better condition. For example, male adults in developing countries travel overseas to work as crew members in cruise ships, or as foreign workers in jobs which local people do not want to take, while female adults go overseas to work as house maids or caretakers to earn more income. As a result, many older persons remain active after their formal retirement and continue making contribution to society.

Furthermore, if young professionals can stay permanently in another country after the expiry of their work permits, two problems will arise. First, the possible brain drain of professionals in developing countries will hinder the economic and social developments of their home countries. Second, since adult children often move their parents overseas to join them, older migrants will experience new cultural and linguistic challenges and must learn how to adjust to new physical and political environments. Conversely, globalisation provides retirees in developed countries with

[31] Ibid., 103.

[32] Ibid., 15.

opportunities to move overseas to settle down because it costs them less money to have a comfortable living style overseas than in their home countries. For instance, it was estimated that about one million British expatriates living overseas received a state pension.[33] Hence, globalisation through migration and movement of people across national borders affects older persons in various ways.

In terms of capital flow, the linkages of financial systems around the world create a ripple effect if one major financial market experiences problems. The most obvious example is the Global Financial Crisis ('GFC') of 2008. Simply put, the GFC was triggered by the bursting of the U.S. housing bubble and Lehman Brothers' filing for bankruptcy, which stemmed from predatory lending to low-income homebuyers and excessive risk taking by financial institutions. The consequential significant declines in the value of retirement saving accounts, investments, savings, and land and housing reduced the value of assets that older persons relied on for their retirement.[34] Moreover, the large negative rates of return of various funds[35] caused many retirees to lose their expected levels of income. Meanwhile, some employers reduced or ceased their contributions to employees' retirement schemes in order to retain jobs.[36] In developing countries, the GFC resulted in wage cuts or caps, reduction or removal of subsidies, reform of old age pensions, and increase of consumption taxes.[37] Furthermore, the World Bank's stance on pension reform has influenced national governments and the International Labour Organization in their advocacy of mean-tested first pension and the promotion of individualised and capitalised private pensions.[38] Thus, if development loans contain conditions of privatisation and deregulation, such as the partial privatisation of healthcare and the deregulation of the domestic financial market, older persons will definitely be affected.

As regards trade and investment, ageing and globalisation clearly intersect with each other. Given the growth of ageing populations around the world, it is expected that bilateral or multilateral negotiations over trade in goods, trade in services, and foreign direct investment will take the needs and wants of older persons into consideration. Under the World Trade Organization ('WTO') agreements, regional free trade agreements or bilateral free trade agreements, countries endowed with different material and human resources and at different stages of economic development can trade in goods that can improve the quality of life of older persons, such as assistive apparatuses and health products for older persons, and provide market access to the nationals of member states in relation to long term care facilities, gerontological services, and private insurance schemes. In fact, the World Bank's belief that the public sector is less efficient in managing new infrastructure activities and private actors should take over public services has been endorsed by multinational corporations in their

33 Ibid., 80. Citing Wallop, Harry. 2010. Four in 10 Retirees Want to Live Abroad. The Telegraph (London), March 6.

34 Ibid., 47.

35 Ibid.

36 Ibid.

37 Ibid., 44.

38 Phillipson (2003).

work with the WTO, which has enforced 20 international agreements, including the General Agreement on Trade in Services ('GATS'), which covers banking, insurance, and financial services.[39] In that sense, population ageing will also affect the dynamics of global trade and foreign direct investment.

6.4 Law and Policy Implications for the International Community

With the expansion of older populations across the globe, population ageing is not merely a national issue. Moreover, globalisation has reduced the distances and differences between nation-states. Given the trend of globalisation, developed and developing countries may adopt a more coordinated approach to tackle population ageing worldwide. In view of the challenges arising from population ageing and the intersection of ageing and globalisation, one question is whether the international community can do anything to leverage these two trends. To attempt answering this question, it would be appropriate to examine what the international community has hitherto undertaken to protect the rights of older persons.

In 1982, the First World Assembly on Ageing was held in Vienna. The First Assembly adopted the Vienna Plan of Action on Ageing, which provided a basis for the formulation of policies and programs on ageing and propounded 62 recommendations for action to address such issues as research; data collection and analysis; training and education; and sectoral areas (including health and nutrition, protection of elderly consumers, housing and environment, family, social welfare, income security and employment, and education).[40] In 1990, the UN General Assembly designated 1 October as the International Day of Older Persons by Resolution 45/106.[41] In the following year, the UN General Assembly adopted a set of 18 principles for older persons into their national programs in terms of independence, participation, care, self-fulfillment, and dignity.[42]

In 2002, the Second World Assembly on Ageing was held in Spain, which adopted a Political Declaration and the Madrid International Plan of Action on Ageing. These two international instruments contained commitments from governments to formulate and implement measures to address the challenges arising from population ageing. More than 100 recommendations were propounded for action based on three priority themes: mainstreaming older persons in development, advancing health and

---

[39] Ibid., 3.5.

[40] United Nations. 1982. Report of the World Assembly on Ageing: Vienna 26 July – 6 August 1982. https://www.un.org/esa/socdev/ageing/documents/Resources/VIPEE-English.pdf.

[41] United Nations. 2021. 2021 Theme: Digital Equity for All Ages. https://www.un.org/en/observances/older-persons-day. Accessed 26 February 2022.

[42] United Nations. 1991. United Nations Principles for Older Persons. https://www.ohchr.org/en/professionalinterest/pages/olderpersons.aspx. Accessed 25 February 2022.

wellbeing into old age, and ensuring enabling and supportive environments.[43] The Second Assembly bestowed on the UN Regional Commissions responsibility for translating the Plan of Action into regional action plans.[44] In essence, the Second Assembly urged States to change attitudes, policies and practices so that older persons are viewed as active participants in the development process rather than as welfare beneficiaries.[45] To ascertain how Regional Commissions and Member States had implemented the Madrid Plan of Action, a global review was undertaken in 2010 to appraise the progress regarding national policies and legislation, data and research, and institutional arrangements pertaining to older persons.[46]

In the 2010s, the UN General Assembly resolved to establish the Open-Ended Working Group on Ageing, whose mandate is to strengthen the protection of the human rights of older persons (Resolution 65/182). The Group is to consider the existing international framework for the human rights of older persons, identify possible gaps, and ascertain how best to address them.[47] Accordingly, the Group provides the primary forum for debate over the adoption of a multilateral human rights treaty in relation to the rights of older persons. Until now, the Group has conducted 12 sessions, with the 13th one to be held in April 2023. The latest major initiative of the international community was the introduction of the UN Decade of Healthy Ageing in 2020. The Decade of Healthy Ageing (2021–2030) is a global collaboration aligned with the last ten years of Sustainable Development Goals and focuses on four areas of action: fostering age-friendly environments, combating ageism, integrating curative, rehabilitative and palliative end-of-life care, and providing access to good quality long-term care.[48,49]

Nevertheless, these international initiatives provide only a fragmentary, non-binding plan of action for the protection of the human rights of older persons. The absence of a multilateral convention on the rights of older persons is in stark contrast to the existence of three UN Conventions—Convention on the Rights of the Child

---

[43] United Nations. 2002. Report of the Second World Assembly on Ageing: Madrid, 8–12 April 2002. https://documents-dds-ny.un.org/doc/UNDOC/GEN/N02/397/51/PDF/N0239751.pdf?OpenElement.

[44] Ibid.

[45] UNFPA and HelpAge International. 2012. n 2, 13.

[46] Ibid., 105–131.

[47] United Nations. 2022, Open-Ended Working Group on Ageing for the Purpose of Strengthening the Protection of the Human Rights of Older Persons. https://social.un.org/ageing-working-group/. Accessed 28 February 2022.

[48] World Health Organization. 2022. What is the UN Decade of Healthy Ageing? https://www.who.int/ageing/decade-of-healthy-ageing. Accessed 25 February 2022.

[49] In 2015, the United Nations adopted 17 Sustainable Development Goals to succeed the Millennium Development Goals. The 17 goals were (1) no poverty; (2) zero hunger; (3) good health and well-being; (4) quality education; (5) gender equality; (6) clean water and sanitation; (7) affordable and clean energy; (8) decent work and economic growth; (9) industry, innovation, and infrastructure; (10) reduced inequalities; (11) sustainable cities and communities; (12) responsible consumption and production; (13) climate action; (14) life below water; (15) life on land; (16) peace, justice, and strong institutions; and (17) partnerships for the Goals. Member States were committed to achieve these goals by 2030.

(1989), Convention on the Rights of Persons with Disabilities (2006), and Convention on the Elimination of All Forms of Discrimination against Women (1979)[50]—that protect the rights of children, persons with disabilities, and women. Apart from the Universal Declaration of Human Rights (1948) and the general protection provided by the International Covenant on Civil and Political Rights (1966) and the International Covenant on Economic, Social and Cultural Rights (1966), only the Convention on the Protection of the Rights of All Migrant Workers and Members of Their Families (1990) explicitly forbids discrimination based on age.[51] Likewise, both the Millennium Development Goals[52] and the Sustainable Development Goals do not expressly address the issue of population ageing or the protection of older persons. Thus, despite the fact that older persons constitute a significant vulnerable group and the percentages of aged persons in the total population are rising in various countries, there is not an international convention that can spearhead a paradigm shift from viewing old age negatively to positively and will outline normative standards to protect the human rights of older persons. An international convention is warranted because 'people everywhere must age with dignity and security, enjoying life through the full realisation of all human rights and fundamental freedoms'.[53]

Currently, climate change is the top priority for the humankind to tackle collectively. The evolution of the developments of international environmental law may illustrate the enormous amounts of time and effort for the world to act collectively. From the 1972 UN Conference on the Human Environment (Stockholm Declaration), the 1992 UN Conference on Environment and Development (Rio Declaration), the 1992 UN Framework Convention on Climate Change, the 2002 World Summit on Sustainable Development (Rio + 10), and the 2012 UN Conference on Sustainable Development (Rio + 20) to the 2015 UN Climate Change Conference with the resultant Paris Agreement on greenhouse gas emission mitigation and financial contributions by developed countries, it has taken over 40 years for the international community to reach an agreement in addition to a framework convention. Although climate change affects people of all ages around the world, population ageing will no longer affect older persons only. Population ageing has economic and social impacts on individual societies as well as on the world. In fact, population ageing will probably reach the same level of urgency as climate change in the coming decades.

---

[50] In 2010, the Committee for the Elimination of All Forms of Discrimination against Women (CEDAW) adopted General Recommendation No. 27 to protect the human rights of older women.

[51] International Convention on the Protection of the Rights of All Migrant Workers and Members of Their Families. 1990. Art. 1(1).

[52] Following the Millennium Summit of the United Nations in 2000, Member States were committed to achieve eight Millennium Development Goals by 2015. Those goals were (1) to eradicate extreme poverty and hunger; (2) to achieve universal primary education; (3) to promote gender equality and empower women; (4) to reduce child mortality; (5) to improve maternal health; (6) to combat HIV/AIDS, malaria, and other diseases; (7) to ensure environmental sustainability; and (8) to develop a global partnership for development.

[53] UNFPA and HelpAge International. 2012. n 2, 16.

Against the background of population ageing, globalisation has impacted, and will continue to impact, many aspects of human life. The interaction and interconnectivity of people, events, phenomena, and developments across the globe should be investigated to ascertain how positive and negative mutual impacts between two concurrent trends should be handled. The discussion above has highlighted the intersection of population ageing and globalisation. Accordingly, not only should population ageing be mainstreamed into national plans, but the international community should also integrate ageing into the global development and human rights agendas.[54] In this way, the role of globalisation in overcoming the challenges and utilising the opportunities posed by population ageing and in promoting economic development and human rights protection around the world can be optimised. If the international community has formulated evidence-based policies, concluded a binding international convention on the human rights of older persons, and integrated population ageing into global development plans, signatories to the convention will translate them into domestic policies, laws, and implementation measures in the light of their respective national circumstances. Hence, it is time for the international community to pursue actively and responsibly an international convention on the rights of older persons and to incorporate population ageing into the next round of discussions on Development Goals.

6.5 Conclusion

This chapter is written to honour Professor John Farrar, who has been a dedicated mentor to many doctoral students and junior academics. Apart from corporate governance, he has a strong research interest in globalisation and its potential impact on the humankind. In this respect, it is sensible to discuss the human dimension of globalisation by pinpointing its intersection with population ageing. Around the world, globalisation is gaining momentum in different domains, and so is population ageing in various countries. Even though the COVID-19 pandemic has accelerated through international travel, globalisation is still regarded as the way forward. In contrast to positive connotations associated with globalisation, ageing often carries with it negative connotations. Although it is self-evident that the issues generated by population ageing cannot be solved by policies and legislation alone, well-thought-out policies and effective legal norms are indispensable to any systematic and efficacious management of population ageing. As such, it is time for the international community to examine the interface of ageing and globalisation and explore what can be done under international law to promote mutually beneficial impacts between these two trends. If the international community takes the lead in promoting an 'age-friendly' world, this move will also affect the scope, direction, and progress of globalisation.

[54] Ibid., 105; Phillipson (2003). n 38, 5.10.

References

Butler, Robert N. 1969. Age-Ism: Another Form of Bigotry. *Gerontologist* 9:243–246
Commerford T (2018) Ageing in the Workforce Feature: How Many Geriatricians Should, at Minimum, be Staffing Health Regions in Australia? *Australasian Journal of Ageing* 37(1):17–22
Phillipson, Chris 2003. Globalisation and the Future of Ageing: Developing a Critical Gerontology. *Sociological Research Online* 8(4):3.2. http://www.socresonline.org.uk/8/4/phillipson.html
Robertson, Roland. 1992. *Globalisation: Social Theory and Global Culture.* London: Sage Publications
Shortt, Sam. 2001. Venerable or Vulnerable? Ageism in Health Care. *Journal of Health Service Research and Policy* 6:1–2
Whitton, Linda S. 1997. Ageism, Paternalism and Prejudice. *DePaul Law Review* 46:453–482

Chapter 7
A Peek Behind the Curtain of Anti-aging Science

Michael Lupton

Abstract Age related conditions are the leading causes of death, and the ever-increasing cost of health care. If the rate of ageing could be reduced it would result in enormous medical and financial benefits, thus pursuit of this holy grail could constitute a win–win situation for both governments and individuals if successful. Myriad genes and pathways are known to regulate ageing in model organisms, and this has spawned a new crop of antiaging companies who are investing in this research in the hope of discovering this holy grail. The challenges and pitfalls of commercialization include reliance on findings from short lived model organisms, poor biological understanding of ageing, and hurdles in performing clinical trials for ageing. However, if even one company succeeds, the impact will be huge.

7.1 Introduction

I consider it a great honour to be invited to contribute a chapter to the Festschrift in honour of my dear friend, mentor, and eminent scholar Emeritus Professor John Farrar. John is renowned for his generosity with his time, knowledge, and his collegiality in aiding younger academics. Many students have also benefitted from his immaculate supervision of their theses which molded them as future academics. He happily shared the depth and breadth of his scholarship with me over countless cups of coffee and the many occasions we broke bread together.

Thank you, John.

The dream of fending-off old age is as old as human civilisation itself. There are an ever-increasing number of people worldwide who now fall into the 60-to-70-year age bracket because of improved public health regimes and personal hygiene.[1] The next step is now to advance the ageing regime beyond its current matrix.

[1] Magalhães et al. (2017).

M. Lupton (✉)
Faculty of Law, Bond University, Gold Coast, Australia
e-mail: mlupton@bond.edu.au

U. Ghori et al. (eds.), *Globalisation in Transition*,
https://doi.org/10.1007/978-981-99-2439-4_7

The goal of developing therapies that preserve health in old age and postpone the onset of age-related diseases is more important than ever. A major incentive is the fact that scientific research has been able to retard ageing in animal models.[2] Their next goal is to transfer this knowledge to achieving similar outcomes for humans via genome editing.[3] Research into gerontology has travelled a long and tortuous path to arrive at its present state of relative credibility.[4] At the onset of the research an important challenge was to establish that there was in fact a biology of ageing which could be distinguished from the pathologies of ageing.[5] The next challenge to embark on is to prove that this distinctive biology, rather than being a process of random entropy was sufficiently patterned to be worthy of in-depth research.[6]

This research revealed the fact that there were indeed some consistent themes in cellular ageing for example the accumulation of oxidative damage, impairment of energy and faulty DNA repair, amongst others.[7] With the benefit of this knowledge came the opportunity of intervening in some of these processes, including the possibility of delaying the ageing process. Amongst the interventions which have been trialed are altering a person's caloric intake, their antioxidant capacity plus exposure to glucocorticoids.[8]

The most prominent development in the field of gerontology, however, has been the emergence of molecular medicine which has opened opportunities for the therapeutic transfer of genes.[9] Gene editing has emerged as a powerful new tool for making precise additions, deletions and alterations to the genome which constitutes an organism's complete set of genetic material. The recent discovery of CRISPR/Cas 9 has made editing of the genome much more precise and efficient. It is also less expensive and flexible in comparison to previous editing procedures. For example, CRISPR/Cas 9 creates the possibility of editing somatic cells to restore normal function in diseased organs plus it extends to editing human germline cells to prevent genetic diseases in future children and their descendants. Gene editing can also be used to achieve 'enhancements' i.e., for changes that go beyond mere restoration or protection of health.[10]

The rapidity with which gene editing has advanced since the advent of CRISPR/Cas 9 has raised concerns about whether appropriate systems are in place to govern this technology and whether societal values will be reflected in how genome editing is eventually applied in practice.[11]

---

[2] Kenyon (2010).

[3] Holliday (2006).

[4] Holliday (2007).

[5] Fernandes et al. (2016).

[6] Kennedy et al. (2014).

[7] Ibid.

[8] Hipkissm (2007).

[9] Magalhães et al. (2004).

[10] Boccardi and Herbig (2012).

[11] National Academies of Sciences, Engineering, Medicine (2017a).

The underlying cause of many human diseases such as atherosclerosis, cancer, cardiovascular defects, cataract, diabetes 2, dementia, macular degeneration, osteoporosis, and excessive muscle loss leading to sarcopenia, all have genetic origins.[12]

The optimal treatments for every disease, irrespective of age, is a social and moral necessity. However, it is far more efficient and cheaper to treat the cause of the diseases e.g., 'old age' rather than to apply a cure for each individual disease flowing from old age. This is the ideal solution for maintaining and improving the quality of human life and its dignity in old age.[13] There is copious evidence which proves that the longevity of a species is its ability to maintain and repair the mechanisms which in turn, repair the damage to its functions and combat its wear and tear. These complex processes of maintenance and repair involve hundreds of genes whose products and their interactions give rise to a 'homodynamic space' or buffering capacity, which in turn ultimately determines an individual's chance to survive in a healthy state.[14]

Theoretically at least a fully functional and well maintained homodynamic could make a biological system immortal. Conversely the progressive shrinkage of the homodynamic space is the universal characteristic of ageing.[15]

7.2 Definition of Ageing

Aging can be defined as progressive deterioration of the physiological function accompanied by an increase in vulnerability and mortality due to age.[16]

Aging can also be defined as being characterised by a time dependent functional impairment of the organism in which several molecular pathways have been demonstrated to play a causal role. Current research efforts are directed at specifically targeting these fundamental ageing events because the researchers postulate that intervening in these molecular pathways could delay or prevent age-related diseases and increase a person's lifespan.[17]

The most promising pathway for intervention is tackling telomere shortening, because it has been identified as one of the primary hallmarks of ageing. The preferred therapy for elongating the telomeres de novo is by adding telomeric repeats on the chromosome ends by using an RNA template which prevents telomere erosion, while telomerase is a reverse transcriptase (TERI) that elongates the telomeres.[18]

Telomeres are the protein-bound structures residing at the ends of chromosomes. They shorten with cell division, while age has a similar shortening effect in some tissues. The application of genetic manipulation of the telomerase in mice found

---

[12] Rattan and Singh (2009).

[13] Rattan (2007).

[14] Ibid.

[15] Yonge (2008).

[16] Angelou (2017).

[17] Lapointe and Hekimi (2010).

[18] Campisi et al. (2007).

that overexpression of telomerase in adult mice resulted in 24% increase in median lifespan without increasing the incidence of cancer.[19]

Anti- ageing science, if it passes its clinical trials, will have huge appeal for the advanced age demographic around the world and that, in turn, will translate into tremendous commercial opportunities if the new start-ups in this field can conquer the challenges and pitfalls involved in creating a business model based on the rapidly evolving anti- ageing science.[20]

7.3 Ageing and Death

The leading cause of death and health concerns worldwide, more especially in industrialised countries, are age-related diseases like heart disease, lung cancer, and neurological diseases. Because of this relationship, the benefits arising from anti-ageing science have enormous potential. Using a model of future health spending in the USA, the effect of delaying ageing by 1–2 years would yield USD 1 trillion in savings over a 50-year period, as opposed to addressing single pathologies such as cancer or heart disease. Rational anti-ageing strategies based on scientific evidence aim to slow down the ageing process by preventing and/or delaying physiological decline and regaining lost functional abilities. An approach of this nature may be of a short duration and directed at one body part at a time, alternatively, the intervention may instead be directed against the ageing process itself.

Along with ongoing cell division, almost all normal human cells undergo progressive telomere shortening. Once telomeres reach a critically shortened length, they will induce a DNA damage signal that is often referred to as replicative senescence or cell ageing.[21] Short term interventions include organ replacement, stem cell injections and external supplementation of for example, hormones. These therapies may result in alleviating some problems relating to the deficiencies of old age but do not mitigate the ravages of the ageing process.

Too short telomeres have the potential to unfold from their presumed closed structure. This in turn leads to genomic instability.[22] On the other hand, in order to achieve long term prevention of old age, the patient will be required to embrace effective gene-based therapies to prevent or reduce the rate of shrinkage of the telomeres that occurs because of the accumulation of unrepaired molecular damage.

In order to repair the damaged telomere in certain special cells, a specialised protein called a 'telomerase' has been developed. A telomerase is responsible for elongating telomeres.[23]

---

[19] Rattan and Singh, n 12, 1–10?

[20] Swain (2019), Scott et al. (2015) and Edd (2019).

[21] Dai et al. (2019).

[22] Ibid.

[23] Ibid.

7.4 Current Anti-ageing Treatments

7.4.1 Introduction

The premise contained in the use of gene therapy is to transfer a healthy transgene to replace an existing malfunctioning gene to prevent a disease from occurring or to prevent the adverse consequences of a disease. The aim is to bring about a recovery from the consequences of such a disease. The aim would be to prevent opportunistic diseases from occurring, thereby helping to arrest the ageing process by focusing on the repair and maintenance of cells.[24]

7.4.2 Gene Therapy for Age-Related Diseases

Advancing age is known to affect a person's metabolism. Examples of this are obesity and type 2 diabetes which are known to be linked to signs of premature cell deterioration and ageing. The most common anti-diabetic medication, metformin, has recently been nominated as also having great promise as an anti-ageing drug which also has the potential of reducing a variety of ageing-related disorders such as cardio-metabolic and neurodegenerative types as well as cancer.[25]

Gene therapy-based approaches also have the potential to counter age-related metabolic impairments via the replacement of faulty genes using the CRISPR/Cas 9 technology. The mice treated with this technique also exhibited the restoration and normalization of the skeletal muscles for 4 months after the treatment.[26]

7.4.3 Neurodegenerative Disorders

Gene therapy holds great promise for treating ageing disorders such as Alzheimer's and Parkinson's diseases. Alzheimer's disease (AD) is characterised by progressive deterioration of a sufferer's cognitive functions (dementia) and is the most common ageing associated brain disorder. The symptoms of (AD) are associated with the accumulation of neuro-fibrillary tangles and extracellular amyloid beta (Ab) plaques in the brain. Current therapies are geared to reducing these symptoms in the brain, by way of gene therapy.[27]

---

[24] Bär and Blasco (2016).

[25] Ibid.

[26] De Magalhães, Stevens and Thorton, n.1.

[27] Verdin (2015).

Parkinson's disease (PD) is the second most common neurodegenerative and movement disorder disease in ageing victims.[28]

The efficiency of gene therapy in treating PD has been confirmed in several Phase 1 clinical trials but were less effective in Phase 2 trials.[29]

7.4.4 Enhancement

Longevity is a polygenic trait, and at present, there is insufficient information available about how many genes and their variants determine the potential longevity of a species or an individual. This fact can be ascribed to the fact that until recently most research in this area has focussed on individual genes/proteins without addressing the possible effects of interactions between them.[30] If researchers were to contemplate an analysis and use of the links between longevity-associated genes and genes involved in age-related diseases, then such a study would be essential to enable researchers to select the potential gene targets for an intervention that would result in an enhancement.[31]

The use of Genome editing technology currently places the emphasis on aiming to treat or prevent diseases and disabilities. The public debate around genome editing has expressed concern at applying the technology to achieve enhancements in human traits and capacities beyond levels considered typical of adequate health, especially since editing for enhancement purposes could involve both somatic and germline cells. Were this technology to be used for this purpose, the public response obtained by researchers from the National Academy of Sciences highlighted and expressed concern in relation to fairness, social norms, personal autonomy and the role of a government.[32] If enhancement were to result in exacerbating social inequalities or in creating social pressure for people to use technologies they would not otherwise choose, it would be inadvisable to use gene editing for this purpose.[33]

The long-established norm regarding the application of medical therapies is that they are sanctioned if they are curative. Using the therapy purely for the purpose of achieving an enhancement cannot be categorised as therapeutic and applying it would therefore conflict with current medical ethics. A further problem arising out of the use of gene enhancements is the difficulty in evaluating the benefit of an enhancement to an individual considering the role that subjective factors play.[34]

In order to instil public confidence in the enhancement technology, a process of extensive public consultation should be launched to clarify the ratio between

---

[28] Ibid.

[29] Hewitt et al. (2012).

[30] Curran and Ruvkun (2007).

[31] Martin et al. (2007).

[32] National Academies of Sciences, Engineering, Medicine (2017b).

[33] Ibid.

[34] Gladyshev (2016).

regulatory rights compared to the benefits flowing from the use of enhancement technology, and with specific reference to the social impacts of its application which will, in turn, inform the extent of governance that needs to be implemented.[35]

The current stance of the National Academy of Sciences and the National Academy of Medicine is to sanction the use of genome editing for the treatment or prevention of disease and disability, but that its use for enhancement purposes should not proceed.[36]

7.5 Genome Editing as an Anti-ageing Therapy

Gene therapy is currently regarded as the most promising treatment option to cure most diseases. Its concept is to replace bad DNA with good DNA. This is done by introducing functional DNA fragments into the patient's target cells to correct the disease inducing mutations. Functional genes can be delivered to replace defective genes and to reduce their toxic products.[37]

A gene therapy approach acts in a direct fashion, by gene editing. It can also be applied in indirect fashion by using viral and non-viral vectors to modulate the genome architecture and its function. By using the gene therapy approach by way of a direct in vivo gene transfer, it permits the targeted delivery of the gene therapy vectors e.g., adenoviral vectors, to the desired site of the malfunctioning gene in the patient.[38]

This mode of delivery is preferred when it is difficult or impossible to use cell cultured approaches especially when the targeted cells consist of neurons which cannot be cultured in vitro in sufficient numbers, or when the cultured cells cannot be effectively re-implanted into the patient's body. Gene therapy based on therapeutic modalities is considered a promising tool, not only for treating monogenic disorders, but also for polygenic complex diseases including age-related ones.[39]

The advent of the CRISPR/Cas 9 technology now allows it to specifically target specific genetic conditions by targeting the site within the gene and the type of mutation that has been inherited.[40] Gene therapy has emerged as a popular application for treating cardiovascular diseases such as atherosclerosis which is a condition frequently associated with old age. This condition is associated with the following symptoms viz systemic oxidative stress and low-grade chronic inflammation. The gene therapy applied targets the two conditions described above and sets out to

[35] Kaser and Frasnian (2018).

[36] National Academy of Medicine, n 32, 3.

[37] National Academies of Sciences, Engineering, Medicine. n 32, 15–25.

[38] Ibid.

[39] Ogle et al. (2001).

[40] Doudna and Charpentier (2014).

rejuvenate the HCPC's (autologous human cardiac stem/progenitor cells) which are susceptible to cardiovascular senescence in elderly people.[41]

In order to achieve highly efficient editing, sufficient quantities of a highly active nucleus with good specificity must be delivered into the nucleus of a cell without activating a toxic cellular response.[42]

Successful gene therapy in ageing persons also includes the use of stem cells and epigenetic interventions.[43] In order to successfully achieve gene manipulation it requires the application of epigenetics to the process. Epigenetics is the sum of the interactions of the faulty genes and the milieu in which those genes happen to operate. Regulated epigenetics and stochastic epigenetics such as modifications of DNA and RNA will effectively determine the success or failure of a gene replacement intervention.[44]

7.6 Can We Characterise Gene Therapy as Being Ethical?

Effective anti-ageing strategies represent a central concern for the individual and society in general. This is because gene editing technology has now been applied to gametes as well as to triploid and diploid human embryos. The ease, speed, and low cost with which this can be achieved via the CRISPR/Cas 9 gene editing technology has been hailed by many scientists as a tremendous breakthrough. There is no doubt that this technology will be applied clinically in the near future for the primary prevention of disease.[45]

The science to achieve a remission of ageing in a human's physiology is thus within reach, should scientists be allowed to offer gene therapy on demand to patients?[46] However, the far-reaching public debate on the area has not yet taken place and until this has occurred there will be no clarity on the ethics of this therapy, its technical limitations, its efficacy and fidelity. It is also implicit in the technical advancement inherent in CRISPR/Cas 9 that the ethics that should guide its use should not occur independently but should complement the actual technology. Instead, the ethics of any disruptive technology should be considered in conjunction with, if not before, the technical development itself.[47]

History has consistently shown that in most cases a technology is developed first, and it is only *ex post facto*, that society will apply its normative rules and

---

41 Vijg and Campisi (2008).

42 Lange, Valter D. The race to control ageing and diseases: Sir2/SirT1 against Ras, Tor and Akt/S6K. *Biochemist* 30(5): 8–13.

43 Rando (2006).

44 Sharpless and DePinho (2007).

45 Porteous (2019).

46 Rattan and Singh n 12, 3–9.

47 National Academies of Sciences, Engineering, Medicine, n 32, 2–10.

react by accepting or rejecting the new technology.[48] We have now reached that tipping point with the CRISPR/Cas 9 technology where ethically we need to decide whether germline editing is acceptable or not. It was not surprising that the 2017 joint report of the 'National Academies of Sciences and Medicine' entitled 'Human Genome Editing: Science, Ethics and Governance' sought to address these issues. The Academies concluded that germline gene editing should be allowed only if it meets certain criteria.[49] The first of which is the absence of 'reasonable alternatives'. However it seems that contemporary IVF with preimplantation genetic diagnosis (PED) aimed at single gene disorders already provide a reasonable alternative for nearly all possible lines of investigation given that this form of editing meets the moral imperative of medical treatment viz that the treatment is therapeutic and would for example likely improve the yield of embryos that would, following gene editing, now be suitable for transfer.[50]

Yet the following questions still arise e.g.

i. What is the difference between a disease and a condition?
ii. Which diseases are considered serious?
iii. What governance infrastructure is required to exercise proper oversight to ensure gene corrections are limited to pathologic variants?
iv. What is the reference population that is to be used to determine the prevalence of a 'normal genotype'?[51]
v. How will a long-term follow-up be conducted effectively?

The authors of the National Academies report speculate that data from CRISPR/Cas 9 experiments on human embryos is expected to inform and improve IVF procedures, embryo implantation rates and reduce the rates of miscarriages. However, the authors are mistaken in their assumptions as CRISPR/Cas 9 will neither improve implantation rates nor decrease the rate of spontaneous abortion unless the genes specifically involved in these outcomes are targeted. This is not the current purpose of such research which is to modify the heritable causes of monogenic diseases.[52]

7.6.1 *Individual Concerns Regarding Genome Editing*

The decision as to whether genome editing should be used in a particular patient will depend on an understanding of whether the safety and efficacy of the treatment, and an evaluation of the anticipated benefits, are reasonable vis-à-vis the risks attached to adverse effects. A treatment to arrest ageing in a patient via a controlled modification

48 Ibid.
49 Ibid., 6.
50 Ibid., 7–9.
51 Ibid., 24–25.
52 Ibid., 24–25.

to specific portions of the DNA e.g., to lengthen or shorten telomeres, will affect the function of the target genes but avoid any changes to other neighbouring genes.[53]

The use of a genome editing treatment whose effects are non-heritable and are restricted to an individual patient may in fact not differ significantly from the use of a traditional drug or a medical device. Gene editing for the purpose of retarding the ageing process cannot, however, be placed in this category as there are no current therapies which can retard the ageing process. There are other justifications which will be discussed infra for using gene editing on non-heritable genes linked to ageing.[54]

Two areas of gene editing which have been barred by legislation in Australia[55] are editing which relates to changes which may be inherited by future generations and those interventions which are aimed at enhancing human capabilities. To mention just one major problem at this stage is the fact that such interceptions would promote gross unfairness and equity in a society that sanctions enhancement practices.[56]

The advent of the CRISPR/Cas 9 system has significantly speeded up the process of potential applications of gene editing and consequently shortened the timeline for discussion of what constitutes the appropriate governance structures to regulate the use of gene editing. As the researchers approaches the point at which they can move to clinical trials the question will then become not whether scientists and clinicians can use gene editing to replace faulty genes, but whether they should be allowed to do so.[57]

7.7 The Consequential Effects of Retarding the Ageing Process

Doctors have a duty to save lives. Administering the optimal treatment for every disease is a social and moral duty owed to every patient.[58]

Old age is a cause of death and given the fact that gene editing will soon enable doctors to intervene in the basic processes of ageing, this treatment, which retards the ageing process, may be the ideal solution for maintaining and improving the quality of human life and the dignity of patients in old age.[59]

The question that must be answered is whether this therapy should be limited to treating patients suffering from illness, disease, or trauma. Or does the doctor's duty to treat an elderly patient extend to manipulating the functions of his/her genes by a process of telomerase gene therapy?[60]

---

[53] Gladyshev (2016).

[54] Ibid.

[55] *Prohibition of Humane Cloning for Reproduction Act 2002* (Cth) s 15 (1).

[56] Ibid.

[57] Kim et al. (2017).

[58] Vaiserman et al. (2017).

[59] Ibid.

[60] Kennedy et al. (2014).

If the answer to this question is in the affirmative, then is it ethical to administer such treatment?[61]

7.7.1 Legislative Regulation of Gene Editing (The Regulatory Framework) Prohibition of Human Cloning for Reproduction Act 2002 (Cth)

The Prohibition of Human Cloning for Reproduction Act 2002 (Cth) (the Act) creates a regulatory framework which:

(a) Provides an efficient and effective system for the application of gene technologies, and
(b) Operates in conjunction with other Commonwealth and State regulatory schemes relevant to GMO's and GM products.

The gene technology regulator is required to issue technical and procedural guidelines in relation to GMO's and to provide information and advice to other regulatory agencies about GMO's and GM products.

A genetically modified organism means an organism that has been modified by gene technology or anything declared by the regulations to be a genetically modified organism but does not include a human being who has undergone somatic gene therapy only.

Section 32 specifies that a person may not deal with a GMO without a licence as to do so constitutes an offence subject to 5 years imprisonment.

In terms of Section 15, the regulator must prepare a risk assessment and risk management plan before issuing a licence to edit a patient's genome. In terms of s 15(1)(a) a person commits an offence if:

(i) The person alters the genome of a human cell in such a way that the alteration is heritable by descendants of the human whose cell was altered; and
(ii) In altering the genome, the person intended the alteration to be heritable by descendants of the human whose cell was altered.

7.7.2 The Gene Technology Act 2000 (Cth)

Section 15 of this Act duplicates the prohibition on heritable editing also found in the Prohibition of Human Cloning for Reproduction Act.

The object of this legislation is spelt out in s 4(a) of the Act viz to: provide an efficient and effective system for the application of gene technologies and, s 4(b)

[61] Kaser and Frasnian (2018).

[to] operate in conjunction with other Commonwealth and State regulatory schemes relevant to GMO's and GM products.[62]

The scope of the Act is thus sufficient to protect the health and safety of people who consent to gene replacement therapy.

The Act is administered via a Ministerial Council (s 21) which is empowered to issue policy principles linked to 'ethical issues which relate to dealings with GMO's and by the Office of the Gene Technology Regulator (see s 27) whose function is to issue licences to applicants who wish to perform gene editing upon a consenting human patient. The Regulator makes decisions in terms of the Act and the polices issued by the Ministerial Council.[63]

The CRISPR/Cas 9 genome editing systems has revolutionised biotechnology and while scientists have been able to alter DNA for several decades by delivering a healthy gene, the early technique which relied on viral vectors produced unwanted side effects, were expensive and cumbersome to use, whereas CRISPR/Cas 9 utilises a naturally occurring enzyme rather than a virus to alter DNA. It consists of two parts, a guide molecule which binds to a specific DNA sequence (the CRISPR part) and an enzyme which cuts DNA[64] (the Cas 9 part).

When the guide molecule finds a particular DNA sequence, it triggers Cas 9 to cut the DNA strand. The system is found naturally in bacteria, which uses it to cut and neutralise invading viral DNA. Once a DNA sequence is cut, the cells own DNA repair mechanisms could be recruited to add, delete, or alter DNA sequences. Because CRISPR has proved to be a remarkably precise and efficient genetic engineering tool, it was first used to effect precise and heritable changes to the DNA of a range of animals and is now being used on human cells. These genome editing tools have the potential to treat diseases that have a genomic basis such as diabetes, leukemia, or old age.[65]

---

[62] Taylor-Sands and Gyngell (2018).

[63] *Gene Technology Act 2000* (Cth) s 27.

[64] Zhang et al. (2017).

[65] Ibid.

7.7.3 Therapeutic Functions Possible with CRISPR/Cas 9

(a) Delete a Gene

Undesirable genes can be deleted from the genome allowing researchers to study the functions specific to a particular gene and to learn about what happens to the cell when the deleted gene is no longer in the genome.[66]

(b) Add a new gene

Desirable genes can be added to the genome, allowing researchers to study their functions within cells. The complimentary genes can also add new functions to the cell.[67]

(c) Activate Dead Genes

The CRISPR/Cas 9 system can be used to reactivate genes which are essential to holding back the advent of old age. This is essential to reversing the anti- ageing process.[68]

(d) Control the Gene Activity Level.

Genes which are overactive can be controlled to produce the correct number of proteins which in turn will help to maintain the correct balance within a cell.[69] This will allow the correcting gene-mediated age-related pathology to function efficiently.

Some of the age-related disorders which can be targeted by the CRISPR/Cas 9 Technology are:

i. Huntington's Disease; prevalent in patients 40 years and older, with more than 5 million cases worldwide.
ii. Alzheimer's Disease; age of onset normally in patients over 65 years old.
iii. Parkinson's Disease; age of onset normally over 50 years of age, with 10 million cases worldwide.
iv. Prostate Cancer; onset normally in persons exceeding 60 years of age, with 1.2 million deaths per annum.
v. Ovarian Cancer; onset age 40 and above, 371,000 cases per annum, and 254,000 deaths per annum.
vi. Breast Cancer; 2.3 million new diagnoses a year, with 685,000 deaths per annum.[70]

---

[66] Ibid.

[67] Rattan, n 13, 3–9.

[68] Ibid.

[69] Magalhães et al., n 1, 1062–1073.

[70] Rando (2006).

7.8 Conditions Required by Law for the Practical Application of Biogerontology to Arrest the Ageing Process in a Patient

7.8.1 Informed Consent

For a doctor to treat any patient, elderly or not, that patient must freely give an informed consent to the proposed genetic editing therapy.[71] A patient must be able to fully understand the proposed editing technology before they can give a valid consent. Genetic editing is not as easy to understand as for example consenting to have a heart valve replaced or excising a melanoma from a patient's leg.[72]

There are clearly concerns whether an 80-year-old patient could understand the information supplied by the doctor regarding the gene editing procedure required by the patient. The doctor would have to monitor very carefully the ability of a patient who has levels of impaired cognition, hearing, speech, and vision, to be able to give informed consent to the genetic editing procedure.[73]

To constitute meaningful and valid consent, the patient's agreement should contain three main elements viz:

i. Sufficient and understandable information must be provided to the patient prior to the consent being offered.
ii. The patient should have the mental capacity to give a free consent.[74]
iii. It would thus be wise for an elderly patient seeking gene replacement therapy to bear the stringency of the consent requirement in mind and not delay giving their consent before it is too late for them to meet this requirement.[75]

7.8.2 Ethical Concerns

Could the use of genetic editing for enhancement purposes/or nontherapeutic purposes give rise to a slippery slope, or should this therapy be confined to purely therapeutic treatment?[76]

It is submitted that the provisions of the Gene Technology Act are geared to manage this technology through policy and regulation in such a way that any lapses into a slippery slope can be avoided.[77]

---

[71] National Academies of Sciences, Engineering, Medicine. N. 32, 1–9.

[72] Allan and Blake (2018).

[73] Ibid.

[74] Ibid.

[75] Ibid.

[76] *The Gene Technology Act 2001* (Cth) ss 4, 15, 27 and 32.

[77] Smith (2020).

7.8.3 Eugenics

The enormous discoveries in the field of genetics triggered by the discoveries made during the Human Genome Project have inevitably raised questions as to whether these discoveries have links to the discredited eugenics policies of the 1930's.[78]

It is, therefore, necessary to address the possibility of whether eugenics on a smaller scale, via genetic editing, could open the door to society accepting the use of genetic editing that goes beyond the limits of retarding the ageing process to include more dangerous forms of racially motivated genetics which hearken back to the Aryan race concept propagated by Nazi Germany. However, to put Nazi genetics into context, it existed in a totalitarian society that did not subscribe to the 'rule of law', nor did they have legislation to regulate how their view of genetics should be confined to therapeutic purposes only.[79]

Nobel prize winner Joshua Lederberg stated that what link might exist differs radically from the 'genocidal' eugenics performed by the Nazis. The revolutionary biologist J. B. S. Haldane characterised genetic editing as a form of positive eugenics. Can gene editing to retard ageing however be deemed to be ethical? Old age can be characterised as a form of illness, and therefore in terms of the accepted ethical test for a therapy, viz whether it is curative, gene editing has the proven ability, for example, to extend the shrunken telomeres that cause dementia.[80]

7.8.4 Economic Inequality

Gene editing is a very expensive form of therapy that will be outside the affordability of most of the population, making it an elitist form of therapy e.g., For example, the cost of using one CRISPR/Cas 9 procedure to repair a single point mutation cost USD 15,000 at Yale University without including the costs of genotyping which will add USD 2,000 to the bill.[81]

The consequences of the very high price of gene editing will be that it will result in a two-tiered aged cohort viz a small group that can afford to retard their ageing process and enjoy a vigorous lifespan for many more years more than most aged citizens in the same society whose bodies have to endure the ravages of ageing and a greatly restricted lifestyle compared to the smaller gene-edited group.[82]

---

[78] Kaser and Frasnian (2018).

[79] National Academies of Sciences, Engineering, Medicine, n 32, 25; Facing History & Ourselves (2020), Grodin et al. (2018); U.S. Holocaust Museum, The Biological State: Nazi Racial Hygiene 1933–1939. https://encyclopedia.ushmm.org/content/en/article/the-biological-state-nazi-racial-hygiene-1933-1939.

[80] *National Academic Press* 'Guidelines for clinical trials involving human germline editing as proposed by the National Academy of Medicine' at 8–9 in box 1.

[81] Cwik (2019).

[82] Ibid.

The high cost of gene editing will therefore worsen the health inequalities between the richer and poorer groups in a society which is inequitable, lacks fairness and is difficult to justify.[83]

7.8.5 Sociological Issues Effected by Retarding Old Age

By extending the life of a person participating in gene editing therapy by retarding their ageing process by for example 20 years, could counteract the cost to all inhabitants of that society.[84]

If the entire society must pay for the indulgence of a few, can it be classed as equitable and therefore ethical?[85] The following examples illustrate the point:

(a) Pensions

The current Actuarial Model on which our pension system is based, is that the average male person retires at 65 years and females at 63 years. Males born between 2017 and 2020 will have a life expectancy of 80.9 years while for females it is 85 years. This translates into a pensionable period of 15.9 years for males and 20 years for females.[86] If gene editing extends the average life expectancy for a participant by 20 years, males will draw a pension for 35.9 years and females for 40 years. The current pension model would not sustain such an additional burden.

It is, therefore, submitted that persons who opt for age extension, should fund their own pension for the extended period of their lives.

(b) Disruption of Proportionality

Parties who live an average lifespan maintain the usual degree of proportionality in their family group between parents and children, grandparents, and grandchildren etc. Parents will normally be 20 years older than their first-born child. Grandparents will be approximately 40 years older than their first grandchild. This allows for the oral transfer of knowledge and experience between generations. This has been the norm for many generations and contributes to the preservation of family and cultural traditions.[87]

(c) Effect on Intergenerational Relationships

A grandparent who resorts to gene editing to extend their life by 20 years will likely outlive their parents and possibly their grandchildren as well, and this will in turn upset the natural intergenerational balance and proportional relationship to the

[83] Kozubek (2016).

[84] Ibid.

[85] Schwartz (2018).

[86] Australian Institute of Health and Welfare, 2019.

[87] Baltaci (2020).

detriment of the family and the help and support of younger family members for older family members.[88]

(d) Home Ownership/Property Rights

Recipients of age retardation will obviously live longer and as such they will occupy their homes for a much longer period. This means that those houses will not enter the property market for an extended period, thus disrupting the normal patterns of occupation prior to recycling into the marketplace. This will result in a shortage of houses for sale and upward pressure on prices.[89]

(e) Increase in Traffic

Because of age retardation the recipients of the therapy will be healthier for much longer and retain their drivers' licences for many more years. This will disrupt the models for traffic planning, road densities and road safety based on current demographic patterns.[90]

(f) Insurance

i. Life Insurance
Age retardation will also have a disruptive effect within the life insurance industry, as it will become a major new factor to consider in pricing a life insurance policy. Those lives insured which are subject to age retardation will live longer and therefore pay premiums for much longer, which means their premiums should be charged at a lower rate than those of non-recipients of gene editing whose lifespan will be in accordance with the usual actuarial tables. Adding for example, 20 years to a person's life will distort the calculated averages in the actuarial tables if sufficient persons resort to age enhancement therapy. Unenhanced persons will still fall within the medians set out in the actuarial tables and be charged accordingly. Enhanced persons who could now live for 20 plus more years, and pay premiums for that extra period, should be entitled to be charged proportionately lower annual premiums.[91]

ii. Health Insurance
The fact that people who are the recipients of gene therapy to retard ageing, does not necessarily mean that they do not require treatment for illness or any traumas they may suffer. What it does mean is that they will be drawing on Medicare or Private Health Insurance for many more years due to their enhancement. This raises the question of the equity inherent in a situation where you have a two-tiered society viz those citizens with extended lives

[88] Ibid.

[89] D. Beattie, 'By the numbers: Australian home ownership and tenancy', 19 August 2019 in Savings.com.au.

[90] Infrastructure Australia (2019).

[91] Money Smart (2021).

due to gene editing, and those whose lives have not been enhanced in any way.[92]

(g) Quality of Life

Where gene therapy is employed to cure dementia, it does have a benefit that extends to society as a whole and is not limited to only the individual who has benefited from the therapy. The therapy would certainly promote the patient's happiness and well-being enabling them to once again become a person who contributes to the economy and who does not have to draw on the public purse by being confined to a home for the disabled.[93]

(h) How to distinguish between the age extended class and those who have not been extended

We have seen in the discussion above that overall, the age extended person's greater life expectancy confers benefits, but also comes at a cost to society.[94] To scale down the extended benefits for those receiving age extensions via gene therapy, and to create economic equity between all citizens, the therapy should not be offered on Medicare but should come at the personal cost of those opting for the benefits.[95]

It is also submitted that those who have received age enhancement benefits should also be registered as members of this class of beneficiaries and be subject to higher rates of taxation to compensate for the additional costs the fiscus is subjected to.[96]

(i) Other restrictions

It is submitted that all gene-editing procedures should be subject to compulsory registration in a register and that the Gene Technology Act should be amended to create such a designated register. The Act should also be amended to reflect the fact that each participant should be limited to only one session of gene editing for age retardation. The Act should also reflect the fact that the therapy should not be performed on an applicant before they reach the age of 70 years. This restriction will give nature an opportunity to bring about the natural death of the person, thereby limiting the numbers of potential applicants.[97]

(j) Summary

A public discussion which will guide a decision on the implementation of gene-editing to retard ageing must be guided by whether the ethical concerns exceed the positive outcomes that flow from gene editing. All aspects of gene editing must be

---

[92] Ibid.

[93] Kass (2003).

[94] Warneck-Silvestrin (2021).

[95] Uddin et al. (2020).

[96] Ibid.

[97] Mallapaty (2019).

implemented in an effective and safe manner, driven by the guidelines which should emerge from the public discussions averted to.[98]

To create a specialist body to drive the process of gene editing forward, the Australian Law Reform Commission recommended the establishment of an independent federal statutory authority to be designated as The Human Genetic Commission of Australia. This body should have the following mandate[99]:

i. To engender public confidence in its findings, decisions, and advice by demonstrating its independence by way of developing and maintaining in-house expertise as well as by cultivating a network of experts and stakeholders who rely on their services.
ii. To ensure that the Commission has sufficient budget resources to enable it to fulfill its mission.
iii. To provide it with sufficient operational flexibility to enable it to deploy its resources when and where needed in the most effective manner.[100] … [T]here is a continuing need for our laws… to be reviewed and revised to address the advances made by human genetic science and technology.

Currently the recommendations of the Law Reform Commission have not yet been implemented and thus no such standing body currently exists in Australia. The United Kingdom is served by The Nuffield Council on Bioethics established in 1991 that reports on ethical issues in the field of biology and medicine. The Nuffield Council has achieved an international reputation for advising policy makers and stimulating debate on bioethics.[101] It is also submitted that there needs to be specific legislation to address the use of genome editing geared to the prevention or removal of age-related diseases rather than relying on current legislation which is very general in nature. Such new legislation must be based on 3 ethical imperatives, viz,[102]

(a) It must represent the potential of age-related genome editing in a conservative way, free of any unwarranted political restraint.
(b) It should reflect the fact that ageing causes suffering, whereas the putative social drawbacks of controlling ageing are subject to dispute.
(c) It should tackle the challenge of fighting ageing without fostering ageism. The major targets at which to direct anti-ageing genetic interventions are as follows[103]:

    i. To repair the damaged macromolecules, for example, by focusing on the DNA repair pathways;
    ii. Increasing the removal of damaged macromolecules, such as proteasomal and lysosomal pathways; and

[98] Australian Law Reform Commission (2010).
[99] Ibid.
[100] Ibid.
[101] Ibid.
[102] Ibid.
[103] Ibid.

iii. By decreasing the source of damaging agents such as reactive oxygen species which are highly reactive chemicals formed from oxygen, such as peroxides and superoxide.[104]

The first two targets imply achieving genetic enhancement or genetic improvement such as repairing or replacing genes related to ageing, while the third target requires the resetting of the metabolic pathways.

Retarding old age via gene-editing can, despite many ethical concerns, be justified on the basis that old age is a form of debilitating disease, for which therapy can be justified, whereas editing for enhancement of strength endurance, appearance or memory cannot be justified as being ethical and hence warranting gene editing.[105]

7.9 The Polygenetic Nature of Aging and Longevity

Gene therapy, or interventions for targeting ageing, differ from the more focused approach where the therapy is directed at one or more specific diseases. Research has revealed that ageing and longevity are amendable to modulation. Researchers have also discovered that the majority of the putative longevity genes need to be switched off or their activity reduced to extend the longevity of the patient. This is necessary even though all these modified genes are also part and parcel of the metabolic processes which have evolved for normal growth, development, and survival. Although the implementation of these genetic interventions to slow down ageing and extend a patient's life span are technically achievable, the epigenetic modulators of ageing and longevity pose a level of complexity that has yet to be fully understood. Targeting polygenic age-related diseases is far more complex than monogenic disorders, because the simultaneous targeting of numerous genes could trigger a cascade of unpredictable events.[106]

7.10 Conclusion

Gene editing involves not only the evolution of the scientific techniques that enable the editing to take place, but also the ethical issues required to determine which techniques are appropriate and should be allowed. This in turn will require agreement on a set of principles necessary to govern its application, to facilitate its appropriate use and to avoid its misuse.[107]

---

[104] Ibid.

[105] Gonçalves et al. (2017), World Health Organization (2021), Fletcher (1983).

[106] Delhove et al. (2020).

[107] Ibid.

Arriving at such appropriate use of the technology and the regulatory mechanisms needed to enforce these limits will vary according to each nation's cultural, political, and legal context. To extend the use of genome editing on a transnational co-operative basis will require ongoing transnational scientific co-operation. In addition, public discussion to facilitate input into policy making should be employed which is a well-used precedent in similar situations.[108]

To sum up, CRISPR/Cas 9 technology is a powerful editing tool which has tremendous therapeutic potential for slowing down the ageing process. The cost of these therapies is likely to be very high initially, which will limit accessibility. But applying a cost benefit analysis, including the savings on the cost of medical care over a person's extended lifetime, could provide justification for using anti-ageing gene therapy. A tight rein on costs would be required to improve the equality of access.[109]

The current generation must, therefore, make sensible decisions regarding the clinical application of human gene-editing technologies especially those that are heritable to prevent far reaching deleterious impacts on generations to come without those generations having consented to having those risks imposed on them.[110]

Our generation, which stands on the cusp of large-scale implementation of this therapy, has an intergenerational moral duty to remain vigilant and alert to the benefits and risks of human genome editing, which must be implemented only when improved governance has been implemented.[111]

Once clinical and human trials of genetic editing are completed it will doubtless become a popular and much sought-after therapy for those who can afford it. Now is the time to improve the governance of this unique therapy for retarding ageing. It is therefore submitted that specific legislation should be passed to regulate gene-editing to retard ageing.

This legislation should include three ethical imperatives:

(i) The potential of ageing research should be presented objectively and without any hype, but also without any unwarranted political constraints.
(ii) It should accept the fact that ageing causes suffering, whereas the putative social drawbacks of the therapy are speculative and contested.
(iii) It should tackle the challenge of fighting ageing on a sound scientific and ethical basis without fostering agism.

7.11 Postscript

In 2005, Elizabeth Parrish the then 42-year-old CEO of Bio Viva, demonstrated her faith in her own company's experimental gene therapies by receiving two treatments. One was to protect against loss of muscle mass which accompanies advancing age.

108 Yotova (2017).

109 Irvine (2019).

110 Sugarman (2015).

111 Jaswal and Jolly (2010).

The second was directed to combating stem cell depletion which brings on diverse age-related diseases and infirmities.

The early data gathered indicates that it is the world's first successful telomere lengthening process via gene therapy in a human patient. All previous applications had been in mice.

Telomeres are short segments of DNA which cap the ends of every chromosome thereby acting as buffers against wear and tear. They shorten with every cell division, which eventually results in them getting to short to protect the chromosomes. This in turn results in cells starting to malfunction and the body to age.

Tests done prior to the administration of gene therapy revealed that Parrish's telomeres were unusually short for her age. This would leave her facing the prospect of her being vulnerable to age associated diseases early in life.

In March 2016, Spectra Cell performed the same tests on Parrish's white blood cells. The tests revealed that her telomeres had lengthened from 6.71 to 7.33 kb, this amounted to a factor of 20 years. The tests thus confirmed that she had become biologically younger.

The findings of the 2016 Spectra Cell tests were independently monitored by the Brussels based non-profit HEALES (Healthy Life Extension Company) and the Bio-Gerontology Research Foundation; a U.K.-based charity committed to combatting age related diseases.

Bio Viva will continue to monitor Parrish's blood for the indefinite future, and they will also be testing new therapies. Time will tell whether the success they achieved with leukocytes can be expanded to also include other tissues and organs for the benefit of future patients.

For now, all the answers to arresting aging lie in the cells of Elizabeth Parrish, 'patient zero', in the quest for restorative gene therapy.

Parrish's self-experimentation without first going through properly supervised human trials has been criticised by fellow scientists in the field of genetic engineering and cannot be accorded the weight they deserve.[112]

References

Allan, Sonia and Meredith Blake. 2018. *Australian Health Law*. Chatswood, NSW: LexisNexis, 181–198, *c* 2017, 116–126.

Angelou, J. 2017. Time to stop getting old. *New Scientist*, 22–23.

Australian Law Reform Commission. 2010. A Human Genetics Commission of Australia. Australian Law Reform Commission. https://www.alrc.gov.au/publication/essentially-yours-the-protection-of-human-genetic-information-in-australia-alrc-report-96/05-a-human-genetics-commission-of-australia/a-human-genetics-commission-of-australia/.

Baltaci, Sehanz. 2020. The Benefits of Intergenerational Relationships. European Commission. https://epale.ec.europa.eu/en/content/benefits-intergenerational-relationships.

[112] Drug Discovery & Development (2016).

Bär, Christian, and Maria A. Blasco. 2016. Telomeres and Telomerase as therapeutic targets to prevent and treat age-related diseases. F1000 Research 20(5): 89, 1–11. https://doi.org/10.12688/f1000research.7020.1
Boccardi, Virginia, and Utz Herbig. 2012. Telomerase gene therapy: a novel approach to combat ageing. *Molecular Medicine* 4(8): 685–687.
Campisi, Judith, and Fabrizio d'Adda di Fagagna. 2007. Cellular senescence: when bad things happen to good cells. *National Review of Molecular Cell Biology* 8(9): 729–740
Curran, Sean P., and Gary Ruvkun 2007. Lifespan Regulation by Evolutionarily Conserved Genes Essential for Viability. *Public Library of Science (PLoS) Genetics* 3(4): 0479–0487.
Cwik, Bryan. 2019. Moving Beyond "Therapy" and "Enhancement" in the Ethics of Gene Editing. *Cambridge Quarterly of Healthcare Ethics* 28(4): 695–707.
Dai, Wei et al. 2019. Cancer Therapy with a CRISPR- assisted telomerase- activating gene–expression system. *Oncogene* 38(21): 4110–4124.
De Magalhães, João Pedro, and Olivier Toussaint. 2004. Telomeres and Telomerase: a modern fountain of youth?' *Rejuvenation Res* 7(2): 126–133.
De Magalhães, João Pedro, Michael Stevens and Daniel Thorton. 2017. The Business of Anti-Aging Science. *Trends in Biotechnology* 35(7): 1062–1073, 1063.
Delhove, Juliette, Ivana Osenk, Ivanka Prichard and Martin Donnelley. 2020. Public Acceptability of Gene Therapy and Gene Editing for Human Use: A Systematic Review. *Human Gene Therapy* 31(1–2): 2–46.
Doudna, Jennifer A., and Emmanuelle Charpentier. 2014. The new frontier of genome editing with CRISPR Cas-9. *Science* 346(6213): 1077.
Drug Discovery & Development. 2016. First Gene Therapy Successful Against Human Aging. Drug Discovery & Development; Rockaway.
Edd Gent. 2019. A New Anti-Aging Therapy is Starting Its First Human Trial – and It Costs $1 million. *SingluarityHub.*
Facing History & Ourselves. 2020. Breeding the New German Race. https://www.facinghistory.org/resource-library/breeding-new-german-race
Fernandes, Maria et al. 2016. Systematic Analysis of the genome reveals links between ageing and age-related diseases. Human Molecular Genetics 25(21): 4804–4818.
Fletcher, John C. 1983. Moral Problems and Ethical Issues in Prospective Human Gene Therapy. Virginia Law Review 69: 515–546.
Gladyshev, Vadim N. 2016. Aging: progressive decline in fitness due to the rising deleteriome adjusted by genetic, environmental, and stochastic processes. *Aging Cell* 15(4): 594–602.
Gonçalves, Giulliana Augusta Rangel and Raquel de Melo Alves Paiva. 2017. Gene Therapy Advances. *Einstein* 15(3): 369–375
Grodin, Michael A., Erin L. Miller and Johnathan I. Kelly. 2018. The Nazi Physicians as Leaders in Eugenics and Euthanasia. *American* Journal of *Public Health* 108(1): 53–57
Hewitt, Graeme, et al. 2012. Telomeres are favoured targets of a persistent DNA damage response in ageing. *Nature Communications* 3(1): 708.
Hipkissm Alan R. 2007. Dietary restriction, glycolysis, hormesis and ageing. *Biogerontology* 8(2): 221–224.
Holliday, Robin. 2006. Aging is no longer an unresolved problem in biology. *Annals of the New York Academy of Science* 1067: 1–9.
Holliday, Robin. 2007. *Aging: The Paradox of Life.* Dordrecht: Springer, 20–32
Infrastructure Australia. 2019. Urban Transport Crowding and Congestion: The Australian Infrastructure Audit 2019 Supplementary report. https://www.infrastructureaustralia.gov.au/publications/urban-transport-crowding-and-congestion.
Irvine, Allison. 2019. Paying for CRISPR cure: The Economics of Genetic Therapies. Innovative Genomic Trust. https://innovativegenomics.org/news/paying-for-crispr-cures/.
Jaswal, P.S, and Stellina Jolly. 2010. Germline Engineering and Future Generations: An Ethical and Legal Outlook. *Journal of the Indian Law Institute* 52(1): 3–15.

Kaser, Daniel J. and J Frasnian. 2018. Crossing the Germline CRISPR-Cas 9 and our responsibility. *Journal of Assisted Reproductive Genetics* 35: 399–402.
Kass, Leon. 2003. Beyond Therapy: Biotechnology and the pursuit of Happiness. Washington, D.C.: *President's Council on Bioethics.*
Kennedy, Brain K. et al. 2014. Geroscience; linking ageing to chronic disease. *Cell* 159(4): 709–713.
Kenyon, Cynthia J. 2010. The genetics of ageing. *Insight Review: Nature.* 464(7288): 504–512, 466.
Kim, Hyojun et al. 2017. CRISPR-Cas 9 Medical Telomere Removal Leads to Mitochondrial Stress and Protein Aggregation. *International Journal of Molecular Science* 18(10): 2093.
Kozubek, J. 2016. *Modern Prometheus: editing the human genome with CRISPR-Cas 9.* Cambridge, United Kingdom: Cambridge University Press.
Lapointe, Jérôme, and Siegfried Hekimi. 2010. When a theory of ageing ages badly. *Cellular Molecular Life Sciences* 67(1): 1–8.
Mallapaty, Smriti. 2019. Australian gene-editing rules adopt 'middle ground'. Nature. https://www.nature.com/articles/d41586-019-01282-8.
Martin, George M. et al. 2007. Genetic determinants of human health span and lifespan: Progress and new opportunities. *Public Library of Science (PLoS) Genetics* 3(7) 1121–1130.
Money Smart. 2021. How life insurance works. Moneysmart.gov.au. https://moneysmart.gov.au/how-life-insurance-works.
National Academies of Sciences, Engineering, Medicine. 2017a. Human Genome Editing: Science Ethics and Governance. Washington D.C.: National Academies Press, p. 3.
National Academies of Sciences, Engineering, Medicine. 2017b. *Human Genome Editing: Science, ethics and governance.* Washington, D.C.: National Academies Press, 8–9.
Ogle, William O., Sapolsky, Robert, M. 2001. Gene Therapy and the Aging Nervous System, Mechanisms of Ageing and Development. 122 (14): 1555–1563.
Porteous, Mathew H. 2019. A new class of Medicines through DNA Editing. *New England Journal of Medicine* 380(10): 947–959.
Rando, Thomas A. 2006. Stem cells ageing and the quest for immortality. *Nature* 441 (7097): 1080–1086
Rattan, S.I.S, and R. Singh. 2009. Progress and Prospects Gene Therapy and Aging. *Gene Therapy* 16(1): 3–9.
Rattan, Suresh I.S. 2007. The science of healthy ageing, genes, milieu and chance. *Annuals of New York Academy of Science* 1114(1): 1–10.
Schwartz, Mark. 2018. Target, Delete, Repair. Stanford Medicine. https://stanmed.stanford.edu/2018winter/CRISPR-for-gene-editing-is-revolutionary-but-it-comes-with-risks.html.
Scott, Christopher Thomas, and Laura De Francesco. 2015. Selling Long Life. *National Biotechnology* 33(1): 31–40
Sharpless, Norman E., and Ronald A. DePinho 2007. How stem cells age and why this makes us grow old. *Nature Review of Molecular Cell Biology* 8(9): 703–713.
Smith, Malcolm. 2020. *Medical Law.* Sydney: LexisNexis Butterworths, pp. 17–41.
Sugarman, Jeremy. 2015. Ethics and germline editing. *Embow Reports* 16(8): 879–880.
Swain, Frank. 2019. Buyer beware of this $1 million gene therapy for ageing. *MIT Technology Review.* https://www.technologyreview.com/2019/12/06/131657/buyer-beware-of-this-1-million-gene-therapy-for-ageing/
Taylor-Sands, Michelle and Christopher Gyngell. 2018. Legality of Embryonic Gene Editing in Australia. *Journal of Law and Medicine* 26(2): 356–373.
Uddin, Fathema, Charles M. Rudin and Sen Triparna. 2020. CRISPR Gene Therapy: Applications, Limitations and Implications for the Future. *Frontiers in Oncology* 10: 1387.
Vaiserman, Alexander M., Alexander K. Koliada and Francesco Marotta. 2017. *Aging Research Reviews* 35: 36–45.
Verdin, Eric. 2015. NAD in Aging, Metabolism and Neurodegeneration. *Science (American Association for the Advancement of Science)* 350 (6265): 1208–1213.

Vijg, Jan, and Judith Campisi. 2008. Puzzles, promises and a cure for ageing. *Nature* 454: 1065–1071.
Warneck-Silvestrin, Larissa. 2021. The promises of CRISPR Genome editing in Biomedicine. LA Biotech.eu. https://www.labiotech.eu/interview/crispr-therapeutics-genome-editing/.
World Health Organization. 2021. WHO Issues new recommendations on human genome editing for the advancement of public health. World Health Organization. https://www.who.int/news/item/12-07-2021-who-issues-new-recommendations-on-human-genome-editing-for-the-advancement-of-public-health
Yonge, Y.D. 2008. The race to control ageing and disease. *Biochemist* 30: 8-13.
Yotova, Rumiana. 2017. Report on Regulation: The Regulation of Genome Editing and Reproduction Under International Law, E.U. Law and Comparative Law. Nuffield Council on Bioethics. https://www.nuffieldbioethics.org/wp-content/uploads/Report-regulation-GEHR-for-web.pdf.
Zhang, Zhao et al. 2017. CRISPR/Cas 9 Genome Editing System in Human Stem Cells: Current status and future prospects. *Molecular Therapy: Nucleic Acids* 9: 230-241.

Chapter 8
John Farrar and His /Jū-bik'wi-ti/ in Legal Education

Laurence Boulle and Ian Edwards

Abstract In our tribute to John Farrar, we reveal his ubiquity in legal education across many institutions and jurisdictions. It first describes his role as teacher and educator, which provides a platform for many of his other contributions. It is followed by brief references to his mountain of scholarship, particularly in commercial law, corporations law and legal education, in all of which he was a published and acknowledged authority in many countries. His educational expertise and comparative scholarship provided the basis for a long and fruitful involvement in policy development and law reform, predominantly in corporations law. John also spent a large part of his career as a manager and leader in different educational institutions at a time of great upheaval in the sector. In a final reflection on the 'knowledge commons', we consider John Farrar's contribution to less formal ways of knowing, such as in mentoring and being available to discuss and advise on many topics with colleagues. Here he could draw on his extensive knowledge in many areas of theory, jurisprudence, politics, and the law. The authors provide some personal anecdotes on his ubiquity in the law and his contributions to society as a Wyse and Compleate Professor.

8.1 Introduction

This contribution focuses on the ubiquity of John Farrar in the world of Legal Education. The overarching theme is the connection between John as educator and the other aspects of law's project in which he has been involved. John was, par excellence, a man of education and an educating man, and he draws into this role experiences and expertise from his legal practice, from scholarship and legal doctrine, from policy

---

Ubiquity—the fact of being everywhere.

L. Boulle (✉) · I. Edwards
Faculty of Law, Bond University, Gold Coast, Australia
e-mail: lboulle@bond.edu.au

I. Edwards
e-mail: iedwards@bond.edu.au

U. Ghori et al. (eds.), *Globalisation in Transition*,
https://doi.org/10.1007/978-981-99-2439-4_8

and law reform work, and from his roles in university administration and management and other institutions supporting and driving legal education. If legal education sits at the heart of the legal ecosystem, John has had a hand in many of the organs that makes law whole.

In its development, the chapter shadows its subject in moving from one jurisdiction to another, from the national to the international, and from the comparative to the global. It ends with reflections on the learned professor's contributions to the legal knowledge commons. It is in essence a celebration of Professor John Farrar, and it gives voice to two of his many professional admirers in relation to his contributions to legal education and legal knowledge.

8.2 John Farrar the Educator

Law's narrative, national and global, can be seen as a combination of the many personal stories of teachers, practitioners, judges, and other law officials performing the complex and complementary tasks which make up law's project. One anecdote in John's personal narrative was encountered on a dusty day in Francistown in northern Botswana near the Zimbabwe border.

The first author was on a marketing trip for a prominent Australian law school. It included visitations, inter alia, to public and private legal practitioners to assess the higher degree needs of local lawyers. In Francistown, the author had arranged to see a prominent lawyer but there was little real progress in the meeting. After a pregnant pause in discussions, he noticed on the wall a testamur from the University of Bristol. This led to enquiries about the practitioner's studies at the Bristol Law School.

The practitioner soon referred to the greatest influence in his legal studies, namely Professor John Farrar, and proudly produced from his shelves an exhibit: an early edition of his professor's work on corporations law. This same text contributed over the years to John's fame in four continents. As John was by now a colleague and friend of the author, the Bristol nexus broke all barriers. A convivial evening was held as we discoursed on different legal topics, many involving our common friend.

John Farrar commenced his teaching career in 1969 as a lecturer in law at the University of Bristol from whence teaching took him many kilometres away, and sometimes back again. In terms of his teaching career John has been engaged in senior positions at many institutions in Australia and beyond. He has held visiting positions at universities in the U.S., U.K., Belgium, Hong Kong, China, Canada and Taiwan. His research in topical areas, such as globalisation and corporate governance, were reflected in the wide ambit of subjects he was asked to teach, and what he taught in such areas was fed into policy, practice, and law reform.

John was no ideologue in terms of his philosophy of legal education.[1] While he was always a master of 'black letter' law, his normal, or one might say natural, approach

[1] Farrar (2010).

was that of law in context, linking legal rules and principles to their social, political and economic context.[2] This approach merges with socio-legal and law and society approaches to the discipline, and later derivatives including inter-disciplinary legal perspectives. The approach is partly a function of what John refers to as the 'complex nature of Law'.[3] At an early stage in his career it made him open to incorporating legal skills into foundational legal education as recommended in the Pearce Report in the late 1980s. He contributed to realising this goal at both the University of Waikato and Bond University, Faculty of Law, when others were dogmatically committed to a 'black-letter' approach. This acceptance can be partially attributed to his close association with legal practice, referred to later.

John was also open to the changing and challenging technologies which confronted all forms of work and education. A decade before the 2020 pandemic, while Dean at Waikato, he accommodated the IT revolution by providing video streaming of lectures to a satellite campus. This provided asynchronous access to legal education to many who could not abandon homes and careers to attend in person: mature students, full-time workers, some re-entering the workforce and those located in regional areas of the country. Despite resistance from other law schools and the profession, this form of teaching and learning, complemented by mandatory face-to-face tutorials, prevailed. The pandemic has rendered it common-place and the 'new normal' is not likely to eradicate it from the student experience. It also fits more closely into changes and adaptations in the legal services industry as a whole, from online court hearings to the conduct of conciliations, to the use of AI data processing in mass litigation.

8.3 Connecting Education with Scholarship

In John Farrar's world view, education and scholarship are conjoint twins, both thriving with combined organs and limbs acting independently. John's dedication to education was evident when, shortly after taking up teaching, he was one of the original signatories to a resolution that formally constituted the Commonwealth Legal Education Association in 1971, to establish 'a body which will promote greater and closer collaboration within fields of legal education'.[4] He researched and published extensively in numerous legal jurisdictions and with multiple issues of works in corporations law and corporate governance. The Farrar ship of scholarship voyaged into numerous areas of legal doctrine and comparative law, all of which had resonance in the classroom.

[2] Ibid., 84. One of the influences in this regard was Otto Kahn-Freund, Professor of Comparative Law at Oxford. John was an original member of the Socio-Legal Group of the Society of Public Law Teachers in the U.K.

[3] Farrar (2018b).

[4] Read (2001).

Reference has already been made to one of his early works. In fact, the first author's initial connection with John was what in contemporary parlance would be known as a virtual one. As a new law teacher his juniority was recognised in being designated to teach Interpretation of Statutes. In searching for inspiration, he was delighted to find in the library a copy of Farrar and Dugdale's *Introduction to Legal Method,*[5] already in its second edition, and was enthused by its section on statutes and their construction. The inspiration was furthered by a later encounter with Guido Calabresi, Dean at the Yale Law School, and his book *A Common Law for the Age of Statutes*[6] published the same year as Farrar and Dugdale's second edition. These experiences prompted unanticipated enthusiasm for teaching a subject which, unobligingly, has poor consumer reviews.[7]

A perfunctory review of the first edition of *Legal Method*[8] dismissed the text in a way which reflected more on the reviewer than the author. In reality, this work influenced legal education in the United Kingdom significantly, and the ripples were felt elsewhere in common law jurisdictions. *Legal Method* and the author survived the hostile review, and thrived in second and third editions, with Tony Dugdale.[9] These works provide insights into the practical methodologies required in law's project and proved to be basic educational resources in different jurisdictions. The links with comparative legal systems and with practitioners, both central to John's educational philosophies, is reflected in the fact that these works were used by both lawyers and judges in different European jurisdictions.[10]

John's later work, *Legal Reasoning,*[11] continued his 'law in context' approach, and was, in the author's own words, based on 'experiences of teaching'[12] in different jurisdictions. This is the voice of the mature educator, reflecting and probing, critiquing and refining, and balancing complex jurisprudential theory with exacting forensic analysis, including multi-jurisdictional case studies. This book also reflects two other dimensions of the Farrar educational project. The first is its humanistic approach to matters legal, for example in his various 'truisms' about human nature. The second is in its appreciation of the regulatory function of law in context, in particular in his depiction of methods of social control achieved through the law.

The nexus between education and scholarship is now taken for granted, despite some Law Schools shifting back to teaching-only staff appointments. There is, however, another source of pressure on the nexus. Industry, it is often said, needs,

---

[5] Farrar et al. (1984).

[6] Calebresi (1984).

[7] It also led to the development of a book proposal, *Statute Law*; it was accepted by a publisher but never saw the light of day.

[8] B D Renton, 'A Method for Legal Method' (1977) 7:3 Kingston Law Review - review of John Farrar, 'An Introduction to Legal Method' (London: Sweet and Maxwell).

[9] Farrar et al. (1984).

[10] John Farrar's comparativist leanings are reflected in one of his very early publications, Farrar (1976).

[11] Farrar (2009). This publication reflected earlier views by the author, for example in Farrar (1997).

[12] Calebresi (1984).

or wants, graduates who are 'work ready', able to fit into the relevant industrial groove. There is a mechanistic assumption behind this claim. In relation to the law, it assumes that technical knowledge of rules and procedures, including how to operate a trust account, is what the 'legal services industry' needs as the contours of practice change. In some jurisdictions, this thinking is evidenced in the emergence of non-university providers of legal education, or rather training, to provide a greater focus on practice realities. However, while there are areas of legal practice which run in well-developed grooves, such as costs and stamp duties, the law's connections with society, economics and individual claimants requires a much broader educational basis for when the rules run out, when they are ambiguous, or where sensitive cost–benefit analyses are required. John Farrar has always upheld the nexus.

8.4 Connecting Education with Policy and Law Reform

John Farrar's early involvement in legal education gave him access to policy development, both in educational design and the law, exemplified by his involvement in the Lord Cross committee in the U.K.[13] recommended by the 'Ormrod Report'.[14] He was nominated as the Society of Public Teachers of Law's representative on this committee, established after the Omrod Report on legal education and with influence in many common law jurisdictions. John had another Cross connection, this time with Rupert, brother of the Lord and twelfth Vinerian professor. Cross's treatise on *Evidence* became a work of authority, including among English judges, and it was published in separate editions in both Australia and New Zealand. John followed in these footsteps in becoming a much-quoted authority by bar and bench in many facets of corporations law in the same three jurisdictions, and others besides. John also shares with Rupert Cross what has been referred to as 'academic wrath' at faulty jurisprudence, although in an altogether more diplomatic way than the earlier scholar.[15]

John's institutional influence on legal education policy was founded in his membership of the New Zealand Council of Legal Education, on two separate occasions, and as a member of the Queensland Attorney-General's Committee on Legal Education. Recognition of his policy contributions is found in John's life membership of the Commercial Law Teachers Association. He served on the executive committee of this body and hosted two of its conferences at Bond University. He was also made an honorary life member of the Australasian Law Teachers Association in 2008 for his services to legal education in several jurisdictions and in the same year honorary life membership of the Corporate Law Teachers Association was conferred on him.

13 Lord Chancellor's Advisory Committee on Legal Education and Conduct (1996).

14 Omrod, Roger Report of the Committee on Legal Education (Ormrod Report) (London: HMSO, 1971) Cmnd 4595.

15 See Glazenbrook (1985).

As a consummate comparativist John Farrar always connected with legal education in multiple jurisdictions, and not only those based on the common law. This reflects what he once referred to as the 'globalisation of the mind'.[16] He, and colleagues Vai lo Lo and Goh Bee Chen, edited a festschrift to his colleague Mary Hiscock, *Scholarship, Practice and Education in Comparative Law*.[17] As the title suggests this book pursues the theme of connectivity in the law involving the work of academics, practitioners and teachers. The Farrar contributions to policy reform in legal education have been positively acknowledged in the literature. An example from New Zealand relates to his role in reforms recommended in the Neil Gold Report in that country relative to curriculum changes and professional legal education.[18]

In relation to his contributions to legal education reform John Farrar always had the advantage of his experience in legal practice. Despite having been in academia since 1969, John was admitted as a legal practitioner in England, New Zealand and Australia. He was in practice before then and spent four years at a leading Wellington law firm, Bell Gully Buddle Weir, first as partner and later as consultant. The education-practice connection was as prominent as that between education and scholarship.

8.5 Mentoring and Supervision in Education

John had an extensive role as supervisor of doctoral, masters and other dissertations, again in a multiplicity of jurisdictions, and as an international external examiner. Thesis supervision can be protracted and painful, with parturition not always guaranteed. At Bond University alone John has from 2006 to date supervised 19 PhD dissertations, continuing well into the emeritus phase of his career. In a recent discussion between the authors and one of his students he was described as 'a titan of corporate governance who was both a supervisor and friend who throughout the journey was able to adapt to the global upheaval caused by the pandemic and provided unwavering support. The ability to adapt that keeps John current, legitimate and timeless.

John Farrar had a less formal role in mentoring new law teachers in the ways and vagaries of teaching, publishing and otherwise forging their careers. In the authors' experience this has occurred extensively at Bond Faculty of Law but can be assumed to have taken place (behind their backs) at other institutions. His guidance is often acknowledged in the literature. For example, a colleague, Ross Buckley, assumed his first academic post at Bond, having practised in Hong Kong and New York and having completed a PhD at the University of New South Wales. In a contribution on legal scholarship for new law teachers he made a handsome acknowledgment of John's influence in his thinking.[19]

[16] Farrar (2018a).

[17] Farrar et al. (2019).

[18] For example, by Lewis (1988).

[19] Buckley (1997).

8.6 Connecting University Management and Education

In a 2015 publication, John Farrar reflected on his time, triumphs, and tribulations in university management.[20] In the article, John observes the shift in university governance from a *gemeinschaft*, or communitarian organisation, to *gesellschaft*, or corporatised form of government.[21] Here the institutional sociology of academia provided evidence of extensive investment in marketing, public relations, 'pathways' programs, engagement with high schools, quality assurance and risk management systems. There was also arguably an over-expansion of law schools, including the establishment of multiple 'branches' of single Schools. By the time John's managerial responsibilities had ended he had had to deal with the Commonwealth Tertiary Quality and Standards Agency, the Legal Services Council, the Commissioner for Uniform Legal Services Regulation, the Admissions Committee set up by the Legal Services Council, core curriculum challenges, the CALD Standards and Teaching and Learning Outcomes. John suggests that within this vast crucible of government, professional and university initiatives one body inadequately consulted was the Council of Australian Law Deans on which he served.[22]

For the record, John Farrar served as Dean and Head of School at three Law Schools in two countries.[23] During the span of time during which he was Dean the position shifted from a 'first among equals' sinecure to an executive management role with responsibility for staffing, budgets, learning and teaching, student recruitment and university administration. For many deans these required the development of new managerial skill sets within short periods of time.

At the University of Waikato, John had decanal responsibility for furthering three foundational, and not always compatible principles, on which the school was based: to provide professional legal education, to teach law in its context, and to develop a bicultural approach to legal education so that Maori perspectives were reflected in the curriculum and other activities. He is modest in his self-assessment of the third principle, which in the history of the school, proved to be a difficult goal.[24] The concept itself shifted from its original purpose, and more contemporary views of both society and education, though the Waikato principles and objectives were of interest to other societies grappling with the challenges of legal education in multi-cultural, ethnic or tribal contexts.[25]

John served as acting Vice-Chancellor at Bond University for two years during which time it went through many financial, reputational and political 'troubles'. He was chief executive when the university had to buy its campus to ensure its independence, part of the shift from public to private funding of legal education

---

[20] Farrar (2015).

[21] See Tonnies (1912).

[22] Farrar (2018a).

[23] He served as Dean or Head of Law at the Universities of Canterbury, Waikato and Bond, and also served as Associate Dean at the University of Melbourne.

[24] Farrar (2010).

[25] Ibid., 87.

that is now commonplace. His steady hand contributed to the institution securing independence by owning its own campus, increasing enrolments, and moving towards financial stability. This laid the foundation for its achievements in education which have been acknowledged, both internally and externally, over the past three decades.

John had specific portfolios in research and quality assurance but leadership in legal education itself was always on the agenda. This was partly a response to the times. New notions of quality assurance, client satisfaction and cross-institutional measurement metrics, not always well-founded, provided new responsibilities for teachers in the age of the corporate institution. Here John had another source of strength, namely his knowledge of regulation and compliance, corporate governance, and business finance, in all of which he had contributed publications. While he had not undertaken training in management and related disciplines, he had taught many students in MBA and other business settings in different jurisdiction. This led to management praxis—where theory meets practice.

The external environment of universities changed significantly during the three decades under discussion. Policies of corporatisation, efficiency and productivity became prominent in the tertiary sector. For many institutions there was a new dependence on overseas students, requiring marketing and regulatory compliance. Ranking systems and competition between universities for student satisfaction and retention were reflected in metrics. Competition in legal education also emerged from publishers, professional bodies, law firms and the College of Law, each claiming different aspects of the prize. Fee-paying students, and prospects of long-term student debt, put greater consumer pressure on law schools, their service delivery, and standards.

8.7 Farrar and the Knowledge Commons

John's involvement in the law as educator, administrator, reformer, and scholar has been long and illustrious. As a scholar, John takes a keen interest and has been and remains a staunch supporter and champion of everything, or at least most things, knowledge-related, and it is in this setting the second author met and got to know him. In 2017, the Bond University Law Library was undergoing a physical and ideological transformation as a result of building renovations and simultaneously, a greater uptake of eBooks. Renovations increased the availability of study spaces and but reduced the size of the print collection. In the second authors opinion, it is fair to say that John approved of the former but maybe less so of the latter. However, John, the reformer knows, accepts, and importantly adapts to change. Not that we knew it at the time, but the shift to eBooks proved to be a saviour in providing the mechanism for continuity of student support during the pandemic years that were to follow. Now to John the librarian, the member of Faculty who regularly beats library staff into the library, stops in for a chat and leaves behind a recommendation of the latest new release titles the library should acquire for its collection. John is and will always be a pre-eminent educator, administrator, reformer, scholar and contributor to the knowledge commons.

The concept of the 'commons' is associated with fields, forests and lakes and denotes that they are public goods for the benefits of all.[26] Over time the commons were appropriated by states or private corporations, denying access to others expect on payment of designated fees. Neo-liberal economic policies and legal structures have prevented restored access to these social and economic assets, despite attempts to reinstate them for community benefits.

All contemporary knowledge is ultimately built on the 'knowledge commons': the insights, writings, technologies, and inventions of others, many long forgotten. However, corporatised universities, as well as the private sector, have contributed to the diminution of the 'knowledge as commons' phenomenon, through the encouragement of copyright, patents, trademarks, commercial in confidence agreements and the commercialisation of 'product'.

Some perspectives suggest how important the knowledge commons are in relation to what is known interstitially, that is between published literature, fee-for-service teaching, and other aspects of education—now seen as a product to be sold to existing and new clients and measured with metrics relating to high-star journals and research impacts. John Farrar the educationalist has both excelled within the knowledge-as-product environment, and outside it. As an educator he has grown the legal knowledge commons with his numerous contributions to students, colleagues, professional bodies, and universities themselves. As a mentor, supervisor, colleague, and policy-adviser he has often stood outside the mercantilist model of education. There are many testaments to these contributions, starting with the Botswana solicitor referred to in the first paragraph.

There were few closed categories or irrebuttable presumptions in this aspect of Professor Farrar's educational contributions, partly because of the diversity of his intellectual interests, the breadth of his reading and the catholicity of his mind. A collegial conversation with him on, say, directors' duties or the business judgment rule, could lead into legal theory, comparative law, social theory, politics and even, for the unaware, theology. Connections in his thought processes mirrored the connections in his professional pursuits, making of John Farrar a Wyse and Compleate Professor.

References

Buckley, Ross. 1997. Legal Scholarship for New Law Teachers. *Legal Education Review* 8(2): 181, 193.

Calebresi, Guido. 1984. A *Common Law for the Age of Statutes*. Cambridge: Harvard University Press.

Farrar, John H and Dugdale, Anthony M. 1984. *An Introduction to Legal Method*. 2nd ed. London: Sweet and Maxwell

---

[26] The concept comes from a much used and misused article by Hardin (1968).

Farrar, John H, Lo, Vai Io, and Goh, Bee Chen. 2019. *Scholarship, Practice and Education in Comparative Law: A Festschrift in Honour of Mary Hiscock*. Singapore, Berlin: Springer.
Farrar, John. 1976. Law Reform Now – A Comparative View. *International and Comparative Law Quarterly* 25:214–228
Farrar, John. 1997. Reasoning by Analogy in the Law. *Bond Law Review* 9(2):149-175.
Farrar, John. 2009. *Legal Reasoning* Sydney: Law Book Co.
Farrar, John. 2010. Living with the Waikato Foundation Principles 20 Years On. *Waikato Law Review* 18: 83–89
Farrar, John. 2015. Reflections on Deanship. *Bond Law Review* 27:139.
Farrar, John. (2018a) The Future of Australian Legal Education: A Comparative View. In Kevin Lindgren, Francois Kunc, and Michael Coper (eds) The Future of Australian Legal Education Thomson Reuters, Australia, p143–155.
Farrar, John. 2018b. The Future of Australian Legal Education: A Comparative View. In *The Future of Australian Legal Education* eds, Lindgren, Kunc, Coper, 143–155. Australia: Thomson Reuters.
Glazenbrook, P R. 1985. The Twelfth Vinerian Professor: Rupert Cross and Criminal Justice. *Oxford Journal of Legal Studies* 5:113–116.
Hardin, Garrett. 1968. The tragedy of the Commons. *Science* 162 (3859): 1243.
Lewis, D Craig 1988. Observations from an Outsider. *Canterbury Law Review* 3:347–356
Lord Chancellor's Advisory Committee on Legal Education and Conduct. 1996. *First report on legal education and training*. https://ials.sas.ac.uk/ukcle/78.158.56.101/archive/law/files/downloads/407/165.c7e69e8a.aclec.pdf.
Read, James S. 2001. A Worthy Association: The early years of CLEA. *Commonwealth Legal Education Review: Newsletter of the Commonwealth Legal Education Association* 88: 8–15.
Tonnies, F.1912. *Gemeinschaft und Gesellschaft*. Fues Verlag, 2 4d

Part II
Globalisation in Transition: Economics Perspectives

Chapter 9
Calculated Compliance in a Globalised World: The Response to Social Licence Compulsions by the Australian Live Export Sector

Umair Ghori

Abstract The Australian live export sector has been under heightened pressure since media reports revealed widespread animal cruelty cases and violations of ethical treatment standards. After multiple reviews, the live export sector was expected to adapt to improved treatment standards. The live export sector must maintain its social licence to operate (SLO) by continuously engaging with the community and other stakeholders. This book chapter draws on the dual-layered social licence regulatory model. It argues that the increased vigilance by stakeholders means that governmental regulatory standards will themselves be subjected to audit by stakeholders and other custodians of SLO. In parallel to the regulated governmental response, the live export sector continues under pressure from the animal rights groups and the larger society to maintain their SLO. This regulation raises interesting issues for businesses, both domestic and foreign owned. The live export industry recognises that, given its controversial history, there are no guarantees that it will have the freedom to operate in the future. Therefore, the live export sector seeks to roll out a normative and cognitive strategy around engagement at the local community level with the media, policymakers, and influential opinion leaders. For foreign investors in the Australian cattle and livestock sector, understanding the dynamics of SLO-based regulation and the underlying normative and cognitive elements is essential to operate under the SLO umbrella.

9.1 Introduction

Emeritus Professor John Farrar's work as a legal practitioner and academic spans five decades. His work in corporate law, the study of globalisation and mentoring other academics inspires my humble contribution to this festschrift.

U. Ghori (✉)
Faculty of Law, Bond University, Gold Coast, Australia
e-mail: ughori@bond.edu.au

U. Ghori et al. (eds.), *Globalisation in Transition*,
https://doi.org/10.1007/978-981-99-2439-4_9

While SLO can be classified as a distinct theme, its sudden impact on the governance of modern corporations and corporate decision-making has captured the attention of policymakers and academics. SLO is the process of empowering communities and stakeholders to grant industry approval to conduct business activities.[1] Since there are no agreed definitions of SLO or any international treaties, the definition in academic literature affords the only real opportunity to understand its nature.

Even when the definitions in the academic literature are considered, the driving factors fall outside the realms of international trade or investment laws. Historically, the primary focus of SLO has been on the mining and natural resources sector.[2] Animal welfare has only begun to emerge as a major consideration under the SLO in recent times.

Where the SLO context is mining operations, the local communities are viewed as the custodians and the issuers of SLO because of their proximity.[3] In the case of animal welfare, the SLO issuance is by animal welfare groups such as *Voiceless* or *Royal Society for the Prevention of Cruelty to Animals* (RSPCA), or even the society at large. It should be noted here that I use the term "custodian" to capture all groups and stakeholders that usually "issue" the SLO. The SLO theory does not strictly use this term, nor is the term usually found in any legislation that acknowledges the existence of SLO. Another point to be kept in mind is that the term "custodian" and its meaning evolves when used in the context of animal welfare. The groups that seek to achieve animal welfare outcomes are referred to as the "custodians" because of their role in issuance, review and critique of government policies and laws affecting the welfare of animals. While the non-legislative and loose nature of the term "custodian" may make things difficult to interpret for the industry, it is an all-encompassing term that acknowledges and captures all types of stakeholders that seek to influence law and policy. The loose classification of the term "custodian", does however, shows how unpredictable and uncertain a fluid SLO concept can be to large-scale businesses, especially when it comes to regulatory compliance.

It is also important for the purposes of this chapter that the broad concept of SLO and its attendant term "custodians" be linked to the aim of animal welfare. Animal welfare is a wide expression covering animal 'uses' such as animal husbandry, racing, harvesting, exploitative farming, processing for human consumption, and live animal exports. SLO regarding animal welfare proposes to cover all the activities as mentioned above. In doing so, SLO becomes the 'voice' of society at large as opposed to the 'voice' of the proximate communities. Animal welfare carries greater, more abstract, and wide-ranging social licence effects than the localised effects in the case of mining activity.

Within the animal welfare sphere, the issue of live exports from Australia to the Asian and Middle Eastern markets has drawn significant media attention. In 2011, disturbing scenes from abattoirs in Indonesia drew widespread shock and

[1] Ghori (2019) and Hampton et al. (2020).

[2] Gehman et al. (2016), Raufflet et al. (2013), Joyce and Thomson (2000) referred to by Hall et al. (2015).

[3] Prno and Slocombe (2012).

condemnation from society at large and animal welfare groups.[4] The Australian Government responded by enacting an immediate export ban on live exports to Indonesia.[5] The ban was in place for a month before being lifted following a backlash from livestock breeders and associated industries.[6]

There is little doubt that live exports are a necessary evil. The sector carries immense importance for the rural Australian economy already ravaged by droughts, bushfires, and other natural disasters. According to industry estimates, Australia's beef cattle exports are worth AUD 1.35 billion annually, and dairy cattle exports are worth AUD 170 million, while sheep exports are valued at AUD 250 million.[7] The Australian Livestock Exporters Council (ALEC) estimates that the live export chain generates 10,000 jobs across Australia.[8] ALEC further claims that live exports support thousands of jobs in Australia and 12,000 direct jobs in Indonesia (the largest importer of live exports from Australia).[9]

Despite the importance of the live export sector, the shocking episodes of animal cruelty give rise to legitimate societal concerns that cannot be swept under the carpet. The uncertain governmental regulatory response in 2011 created a silver lining that compelled the live export industries to work with the government and community groups to improve animal welfare outcomes in the live export sector.[10] The outcomes in Australian exports of live animals cover the export process and extend to the transport and slaughtering processes. In doing so, the Australian live export sector began balancing its economic interests and foreign buyers' demands while meeting governmental regulatory standards and societal expectations under the watchful eye of the media.

This chapter offers a concise discussion of the SLO concept in relation to the Australian live export sector. Following the introduction, Part 9.2 discusses the dual-layered application of the SLO covering live exports from Australia. The dual-layered SLO model is based on the institutional theory. It seeks to highlight how regulation utilises a cognitive and normative strategy to demonstrate compliance to the custodians of the SLO. Part 9.2 of the chapter also looks at the Export Supply Chain Assurance System (ESCAS) program as a regulatory mechanism, and the industry led response, the Livestock Global Assurance Program (LGAP), to improve animal welfare outcomes. Part 9.3 of the chapter briefly discusses the industry self-regulation option whereby an industry-owned entity (AniMark) seeks to establish a control and surveillance mechanism that wrests control away from the traditional custodians of SLO. The certainty and predictability of the industry-led solution is the preferred

---

[4] ABC Four Corners (2011) and Parliament of Australia (2016).

[5] Parliament of Australia. Ibid; Blanchett and Zeller (2012).

[6] ABC News (2011).

[7] Australian Livestock Exporters' Council (ALEC) (2021).

[8] ALEC. Ibid.

[9] ALEC. Ibid.

[10] Department of Agriculture, Water and Environment (DAWE), Australian Government. Live animal export trade. https://www.awe.gov.au/agriculture-land/animal/welfare/export-trade. Accessed 13 February 2022.

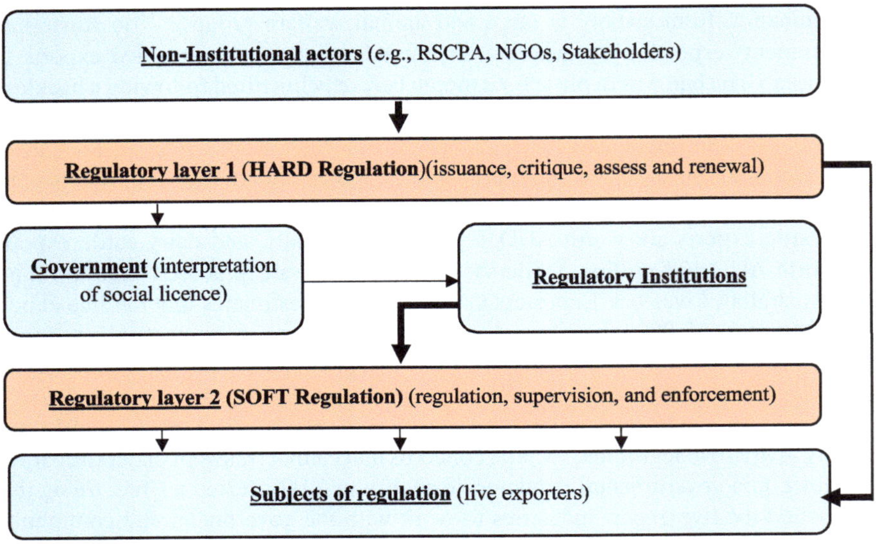

Fig. 9.1 Dual-layered regulation based on social licence narrative

outcome sought by the Australian live export sector because SLO intrudes at several regulatory levels. Part 9.4 concludes.

9.2 The Application of the Dual-Layered Model of SLO to the Australian Live Export Sector

A dual-layered model of SLO (illustrated in Fig. 9.1) occurs where non-institutional actors, the usual custodians of SLO (such as *Voiceless, Animals Australia,* or RSPCA), prompt the Government to adopt regulatory measures.

The ensuing regulation is justified based on the SLO. However, the regulation by the custodians of the SLO continues even after a governmental regulatory measure is implemented. When this process occurs, any institutional regulation is conducted within the defined framework of the regulatory response (e.g., guidelines or rules issued by a government body). At the same time, the custodians of the SLO continue to critique, assess, and 'renew' the efficacy of the regulatory repose and the compliance by the target seçtor. Therefore, the dual-layered model consists of both 'soft' and 'hard' regulation by the institutions and non-institutional actors.[11]

To illustrate the dual-layered model, the Australian Government's short-lived export ban in 2011 provides a suitable example. After the images of cruelty from

[11] Ghori. n 1. 55–89.

abattoirs in Indonesia were released in the media,[12] the emerging non-institutional responses from animal rights groups and society drove government institutions' regulatory response.

The response by the government institutions can be divided into two stages. In the first stage, the Government imposed a knee-jerk export ban following revelations of animal abuse by non-institutional actors. The negative effects of the export ban were immediately felt by businesses and industries linked to the live export sector.[13] The effects were also felt in Indonesia, a highly populated country, and a major importer of live cattle from Australia.[14]

The second stage of the dual-layered SLO model involves the institutional actors (the Government) adapting to the critique of the governmental policies by the non-institutional actors, i.e., the industry interests and the concerned societal groups. The institutional actor aims to balance two competing compulsions, i.e., economic considerations and humane treatment of animals.

9.2.1 Supply Chain Assurance

Following the lifting of the export ban, the Australian Government extended an assistance package to the affected producers and related businesses. The Australian Government introduced a new export permit requirement through the Export Supply Chain Assurance System (ESCAS) framework.[15] The ESCAS is in addition to legislative frameworks and industry standards already in place. The current Act and Regulations that relate to licences to export livestock and Orders that relate to specific export destinations are covered by the *Export Control Act 2020, Export Control (Animals) Rules 2021; Australian Standards for the Export of Livestock (ASEL) 3.2*. The ESCAS is based on four operating principles: animal welfare, traceability, control in the supply chain, and independent audit of the export processes.

The ESCAS enabled the resumption of exports of live animals in August 2011 and was later expanded to cover major foreign export markets for Australian live exports, such as China, Vietnam, and countries in the Middle East.[16] The ESCAS acts as an assurance system that covers animal welfare considerations under the *World Organisation for Animal Health* (OIE) recommendations, control of the supply chain,

---

[12] ABC Four Corners. n 4; Parliament of Australia. n 5. 7–30.

[13] Willingham (2011) and Arthur (2011).

[14] Roberts (2011).

[15] Parliament of Australia. n 4; DAWE, Australian Government. Australian Standards for the Export of Livestock. https://www.awe.gov.au/biosecurity-trade/export/controlled-goods/live-animals/livestock/australian-standards-livestock/reviews-updates.

[16] Parliament of Australia. n 4.

traceability of the stock through the supply chain, and independent supply chain audit in the importing country.[17]

The ESCAS system mandates that the exporter must obtain prior approval, which is granted based on the exporter demonstrating that the handling of the livestock up to the point of slaughter is following the OIE recommendations for animal welfare.[18] The ESCAS lodgment by the exporter must include results of an independent audit that demonstrates conformity with the OIE animal welfare recommendations throughout the supply chain.[19]

The ESCAS has been the subject of two major reviews in its decade-long existence. In the first major review of the ESCAS system, conducted in 2015 (the 'ESCAS Report'), the Australian Government acknowledged lax outcomes and episodes of poor treatment of animals. The Australian Government attributed the lapses to the system being relatively new and because it had been implemented after a short development time.[20] The ESCAS report further acknowledged that the implementation of the system was rigid and complex but claimed that the introduction of the system had contributed to the 'continuation of the livestock export industry'.[21] The ESCAS system continued to receive criticism from the RSPCA and other stakeholders. At the same time, the Department of Agriculture noted that certain breaches resulted in animals ending up in non-approved abattoirs.[22]

In the second, more detailed review of the ESCAS in June 2021, the Inspector-General of Live Animal Exports (IGLAE) reported that the business processes from industry and departmental perspectives were outdated.[23] The 2021 ESCAS Review found that there were still instances of loss of control and traceability at 'low but chronic levels'.[24] The recommended solution to the problem by the IGLAE was, firstly, to use recording, scanning, and tagging technology to maintain control over the supply chain. Secondly, proportionate regulatory sanctions were directed towards poor-performing exporters.[25]

One acknowledged challenge by the IGLAE in the 2021 ESCAS Review was that surveillance, inspection, and audits of non-compliance by the exporters depend on the willingness of the industry, animal welfare organisations, and the community interested in animal welfare outcomes.[26] In the case of ESCAS, the IGLAE noted that the department could not conduct surveillance, inspection, and audits in

---

[17] Department of Agriculture and Water Resources (DAWR), Australian Government. Exporter Supply Chain Assurance System (ESCAS). http://www.agriculture.gov.au/export/controlled-goods/live-animals/livestock/information-exporters-industry/escas. Accessed 13 February 2022.

[18] DAWR. Ibid.

[19] DAWR. Ibid.

[20] Australian Government (2015).

[21] Australian Government. Ibid.

[22] Locke (2016).

[23] Inspector-General of Live Animal Exports (IGLAE), Australian Government (2021).

[24] IGLAE. Ibid.

[25] IGLAE. Ibid.

[26] IGLAE. Ibid.

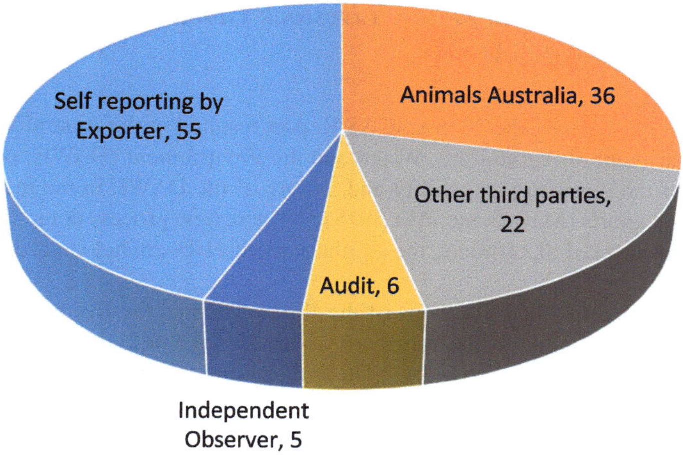

Fig. 9.2 Sources of Compliance Investigations (2015–2020), Table 5, ESCAS 2021 review, 36

the importing sovereign nations.[27] This observation is an acknowledgment by the institutional actors that the execution of regulatory measures in the live export sector greatly depends on the initiative and vigilance of the non-institutional actors.

According to the 2021 ESCAS Review, out of 124 reports of non-compliance with ESCAS, 47% were reported by third parties, with over 62% of the third-party reports coming from animal welfare organisations.[28] Figure 9.2 presents the breakdown of the sources of compliance investigations and the number of reports. The contrast between institutional mechanisms (e.g., audit) and non-institutional actors is striking. Only six instances of non-compliance were found by an audit under ESCAS, while non-institutional actors (excluding the exporters themselves) accounted for 63 out of 124 complaints (50.28%). The exporters self-reported 55 out of 124 complaints, demonstrating their commitments to ESCAS and OIE animal treatment standards.

The data presented in Fig. 9.2 further reinforces the fact that non-institutional actors are not only content in being limited to a custodian role in issuing the SLO to the live export sector but have taken upon themselves to invigilate the process of compliance by the exporters and the importers. The regulators (institutional actors) and the subject of regulations (the live export sector) have acquiesced to this role.

[27] IGLAE. Ibid.

[28] IGLAE. Ibid.

9.2.2 Industry-Led Solution: Livestock Global Assurance Program (LGAP)

The criticism following the 2015 ESCAS Report resulted in the Australian Government Department of Agriculture, Water, and the Environment (DAWE) performing a review of the regulatory capability and culture of the DAWE in the regulation of live animal exports (May–September 2018).[29] The review process demonstrates that under a dual-layered SLO model, the regulator themselves are held to account by the custodians of the SLO.

At the same time, the custodians of the SLO prompted the live export sector to endorse the implementation of a third-party assurance scheme known as the Livestock Global Assurance Program (LGAP).[30] The industry endorsement came in April 2018, even though the Australian Government pledged to implement the LGAP system in 2016 and issued an USD 8.3 million grant in May 2017.[31] The LGAP has been hailed as a 'world-first audit and assessment program for livestock exports'.[32] The LGAP is a voluntary certification program based on international precedents and research. The LGAP scheme covers the welfare of live export animals in the overseas markets from the point of disembarkation to the point of slaughter.[33] The LGAP, however, does not cover pre-export processing such as sourcing, on-farm preparation of livestock, land transport of livestock, and the transport by sea or air.[34]

The Australian standards cover the gap left by LGAP for the Export of Livestock (ASEL). The ASEL is the Australian Government regulatory standard covering minimum animal health and welfare conditions that the exporters must adhere to.[35] The ASEL represents specialised delegated legislation under the *Export Control Act 2020* and *Export Control (Animals) Rules 2021*. The ASEL is constantly subject to renewal and updates considering stakeholder feedback. For example, ASEL 3.2 (the most recent version) has also received criticism from *Animals Australia* in its submission to the 2021 update of ASEL. *Animals Australia* considers the risks to animal welfare in live exports as so serious that it advocates an outright ban.[36] In its submission on ASEL 3.2, *Animals Australia* supported the new definition of 'animal welfare' in line with the OIE Terrestrial Animal Health Code 2021, which includes an animal's 'mental state'.[37] The OIE revised definition of animal welfare is defined

---

[29] DAWE, Australian Government (2018).

[30] ALEC (2017).

[31] DAWE, Australian Government (2020a), ALEC. Ibid.

[32] Major (2021).

[33] AniMark (2020a).

[34] AniMark. Ibid.

[35] DAWE (2020b).

[36] Animals Australia (2021).

[37] Animals Australia. Ibid.

as 'the physical and mental state of an animal in relation to the conditions in which it lives and dies'.[38]

Similarly, the *Veterinary Institute of Animal Ethics* (VIAE) also voiced its support for the revised definition of 'animal welfare'. VIAE stated in its submission that the acknowledgment of the mental state of an animal provides an overriding framework against which standards for live exports should be revised.[39] The *Veterinary Institute of Animal Ethics* further advocated a permanent ban of the live export sector based on livestock conditions and deaths in the live export chain.[40]

The strong opposition by the custodians of SLO against the live export process creates complicated challenges for the industry. The response by the industry involves a delicate balancing act whereby the stakeholders seek on the one hand, to comply with governmental regulation such as ASEL. On the other hand, the stakeholders seek to acknowledge community expectations and critique by the non-institutional custodians of SLO. One possible solution from the industry stakeholders is the self-regulation option discussed in the following part of this chapter.

9.3 The Industry Self-regulation Option

The LGAP and ESCAS are intrinsically linked. Interested live export businesses can access LGAP and utilise its facilities to demonstrate compliance with the regulatory standards under the ESCAS.[41] The LGAP reflects the principles of the ESCAS and does not replace ESCAS, which remains the governmental regulatory framework.[42] In other words, participation in the LGAP constitutes an 'alternative pathway' for exporters to demonstrate their adherence to the ESCAS.[43]

The LGAP is an industry-led solution. It is operated by AniMark, an independent Australian public company limited by guarantee, specialising in developing and adopting standards-based certification programs (LGAP).[44] AniMark has received an *Exporter Supply Chain Assurance Operator Approved Arrangement* from the Department of Agriculture, Water, and the Environment to provide LGAP to the live export sector.[45] AniMark proponents claim that participation under the LGAP is purely voluntary, and AniMark will have greater international reach and influence throughout the supply chain than any sovereign government.[46]

---

[38] OIE (2022).

[39] Veterinary Institute of Animal Ethics (VIAE) (2021).

[40] VIAE. Ibid.

[41] AniMark. n 33.

[42] AniMark. n 33.

[43] AniMark. n 33.

[44] AniMark. n 33.

[45] AniMark. n 33.

[46] AniMark. n 33.

9.3.1 Response by the Industry

The AniMark initiative represents a controlled response by several actors involved in the live export business. The initiative allows the live export sector to retain control over the compliance and certification system. The AniMark-led LGAP scheme is driven by stakeholders such as the Australian Livestock Exporters' Council (ALEC), Cattle Council of Australia (CCA), Goat Industry Council of Australia (GICA), and Sheep Producers Australia (SPA).[47]

The stakeholders mentioned above are not comfortable with non-LGAP ESCAS certification. According to the industry submission in response to the *Third-Party Assurance Scheme for Exported Livestock: Consultation Regulation Impact Statement* (RIS), the LGAP system will be undermined if too many 'potential complications arise from having ESCAS approved but non-LGAP accredited facilities operating within supply chains.'[48]

The live export stakeholders praise the ESCAS system as 'novel' and the only system in the world designed to regulate animal welfare throughout the supply chain across international borders.[49] The live export industry claims that the LGAP system addresses the weakness in enforcing Australian Government regulations (ESCAS) on animal welfare.[50] There are strong jurisdictional grounds whereby the government of an importing country can object to enforcing the Australian Government's regulatory standards on its soil and animal markets. Accordingly, the use of a voluntary industry-led solution makes sense for the industry stakeholders (the target of SLO) because of two primary reasons:

1. Participation by the importers and meat processors in the LGAP is voluntary; and
2. Implementation of a voluntary, industry-led program enables the stakeholders in the live export sector to demonstrate compliance to the custodians of SLO.[51]

However, in the current scenario, the RSPCA (acting as a custodian of the SLO) expressed its dissatisfaction with the industry-led solution proposed by live export stakeholders. According to the RSPCA submission to the *Third-Party Assurance Scheme for Exported Livestock: Consultation Regulation Impact Statement* (RIS) in January 2020, the proposed AniMark implemented LGAP scheme is a form of 'industry self-regulation' where a third-party provider, an industry-owned company (AniMark), is granted a 'quasi-regulator' status.[52]

The RSPCA, in its submission, argues that the industry self-regulation approach transfers function like approval of new supply chains, investigation of non-compliance with ESCAS, imposition of penalties to a third-party provider instead

[47] ALEC (2020).
[48] ALEC. Ibid.
[49] ALEC. Ibid.
[50] ALEC. Ibid.
[51] AniMark (2020b).
[52] RSPCA (2020).

of a governmental regulator.[53] The RSPCA claims that the industry self-regulatory model under AniMark will dilute animal welfare and undermine the integrity of the regulatory framework because the Australian Government will lose direct oversight over the live export compliance process.[54] Furthermore, AniMark, a private company owned by the industry stakeholders, is not subject to Australian Freedom of Information laws or Parliamentary oversight committees.[55]

In essence, the RSPCA arguments are based on the notion of independence between the regulator and the regulated, along with avoidance of regulatory responsibility to the very industry that requires robust oversight to reduce animal abuse cases. The RSPCA endorses an approach whereby the Australian Government exercises direct oversight on the exporters through the supply chains in the importing economies.[56] In other words, the buck stops with the exporters who must ensure that the supply chain actors within the importing economies adhere to Australian Government standards such as the ESCAS and ASEL 3.2.

At the time of writing this chapter, COVID-19 related challenges led to the suspension of the LGAP rollout in the major export markets of Indonesia, Vietnam, and Saudi Arabia.[57] According to Mark Harvey-Sutton (the CEO of ALEC), the LGAP can only be effective if there is a partnership between the exporters and the importers.[58] The LGAP implementation remains uncertain due to the evolving state of the COVID-19 pandemic.

On a macro scale, the live export sector remains under constant pressure from animal rights groups and society to maintain their SLO.[59] Regardless of the regulation adopted by the Government, the 'soft' regulation by animal rights groups raises interesting issues for domestic and foreign businesses. Livestock exporters recognise that given the chequered history of the sector, there are no 'guarantees that the industry has greater freedom to operate in the future'.[60] Therefore, the live export sector seeks to roll out a normative and cognitive strategy around 'engagement at local community level, with the media, policymakers, and influential opinion leaders'.[61] According to W. Richard Scott's analysis, socio-political legitimacy of institutions can be divided into regulative, normative, and cognitive components. The normative component is the social norms, values, beliefs, and assumptions in a society.[62] Normative components of institutions define what is appropriate for the stakeholders in a society. The cognitive component is the common general perceptions of factors

[53] RSPCA. Ibid.
[54] RSPCA. Ibid.
[55] RSPCA. Ibid.
[56] RSPCA. Ibid.
[57] Major. n 32.
[58] Major. n 32.
[59] Bettles (2017).
[60] Bettles. Ibid.
[61] Bettles. Ibid.
[62] Scott (1995).

that are typically taken for granted in a society. The cognitive component of institutions reflects the structures and symbolic systems shared among individuals in a society or a nation society.[63]

For the stakeholders, such as road transporters, holding yards, shipping companies, abattoirs, and meat processors, alongside the Australian cattle and livestock sector, understanding the dynamics of 'soft' regulation and the underlying normative and cognitive elements is essential to continue to operate under SLO.[64] The understanding of the 'soft' regulation and vigilance is in addition to the governmental regulation (such as ESCAS), which, in turn, refers the operators/businesses back to the importance of maintaining SLO.

Figure 9.3 illustrates the complicated regulatory picture if the non-institutional actors can 'soft' regulate the live export sector. At all levels of the regulatory picture, the custodians of the SLO (non-institutional actors such as RSPCA, Animals Australia, Voiceless, or other societal groups) can affect the level and scale of regulation. The non-institutional response to questions of regulation is mainly cognitive and normative. Even where the non-institutional response is exhortative and non-binding, recent developments have demonstrated that it acts as a precursor to a regulatory response by the Government (institutional response).

When the submissions and statements of the non-institutional actors are considered in drafting the latest regulatory standards, the live export industries must comply with a dual-layered standard (see Fig. 9.1). Any legislated institutional response is juxtaposed with SLO-based oversight for the live export sector (see Figs. 9.2 and 9.3). However, only the institutional layer is prescriptive and tangible because it prescribes concrete factors for compliance by the livestock exporters. For example, ASEL 3.2 prescribes specific standards such as body condition score for export of animals for slaughter[65] or vessel preparation requirements for exports by sea.[66]

The SLO's second layer (see Fig. 9.1) remains unlegislated and abstract. The live export sector must constantly 'renew' the SLO. The challenge here is that the renewal of SLO is not cyclical or at regular intervals but is more episodic and unpredictable.

9.3.2 *Vigilance of the Supply Chain*

Another challenge for live export comes in cross-border vigilance of the entire supply chain. While the livestock remains within the Australian territory, 'hard' regulation under Australian laws can easily be applied to the processors and the live export businesses. However, once the live export shipment is loaded, the enforcement of SLO becomes a complicated proposition for both the non-institutional

---

63 Scott. Ibid.

64 Stanley (2017), Department of Parliamentary Services, Parliament of Australia (2014).

65 DAWE, Australian Government (2021).

66 DAWE, Australian Government. Ibid.

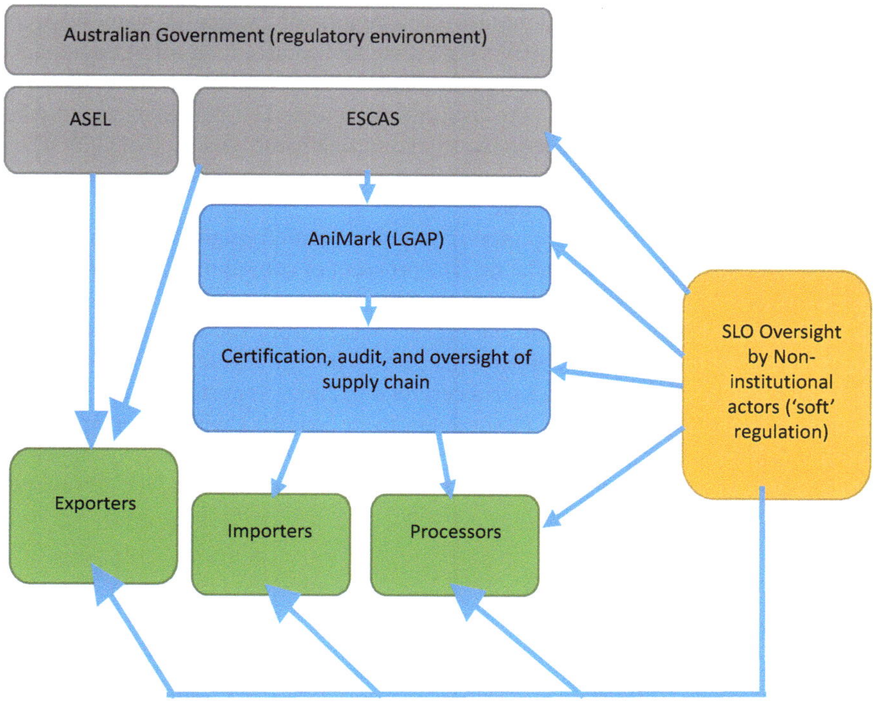

Fig. 9.3 The intrusion of SLO Soft Regulation into the AniMark and LGAP system

actors and the exporters. Figures 9.2 and 9.3 illustrate the oversight exercised by the non-institutional actors over the exporters, importers, and processors.

The non-institutional actors have made in-roads into the regulatory picture following the 2011 revocation of the live export ban by the Australian Government. After the revocation, the government regulators consistently sought to understand the broad SLO and its application to the ESCAS from the interpretation of the animal rights groups and the civil society concerned about animal welfare. For the live export business, a dual-layered SLO regulation environment may prove to be more difficult, unpredictable, and costly than a direct regulatory model whereby the Government prescribes standards by interpreting the SLO.

It is also noteworthy that while the animal rights groups may represent a single pedigree of SLO custodians, the views within the society at large may fluctuate because non-institutional responses by stakeholders may not always be uniform or on the same level. The divergence in views is observable in situations where one group of non-institutional actors advocates for a total ban on live exports. In contrast, another group may favour live exports because of potential employment opportunities or business development in the rural economies, subject to animal welfare standards. Both non-institutional actors may rely on cognitive and normative arguments to support their stance.

The AniMark system and the industry self-regulation option, in many respects, represent an attempt by the industry to calculate and control its level of compliance with the SLO. In doing so, the live export stakeholders capitalise on the disparity within the SLO response from non-institutional actors. The delicate state of rural Australian economies dependent on livestock farming in the backdrop of COVID-19 and extended periods of drought further reinforces the sympathetic response from the industry towards its stakeholders.

However, for the overseas importers, compliance with foreign custodians of SLO represents an unprecedented headache. The prospect of complying with alien values, increased cost of imports, handling, processing of animals, and its overall effects on the business bottom line could put off businesses from sourcing livestock from Australia altogether. If the cost of compliance with foreign regulatory standards such as ASEL, ESCAS, or LGAP crosses a certain threshold, importing businesses may shift their sourcing preferences to suppliers from countries with lesser regulatory overhang. Such a shift would be disastrous for the Australian live export sector, while it would be a long sought-after triumph for the animal rights groups and non-institutional actors.

9.4 Conclusion

The cross-border application of SLO is an emerging trend within globalisation. Importing businesses are justifiably concerned about an unlegislated concept that can impact businesses in the short and long term and where the regulatory contours are difficult to gauge. The non-institutional actors are key drivers of review and policy change in the live export sector. The governmental regulatory responses, such as the 2018 *Review of the Regulatory Capability and Culture of the Department of Agriculture and Water Resources in the Regulation of Live Animal Exports, the 2021 update of ASEL, and the Review of the ESCAS* program (June 2021), have all been the result of concerted campaigns initiated by the custodians of SLO.

The campaigns launched by the custodians of SLO and the response by the Government create interdependency[67] between the two actors that are illustrated in the hierarchy of the dual-layered model (see Fig. 9.1 and the accompanying discussion). Within this interdependency, the custodians of SLO seek to paint a picture of cruelty to animals and corporate greed to tap into the emotional and moral pulse of the society at large. Economic facts and figures associated with live exports are deliberately overlooked or disregarded as secondary. The language used by the custodians of SLO may overlap with existing normative values and negative perceptions of businesses in the society, reinforcing a picture of harm and distress.[68]

---

[67] Murphy-Gregory (2018).

[68] Murphy-Gregory. Ibid. 320, 332.

Using imagery, videos, and emotive expression, the non-institutional actors seek to obtain a seat at the regulatory table.[69] Such an SLO strategy is termed a 'discursive method' to query the adequacy of governmental regulations.[70] The governmental organisations feel compelled through a combination of public pressure and the need for effective regulation to consider the inputs of the SLO custodians. The final regulatory standards are still determined and executed by the government (institutional actors). Therefore, the regulatory hierarchy remains intact between the regulators and the regulated.

For the live export sector, responding to the critique of the SLO and compliance with the mandatory standards presents a double challenge. The industry faces uncertainty and the challenge of containment of the flexible and non-cyclical nature of SLO. While the live export sector may prefer the certainty of a legal licence, the difficulty in measuring SLO means that the industry stakeholders would be keen to contain the boundaries of SLO-based regulation.

Containment is important for the industry for several reasons:

(a) Minimisation of compliance costs.
(b) Certainty enables efficient planning.
(c) Conversion of an intangible set of values to a tangible standard.
(d) Continued maintenance of legitimacy, assurance, and reporting mechanisms.

The impact of the factors mentioned above carries direct relevance for the subsistence of the live export sector. Accordingly, the industry interest would be better served in the form of a prescriptive legal licence instead of the non-prescriptive and fluid SLO.

Containment is also important for the live export sector. Unlike the mining SLO issued by the local communities, the custodians of SLO are not located locally and may be more ideologically diverse. One academic view is that where there is an assortment of stakeholder interests, preference should be given to those most directly impacted.[71] Another view is that SLO recognition is simultaneous because distant stakeholders can affect localised issues, impacting the business reputation both nationally and internationally.[72] Both views carry important consequences for the live export sector.

If Fig. 9.2 and the observations of the IGLAE in the 2021 ESCAS Review are taken as an indicator, it seems that the live export sector has accepted the notion that Australian livestock deserves high standards of treatment in the importing markets. Accordingly, the LGAP system maintained by AniMark can be seen as an attempt by the live export sector to introduce an industry-led level of certainty to the export of livestock from Australia.

Given enough time and continuous review and vigilance, the LGAP system could minimise compliance costs and bring certainty to the sector that is already subject

---

[69] Sim (2021).

[70] Murphy-Gregory. n 67. 332.

[71] Moffatt et al. (2016).

[72] Morrison (2014) and Zhang et al. (2015).

to several layers of regulatory requirements. The live export industry would likely accept this as a tangible regulatory outcome that is preferable to SLO regulatory models driven by non-institutional actors.

References

ABC Four Corners. 2011. A Bloody Business. https://www.abc.net.au/4corners/a-bloody-business---2011/2841918. Accessed 16 February 2022

ABC News. 2011. Governments Lifts Live Cattle Export Ban. ABC News, July 6. https://www.abc.net.au/news/2011-07-06/government-lifts-live-cattle-export-ban/2784790

ALEC. 2017. Livestock Exporters Welcome Federal Commitment for LGAP implementation. https://auslivestockexport.com/images/pdfs/Media-Budget-LGAP-09052017-FINAL.pdf. Accessed 18 February 2022

ALEC. 2020. Submission by ALEC in Response to Third Party Assurance Scheme for Exported Livestock: Consultation Regulation Impact Statement. https://haveyoursay.awe.gov.au/third-party-assurance-escas. Accessed 21 February 2022

Animals Australia. 2021. Animals Australia's Submission Re: Feedback on the Draft ASEL 3.2. https://www.awe.gov.au/sites/default/files/documents/asel-submission-animals-australia.pdf. Accessed 18 February 2022

AniMark. 2020a. Livestock Global Assurance Program. https://www.animark.com.au/programs/. Accessed 19 February 2022

AniMark. 2020b. Submission by AniMark in Response to Third Party Assurance Scheme for Exported Livestock: Consultation Regulation Impact Statement. https://haveyoursay.awe.gov.au/third-party-assurance-escas. Accessed 21 February 2022

Arthur, Chrissy. 2011. Outback Families Still Recovering from Cattle Exports Ban. ABC News, November 23. https://www.abc.net.au/news/2011-11-23/outback-families-still-recovering-from-cattle-exports-ban/3688282

Australian Government. 2015. Exporter Supply Chain Assurance System. http://www.agriculture.gov.au/SiteCollectionDocuments/biosecurity/export/live-animals/livestock/escas/escas-report.pdf. Accessed 3 February 2022

Australian Livestock Exporters' Council (ALEC). 2021. Economic Impact of Livestock Export Trade. https://auslivestockexport.com/about-alec/economic-impact. Accessed 12 February 2022

Bettles, C. 2017. Celebrity Punch Needed to Safeguard Live Exports Social License. Farmonline. https://www.farmonline.com.au/story/4629860/celebrity-punch-needed-to-safeguard-live-exports-social-licence/. Accessed 11 February 2022

Blanchett, J., and B. Zeller. 2012. No Winners in the Suspension of the Livestock Trade with Indonesia. *University of Notre Dame Australia Law Review* 14: 55, 57–61

DAWE, Australian Government. 2018. Submission to the Review of the Regulatory Capability and Culture of the Department of Agriculture and Water Resources in the Regulation of Live Animal Exports. https://www.awe.gov.au/agriculture-land/animal/welfare/export-trade/independent-review-of-regulation/submissions. Accessed 9 January 2022

DAWE, Australian Government. 2020a. 2020a–25 ESCAS Auditing Requirements – LGAP. https://www.awe.gov.au/biosecurity-trade/export/controlled-goods/live-animals/advisory-notices/2020a/2020-25. Accessed 18 February 2022

DAWE, Australian Government. 2020b. Australian Standards for the Export of Livestock. https://www.awe.gov.au/biosecurity-trade/export/controlled-goods/live-animals/livestock/australian-standards-livestock. Accessed 18 February 2022

DAWE, Australian Government. 2021. Australian Standards for the Export of Livestock 3.2. https://www.awe.gov.au/sites/default/files/documents/asel-3-2-a4.pdf. Accessed 22 February 2022

Department of Parliamentary Services, Parliament of Australia. 2014. Foreign Investment in Australian Agriculture (Research Paper Series 2013–14). https://parlinfo.aph.gov.au/parlInfo/download/library/prspub/3006295/upload_binary/3006295.pdf;fileType=application/pdf
Gehman, J., D. Thompson, D. Alessi, D. Allen, and G. Goss. Comparative Analysis of Hydraulic Fracturing Wastewater Practices in Unconventional Shale Development: Newspaper Coverage of Stakeholder Concerns and Social Licence to Operate. 2016. *Sustainability* 8: 912
Ghori, Umair. 2019. Encroachment of Social Licence in Australia's Trade and Investment. *University of Western Australia Law Review* 46(1): 55–89
Hall, N., K. Lacey, S. Carr-Cornish, and A-M. Dowd. 2015. Social Licence to Operate: Understanding How a Concept has been Translated into Practice in Energy Industries. *Journal of Cleaner Production* 86: 301, 301-302
Hampton, J.O., B. Jones, and P.D. McGreevy. 2020. Social License and Animal Welfare: Developments from the Past Decade in Australia. *Animals* 10: 2237. doi:https://doi.org/10.3390/ani10122237
Inspector-General of Live Animal Exports (IGLAE), Australian Government. 2021. Review of the Exporter Supply Chain Assurance System (ESCAS)
Joyce, S., and I. Thomson. 2000. Earning a Social Licence to Operate: Social Acceptability and Resource Development in Latin America. *Canadian Mining and Metallurgical Bulletin* 93: 49–53
Locke, Sarina. 2016. Livestock exporters argue animal welfare standards improved at their expense, while RSPCA slams Government report. ABC News, 10 March. http://www.abc.net.au/news/rural/2016-03-10/rspca-slams-animal-welfare-breaches-of-exports/7235816
Major, Tom. 2021. Live Export Industry Pauses Plans for New Monitoring Program Roll-out. ABC News, September 15. https://www.abc.net.au/news/rural/2021-09-15/live-export-industry-lgap-hold-welfare-sheep-cattle/100461036
Moffatt, K., J. Lacey, A. Zhang, and S. Leipold. 2016. The Social Licence to Operate: A Critical Review. *Forestry* 89:477–488, 481. doi:https://doi.org/10.1093/forestry/cpv044
Morrison, John. 2014. *The Social License: How to Keep your Organization Legitimate*. Palgrave Macmillan, London
Murphy-Gregory, H. 2018. Governance via Persuasion: Environmental NGOs and the Social Licence to Operate. *Environmental Politics* 27(2): 320, 332–335
OIE. Animal Welfare. 2022. https://www.oie.int/en/what-we-do/animal-health-and-welfare/animal-welfare/. Accessed 17 February 2022
Parliament of Australia. 2016. Live Export: A Chronology. https://parlinfo.aph.gov.au/parlInfo/download/library/prspub/4700032/upload_binary/4700032.pdf. Accessed 12 February 2022
Prno, J., and S. Slocombe. 2012. Exploring the Origins of Social Licence to Operate in the Mining Sector: Perspectives from Governance and Sustainability Theories. *Resources Policy* 37: 346, 346–347
Raufflet, E., S. Baba, C. Perras, and N. Delannon. 2013. Social License. In *Encyclopedia of Corporate Social Responsibility*, ed. S. Idowu, N. Capaldi, L. Zu, and A.D. Gupta, 2223–30. New York: Springer
Roberts, Georgia. 2011. Indonesia to Slash Aussie Beef Imports. ABC News, December 15. https://www.abc.net.au/news/2011-12-15/indonesia-to-slash-beef-imports/3733776
RSPCA. 2020. Submission by RSPCA in Response to Third Party Assurance Scheme for Exported Livestock: Consultation Regulation Impact Statement. https://kb.rspca.org.au/wp-content/uploads/2020/04/2020-01-17-RSPCA-Australia-submission-Third-Party-Assurance-Scheme-RIS.pdf Accessed 5 December 2022
Scott, W.R., 1995. *Institutions and Organizations*. Sage Publications
Sim, T. 2021. DAWE Investigating new reports of Alleged ESCAS Non-compliance in UAE. Sheep Central. https://www.sheepcentral.com/dawe-investigating-new-reports-of-alleged-escas-non-complaince-in-uae/. Accessed 13 February 2022

Stanley, Michelle. 2017. Foreign Investment Flagged as Answer to Australia's Livestock Shortage. ABC News, February 27. http://www.abc.net.au/news/rural/2017-02-27/foreign-investment-answer-to-australias-livestock-shortage/8301960

Veterinary Institute of Animal Ethics (VIAE). 2021. Submission by Veterinary Institute of Animal Ethics – Feedback on the Draft 2021 update of the ASEL Consultation Paper. https://www.awe.gov.au/sites/default/files/documents/asel-submission-sentient.pdf. Accessed 17 February 2022

Willingham, R. 2011. Farmers worried as Indonesia plans to cut beef imports. The Sydney Morning Herald, December 16. https://www.smh.com.au/environment/conservation/farmers-worried-as-indonesia-plans-to-cut-beef-imports-20111216-1ox74.html

Zhang, A., K. Moffat, J. Lacey, J. Wang, R. Gonzalez, and K. Uribe et al. 2015. Understanding the Social Licence to Operate of Mining at the National Scale: A comparative study of Australia, China and Chile. *Journal of Cleaner Production* 108: 1063–1072

Chapter 10
Towards More Effective and Inclusive Globalisation Strategies in International Tax: The Use of Peer Reviews in Evaluating Tax Treaty Dispute Resolution Mechanisms

Michelle Markham

Abstract The Organisation for Economic Cooperation and Development (OECD)/G20 Base Erosion and Profit Shifting Project, initiated in 2013, delivered 15 final Actions in 2015. These actions represent countermeasures to serious risks to tax revenues, tax sovereignty and tax fairness because of globalisation and constitute the most far-reaching and fundamental changes to international tax rules in over a century. They exemplify globalisation in transition, as they reflect the realisation that international tax solutions now require dialogue on a global basis. To this end, an Inclusive Framework was established in 2016, to ensure that both developed and developing countries could participate on an equal and collaborative basis in reviewing and monitoring the new tax rules, including the implementation of new minimum standards on tax treaty dispute resolution. This chapter will examine and evaluate the innovative new peer review process in relation to Action 14, which seeks to improve tax treaty related disputes between jurisdictions. It will critically analyse the outcomes of this process in terms of its efficiency and effectiveness in improving international dispute resolution mechanisms on a global basis.

> Globalisation has involved increased flows of goods, services, and capital as well as interconnectedness, movements of people and exchange of ideas. We recognise that globalisation has advanced at a rapid pace in recent decades with some high growth emerging economies becoming major economic players. We recognise that we must improve our understanding of the impact of globalisation, but also note that, in recent decades, we have seen hundreds of millions of people lifted out of poverty and that many others have benefited from higher productivity, global economic growth and an increase in the range and affordability of goods and services.[1]

[1] OECD (2017).

M. Markham (✉)
Faculty of Law, Bond University, Gold Coast, Australia
e-mail: mmarkham@bond.edu.au

U. Ghori et al. (eds.), *Globalisation in Transition*,
https://doi.org/10.1007/978-981-99-2439-4_10

10.1 Introduction

In his seminal work on globalisation, Emeritus Professor John Farrar describes this term as connoting 'internationalisation and, to some extent, standardisation'.[2] This chapter will consider recent moves in the international tax arena towards the standardisation of tax dispute resolution mechanisms, with the aim of facilitating tax certainty by making them more effective, coherent, and transparent.

In the OECD/G20 Action Plan on Base Erosion and Profit Shifting ('BEPS Action Plan'), the OECD describes itself as a 'unique forum where governments work together to address the economic, social and environmental challenges of globalisation'.[3] The OECD recognises the benefits that globalisation has brought to domestic economies, particularly in encouraging trade and increased foreign direct investments in many countries, leading to positive outcomes such as job creation, innovation and growth.[4]

In the specific context of tax on companies, globalisation may have both a positive and a negative effect on a jurisdiction's corporate tax regime. There can be no doubt that access to the global marketplace, with its concomitant exchange of goods, ideas, services, and technology is beneficial to a country's fiscus, but there are also potential risks in global engagement.

The notion of taxation is inextricably linked to national sovereignty, in that each nation has the sovereign right to design its own tax system. While taxation is acknowledged to be at the core of a country's sovereignty,[5] the lack of alignment between national tax systems means that there can be discordance between systems, resulting in the inequitable result of double taxation[6] in certain situations, or in the equally inequitable result of corporate income not being taxed at all, or only being taxed at a nominal rate, in other situations. This lack of alignment is exacerbated by increasing globalisation, a corollary of which has been an exponential rise in trade and cross-border transactions. The existing international standards have sought to address this lack of global alignment while respecting sovereignty, but gaps and loopholes remain.[7]

These gaps and loopholes can be used by multinational enterprises[8] in their tax planning strategies to undertake base erosion and profit shifting. The erosion of a

[2] Farrar and Mayes (2013).

[3] OECD (2013a).

[4] Ibid.

[5] Ibid.

[6] Double taxation is defined by the OECD as follows: 'Double taxation is juridical when the same person is taxed twice on the same income by more than one state. Double taxation is economic if more than one person is taxed on the same item.' See: <https://www.oecd.org/ctp/glossaryoftaxterms.htm>.

[7] OECD, above n 2.

[8] Defined by the OECD as a 'Company or group of companies with business establishments in two or more countries.' See OECD Glossary of Tax Terms <https://www.oecd.org/ctp/glossaryoftaxterms.htm≥ . Accessed 25 January 2022.

country's tax base 'constitutes a serious risk to tax revenues, tax sovereignty and tax fairness for OECD member countries and non-members alike'.[9] In recent years, the OECD has highlighted the significant problems occurring when a country's tax base is eroded by profit being artificially shifted from a high-tax country to a low-tax country where there is little or no economic activity. This issue is of great concern to developing countries, as their 'higher reliance on corporate income tax means they suffer from BEPS disproportionately'.[10]

At its core, globalisation involves economic integration.[11] As economies become more interconnected, a need has arisen to design a new set of internationally coherent standards with regards to corporate income taxation, to put an end to base erosion and profit shifting. Through its BEPS Action Plan, the OECD has sought to develop global tax standards reinforced through strong peer review mechanisms to provide a level playing field for all jurisdictions, declaring that: 'It is time for better globalisation, more inclusive globalisation, globalisation that regains its ultimate sense of improving all people's lives.'[12]

In an increasingly globalised world, unilateral action does not result in optimum outcomes, especially in the international tax arena. The OECD's establishment of an Inclusive Framework, encompassing both developed and developing nations, serves as recognition of the fact that globalisation is in transition. This transformational era necessitates a globally coherent, consistent, transparent, and unified approach that facilitates tax certainty for all taxpayers, and that contributes to the free flow of trade and investment.

10.2 The Establishment of the Inclusive Framework

The OECD/G20 Inclusive Framework on BEPS ('Inclusive Framework') was established in Kyoto, Japan, in June 2016 with an initial membership of 89 countries and jurisdictions.[13] The call for an Inclusive Framework was based on a growing realisation that in order to establish truly global standards, a multilateral collaborative framework beyond the OECD and G20 countries was required. As early as 2011, it was recognised that the OECD, which had formerly been identified as a 'club of rich, industrialised nations' was embarking on a more inclusive policy, engaging more widely with non-members, especially emerging powers and developing countries.[14]

This more inclusive policy attests to globalisation being in a state of transition, as meaningful reform and international tax solutions now require dialogue on a global basis. Membership in the Inclusive Framework has increased exponentially

---

[9] OECD (2013b).

[10] OECD. What is BEPS? <https://www.oecd.org/tax/beps/about/>. Accessed 22 January 2022.

[11] Al-Rodhan et al. (2006).

[12] Gurría (2017).

[13] OECD (2021a).

[14] Clifton and Díaz-Fuentes (2011).

since its inception, as the OECD/G20 has sought to involve all interested countries in the implementation of the BEPS agenda. As at the end of January 2022, the Inclusive Framework includes 141 members,[15] with the northwest Africa country of Mauritania being the latest to join in November 2021.[16] An examination of this membership reveals that approximately one-third are developing countries, and 49 members are low- or middle-income countries that are not members of either the OECD or G20 and are not jurisdictions considered to be financial centres.[17]

The OECD has noted that

> [f]eedback from developing countries indicates strong support for the BEPS agenda, although some have noted that the BEPS Actions may not reflect their highest priorities given that they were not able to participate fully in the process prior to the establishment of the Inclusive Framework.[18]

The establishment of the Inclusive Framework was thus a watershed moment for the participation of developing countries in the BEPS reforms.

While not all 15 Action Items outlined in the OECD's BEPS Action Plan may be high on the agenda of pressing international tax issues for developing countries, one Action may be of universal importance to all jurisdictions: BEPS Action 14: Make dispute resolution mechanisms more effective ('Action 14'). The General Assembly and the Economic and Social Council of the United Nations, as well as the United Nations Conference on Trade and Development, have frequently affirmed the desirability of promoting greater inflows of foreign investment to developing countries, with the proviso that this is carried out in a politically acceptable and economically and socially beneficial way.[19] The United Nations has recently commented that while all countries that rely on income taxes have a vested interest in both minimising international tax disputes and in ensuring that such controversies are resolved fairly and effectively, this is a particularly important issue for developing countries. Such countries are seen to be more reliant on attracting and maintaining foreign direct investment, and thus the implementation of updated and more efficient and effective measures for avoiding and resolving tax disputes is an essential issue with respect to the sustainable development of such countries.[20]

Inclusive Framework members have agreed to make their national dispute resolution mechanisms more effective by the adoption of the Action 14 minimum standard. This includes a strong political commitment to resolve disputes effectively and efficiently through the Mutual Agreement Procedure ('MAP'), a double tax treaty mechanism designed to resolve difficulties arising out of the interpretation or application of a treaty. The MAP Article in double tax treaties (treaties entered for the purpose of the elimination of double taxation with respect to taxes on income and on capital and

---

[15] OECD/G20 Members (2021).

[16] OECD (2021d).

[17] OECD, above n 13.

[18] Ibid.

[19] United Nations, United Nations Model Double Taxation Convention between Developed and Developing Countries 2017 Update (13 October 2017).

[20] United Nations (2021).

the prevention of tax evasion and avoidance) empowers designated country representatives, known as competent authorities, to interact to resolve double taxation disputes and conflicts of interpretations between treaty partner countries on the tax treatment of their activities. This process was designed to ensure that taxpayers entitled to the benefits of the treaty are not subject to taxation which is not in accordance with the terms of the treaty. The MAP is contained in Article 25 of both the OECD and United Nations' Model Tax Conventions.

Under the Action 14 Terms of Reference, the performance of a jurisdiction's MAP regime is assessed in relation to four key areas: (A) preventing disputes; (B) availability and access to MAP; (C) resolution of MAP cases; and (D) implementation of MAP agreements. The Assessment Methodology for these Terms of Reference established by the OECD involves a two-stage peer review and monitoring process. In Stage 1, an Inclusive Framework member's implementation and application of the minimum standard via its MAP legal framework is reviewed, and recommendations are made to address any discrepancies or shortcomings. This is followed by Stage 2, where the actions taken by the jurisdiction in response to these recommendations are evaluated.[21]

This commitment by Inclusive Framework members includes the establishment of an effective monitoring mechanism to ensure that this minimum standard is met by all the jurisdictions involved, ensuring that progress is made towards rapidly resolving disputes on a global basis.[22] Furthermore, it includes an obligation on each jurisdiction to provide timely and complete reporting on dispute resolution via a MAP Statistics Reporting Framework.[23] There is an emphasis on increased transparency on the part of members of the Inclusive Framework,

From a globalisation in transition perspective, while all Inclusive Framework members are required to comply with the Action 14 minimum standard with regards to dispute resolution, several developing countries do not have large numbers of MAP cases. For example, Oman, designated by the United Nations as a developing economy in 2021,[24] has no experience with resolving MAP disputes, as it has not been involved in any such cases.[25] While Oman nevertheless elected to undergo the Stage 1 peer review, certain lower capacity developing countries with low numbers of MAP cases are considered eligible by the OECD to defer their Action 14 peer review. In fact, as at 30 June 2021, 40 developing countries (85% of the countries in the Inclusive Framework that were designated as developing countries at that date) had opted to defer their Action 14 peer review.[26] Furthermore, other developing countries that have subsequently joined the Inclusive Framework are expected to request a deferral of

---

[21] OECD (2016a).

[22] OECD (2016b).

[23] OECD, above n 21.

[24] United Nations., Table C Developing economies by region. World Economic Situation and Prospects 2021, Statistical Annex.

[25] OECD (2021b).

[26] OECD. 2021, above n 23; See also Box 1.5. BEPS Action 14: MAP, Source: OECD, based on the review of the implementation of the BEPS package as at 1 June 2021, 20.

their Action 14 Peer Review in the near future. However, the OECD has emphasised the importance of taking into account that: 'as domestic compliance programmes expand, having a well-functioning MAP process will become increasingly important to sound tax administration and investor confidence'.[27] As countries metamorphose from developing countries into developed countries, perhaps by way of becoming economies in transition,[28] so the relevance of adhering to the Action 14 minimum standards will increase.

10.3 The Peer Review Process

The peer review process under Action 14 allows for commentary not only from the jurisdiction being assessed and peer jurisdictions, but also from taxpayers. It may consequently be regarded as a truly inclusive process, facilitated by the OECD Forum on Tax Administration MAP Forum ('FTA MAP Forum'). In its Strategic Plan, the determination was made that

> *the MAP Forum shall work in accordance with a multilateral strategic plan to collectively improve the effectiveness of our mutual agreement procedures in order to meet the needs of both governments and taxpayers and so assure the critical role of those procedures in the global tax environment.*[29]

The FTA MAP Forum is therefore a unique vehicle to ensure the collaboration of all competent authorities to improve the effectiveness of dispute resolution mechanisms, to the benefit of both tax administrations and taxpayers.

Although the OECD is an international organisation with the capacity to provide binding norms to its member states, in practice its governance is almost only through a soft law approach of diffusing principles and policy solutions, especially with respect to tax matters.[30] Hard law, imposing binding, legally enforceable obligations reinforced by sanctions, is rarely used. The soft law tool utilised for the Action 14 minimum standard is the peer review process.

This process has been described as:

> *the systematic examination and assessment of the performance of a State by other States, with the ultimate goal of helping the reviewed State improve its policy making, adopt best practices, and comply with established standards and principles. The examination is conducted on a non-adversarial basis, and it relies heavily on mutual trust among the States.*[31]

---

[27] Ibid.

[28] The UN *World Economic Situation and Prospects 2021*, Statistical Annex, above n xxiv, designates countries as Developed Economies, Economies in Transition, Developing Economies by Region, and Fuel- Exporting Countries.

[29] OECD. Multilateral Strategic Plan on Mutual Agreement Procedures: A Vision for Continuous MAP Improvement Multilateral Strategic Plan on Mutual Agreement Procedures. https://www.oecd.org/tax/forum-on-tax-administration/publications-andproducts/map-strategic-plan.pdf; Adopted at the Ninth Meeting of the Forum on Tax Administration 23–24 October 2014, Dublin, Ireland.

[30] Vega (2012).

[31] Pagani (2002).

While this facilitative soft law process lacks legal sanctions, in the context of globalisation in transition there may be advantages to the application of such a non-adversarial process to an international collaboration of jurisdictions with a diverse membership of both developed and developing countries, such as the Inclusive Framework. Soft law instruments are reputed to cope better with diversity, as well as imposing lower 'sovereignty costs' on states in sensitive areas.[32] The peer review process has been described as a more effective and legitimate system in enabling state compliance in an international law context, in that 'acceptability replaces command, peer pressure replaces sanctions, and learning replaces enforcement of traditional compliance monitoring systems'.[33]

This does not mean that the value of compliance is diminished. Indeed, an expert commentator has stated that monitoring and enhancing compliance by countries with internationally agreed policies, standards and principles is an important function of the peer review process.[34] However, in certain contexts the soft law nature of peer reviews can be more successful than a traditional hard law enforcement mechanism in encouraging and enhancing compliance. For example:

> *examiners in a peer review have the flexibility to take into account a country's policy objectives, and to look at its performance in a historical and political context. Peer review can therefore assess and encourage trends toward compliance even among relatively poorly performing countries, while noting negative trends in countries that may presently have a higher performance record. Peer review can also tend to enhance compliance by helping to clarify differences in policy positions among countries, thereby leading to the resolution of those differences.*[35]

Peer reviews may therefore have a positive effect on countries that are far from meeting the OECD's minimum standard, in that their experience is contextualised, with the emphasis being on helping the examined state to improve its performance within that policy field. They can be described as representing a dual challenge and a most complex balancing act in that they 'must be critical of a country's activity, while fully respecting its culture'.[36]

As peer pressure replaces sanctions in the peer review process, there is a danger that outlier states will simply ignore the pressure exerted by others in the cohort. In this regard, peer pressure has been described as 'most effective in "laggard" states, because a country seldom wants to risk losing its credibility and being seen in an unfavourable light among its peers'.[37] With the Action 14 peer reviews, there is not only pressure from peers. As the reports are published, they are also open to international public scrutiny, adding to the social and political accountability pressure on recalcitrant jurisdictions.

---

[32] Shaffer and Pollack (2010).

[33] Dimitropoulos (2016).

[34] Pagani, above n 31, 21.

[35] Ibid., 21–22.

[36] Guilmette (2007).

[37] Lehtonen (2020)

10.4 An Inclusive Globalisation Strategy?

As at the end of January 2022, all Stage 1 Action 14 peer reviews, i.e. 82 Stage 1 peer reviews, had been finalised.[38] While all the countries designated as developed economies by the United Nations in 2021 (except for Cyprus) undertook these peer reviews, three countries designated as economies in transition also participated, namely, Serbia, Kazakhstan and the Russian Federation.[39] In addition, countries designated developing economies by the United Nations from the regions of North Africa, Southern Africa (the sole participant being South Africa), East Asia, South Asia (the sole participant being India), Western Asia, Latin America and the Caribbean, Mexico and Central America (the sole participant being Mexico) and South America were also reviewed.[40]

At this time, 60 Stage 2 peer reviews had been finalised.[41] The Stage 2 peer reviews had been conducted mainly in relation to the developed economies, but also included two economies in transition (Serbia and the Russian Federation), as well as twelve developing economies. South Africa was the only African country designated a developing economy to undergo a Stage 2 peer review at this time, the other developing economies taking part being Asian countries (including China and India), with Mexico, Argentina, Chile, and Colombia participating from Latin America.

The countries participating in both Stage 1 and Stage 2 of the BEPS Action 14 peer review process are thus broad-ranging and diverse, both in size[42] and developmental stage. Although participation by developed economies predominates, these jurisdictions do not necessarily have the most extensive tax treaty networks when compared with economies in transition or developing economies. Of the seven countries dubbed 'major developed economies' by the United Nations,[43] also known as the G7, the United Kingdom admittedly has double taxation treaties with over 125 countries,[44] and France has entered 120 such treaties.[45] At the other end of the spectrum the U.S. has over 50 tax treaties,[46] as has Australia.[47] However, large developing economies also have large tax treaty networks, for example, the People's Republic of China has

---

[38] OECD. OECD Action 14 Mutual Agreement Procedure <https://www.oecd.org/tax/beps/beps-actions/action14/>.

[39] United Nations. Table A Developed economies and Table B Economies in transition (above n 24).

[40] Ibid., 126.

[41] OECD, above n 38.

[42] It should be mentioned that many smaller countries not categorised by the United Nations in its UN *World Economic Situation and Prospects 2021*, Statistical Annex are part of the OECD's Inclusive Framework, for example Andorra, Aruba, Jersey, Monaco and the Cayman Islands.

[43] United Nations, above n 39.

[44] OECD (2019).

[45] OECD (2020).

[46] OECD, above n 44.

[47] OECD (2021c).

a very large tax treaty network with over 100 tax treaties,[48] and India has almost 100 tax treaties.[49] Economies in transition may also have as many tax treaties as developed countries, for example, Kazakhstan has over 50 tax treaties,[50] Serbia has more than 60 tax treaties,[51] and the Russian Federation has almost 90 tax treaties.[52] Certain developing countries do have a modest tax treaty network by comparison. For example, Colombia has entered only 15 tax treaties.[53]

As the Action 14 peer reviews have been subscribed to by developed and developing countries, both large and small, as well as economies in transition, they can be said to be effective as an inclusive globalisation strategy, bearing in mind that it is anticipated that developing nations that form the Inclusive Framework will in future elect to participate in the peer reviews, as this was a public undertaking made at the time they joined.

10.5 Conclusion: Are Peer Reviews an Effective Globalisation Strategy at a Time of Transition?

The final question remains as to how effective the Action 14 peer reviews have been as a globalisation strategy in evaluating and improving dispute resolution mechanisms, at a time when globalisation is in a transitional stage. The peer reviews reveal that no country, regardless of their designation as developed, developing, or in transition, is currently completely compliant with the Action 14 Minimum Standard.

Has any progress been made in improving dispute resolution mechanisms since the peer reviews were instigated? The OECD reports that: 'As a result of the peer review, there has been a significant increase in the number of resolved MAP cases in almost all jurisdictions under review, and access to MAP has been expanded and streamlined'.[54] It is, therefore, clear that a positive transformation is taking place.

Although the number of MAP cases being resolved has increased, so has the number of MAP cases being initiated, placing a strain on current competent authority resources. The peer review process is credited with encouraging the streamlining of competent authority processes by several jurisdictions in order to facilitate the swifter resolution of MAP cases. Nevertheless, a lack of necessary resources has been noted as a concerning trend[55] in countries at all stages of economic development, but particularly for developing countries.

48 Ibid.

49 Ibid.

50 Ibid.

51 OECD (2022).

52 OECD, above n 47.

53 Ibid.

54 OECD (2021e).

55 Ibid.

Since the commencement of the Action 14 peer reviews, many jurisdictions have introduced or updated their MAP guidance, and the number of Inclusive Framework MAP profiles appearing on the OECD website now covers over 100 jurisdictions.[56] The peer review process appears to have been instrumental in achieving significant advances in improving dispute resolution mechanisms, however, to date it has not been an unqualified success. The recommendations made in respect of the Stage 1 reports reveal that many deficiencies in tax treaties in relation to the MAP Article remain, and the reviews highlight the fact that many MAP practices and policies are not in line with the minimum standard. Although several jurisdictions have made progress in improving their dispute resolution mechanisms, the results are uneven. The peer reviews have provided an invaluable opportunity to identify problem areas across all the participating jurisdictions. However, the peer reviews reveal that the degree to which countries have addressed deficiencies identified varies from those addressing and resolving almost all of these, to those countries who have not yet addressed any of these.

From a globalisation in transition perspective, perhaps the transparency necessitated by the peer review process has been one of its greatest benefits, as all jurisdictions (and all taxpayers) are able to evaluate the progress (or lack thereof) made by the 141 members of the Inclusive Framework. Peer reviews have sometimes been referred to as 'an instrument of global governance',[57] with peer pressure being exerted by all members. The comment has been made that: 'If the OECD peer reviews have an influence, they do so not because of a "shadow of hierarchy", but rather thanks to a "shadow of image"—the fear of loss of face in front of a set of like-minded peers'.[58]

A concept known as the 'tax paradox'[59] has been attributed to the OECD, in that countries need to cooperate with each other to protect their own interests. In other words, multilateral cooperation is essential for countries to retain their own tax sovereignty, and this collaboration has been described as 'the driving force of the inclusive framework.'[60] At this time of globalisation in transition, it is in the direct interests of all Inclusive Framework members to cooperate in advancing the successful implementation of the Action 14 minimum standard, to together achieve a fairer and more inclusive tax system.

In the words of the OECD Ministerial Council:

> *Given the challenges raised by globalisation, we encourage the OECD to continue strengthening and disseminating its standards and developing advice on better policies and best practices that benefit economies beyond its membership...We reaffirm our commitment for the OECD to remain open and inclusive, recognising that it is not size but the quality of the Organisation's work that will determine its impact and effectiveness.*[61]

---

[56] Ibid.

[57] Ashoff (2013).

[58] Lehtonen, above n 37.

[59] Soong Johnston, Stephanie, cited in Goulder (2021).

[60] Ibid.

[61] OECD (2018).

References

Al-Rodhan, Dr. Nayef R.F. and Gérard Stoudmann. 2006. Definitions of Globalisation: A Comprehensive Overview and a Proposed Definition. Program on the Geopolitical Implications of Globalisation and Transnational Security, Geneva Centre for Security Policy.

Ashoff, Guido. 2013. 50 years of peer reviews by the OECD's development assistance committee: an instrument of quality assurance and mutual learning. Briefing Paper No. 12/2013, *Deutsches Institut für Entwicklungspolitik* (DIE), Bonn

Clifton, Judith and Daniel Díaz-Fuentes. 2011. From 'Club of the Rich' to 'Globalisation à la carte'? Evaluating Reform at the OECD. Universidad de Cantabria, Spain, MRPA Paper No. 33053 (31 August 2011).

Dimitropoulos, Georgios. 2016. Compliance through Collegiality: Peer Review in International Law. *Loyola of Los Angeles International and Comparative Law Review* 37:279.

Farrar, John H. and David G. Mayes. 2013. Globalisation, the crisis and the state: introduction. In *Globalisation, the Global Financial Crisis and the State,* ed. John H. Farrar and David G. Mayes, 1. Cheltenham: Edward Elgar Publishing.

Guilmette, Jean-H. 2007. The power of peer learning: Networks and development cooperation. Academic Foundation, 193.

Gurría, Angel. 2017. Better Policies Series, Fixing Globalisation: Time to Make It Work for All. OECD (27 April 2017).

Lehtonen, Markku. 2020. Harder governance built on soft foundations: experience from OECD peer reviews. *Journal of Environmental Policy & Planning* 22:815. https://doi.org/10.1080/1523908X.2020.1793746.

OECD. 2013a. Action Plan on Base Erosion and Profit Shifting <https://doi.org/10.1787/9789264202719-en>.

OECD. 2013b. Addressing Base Erosion and Profit Shifting. <https://doi.org/10.1787/9789264192744-en>.

OECD. 2016a. BEPS Action 14 on More Effective Dispute Resolution Mechanisms – Peer Review Documents. OECD/G20 Base Erosion and Profit Shifting Project <www.oecd.org/tax/beps/bepsaction-14-on-more-effective-dispute-resolution-mechanisms-peer-review-documents.pdf>.

OECD. 2016b. BEPS Project Explanatory Statement: 2015 Final Reports. OECD/G20 Base Erosion and Profit Shifting Project <https://doi.org/10.1787/9789264263437-en>.

OECD. 2017. Making Globalisation Work: Better Lives for All. Ministerial Council Statement, Meeting of the OECD Council at Ministerial Level, Paris (30–31 May 2018) <https://www.oecd.org/mcm/documents/C-MIN-2017-9-Final-EN.pdf>.

OECD. 2018. Making Globalisation Work: Better Lives for All, OECD 2017 Ministerial Council Statement, Meeting of the OECD Council at Ministerial Level. 30-31 May 2018

OECD. 2019. Making Dispute Resolution More Effective – MAP Peer Review Report, United Kingdom (Stage 2): Inclusive Framework on BEPS: Action 14. OECD/G20 Base Erosion and Profit Shifting Project, <https://doi.org/10.1787/33e2bf3d-en>.

OECD. 2020. Making Dispute Resolution More Effective – MAP Peer Review Report, France (Stage 2): Inclusive Framework on BEPS: Action 14. OECD/G20 Base Erosion and Profit Shifting Project. <https://doi.org/10.1787/a5d1cab8-en>

OECD. 2021a. Developing Countries and the OECD/G20 Inclusive Framework on BEPS: OECD Report for the G20 Finance Ministers and Central Bank Governors (13 October 2021a). <https://www.oecd.org/tax/beps/developingcountries-and-the-oecd-g20-inclusive-framework-on-beps.htm>.

OECD. 2021b. Making Dispute Resolution More Effective – MAP Peer Review Report, Oman (Stage 1): Inclusive Framework on BEPS: Action 14. OECD/G20 Base Erosion and Profit Shifting Project. <https://doi.org/10.1787/19b019f8-en>

OECD. 2021c. Making Dispute Resolution More Effective – MAP Peer Review Report, Australia (Stage 2): Inclusive Framework on BEPS: Action 14. OECD/G20 Base Erosion and Profit Shifting Project. https://doi.org/10.1787/da7fc990-en

OECD. 2021d. Mauritania joins the Inclusive Framework on BEPS and participates in the agreement to address the tax challenges arising from the digitalisation of the economy (4 November 2021d). <https://www.oecd.org/tax/mauritania-joins-the-inclusive-framework-on-beps-and-participates-in-the-agreement-to-address-the-tax-challenges-arising-from-the-digitalisation-of-the-economy.htm>.

OECD. 2021e. OECD/G20 Inclusive Framework on BEPS Progress report July 2020 – September 202. September 30

OECD. 2022. Making Dispute Resolution More Effective – MAP Peer Review Report, Serbia (Stage 2): Inclusive Framework on BEPS: Action 14. OECD/G20 Base Erosion and Profit Shifting Project. https://doi.org/10.1787/577cb1f7-en

OECD/G20 Members. 2021. Inclusive Framework on BEPS <https://www.oecd.org/tax/beps/inclusive-framework-on-beps-composition.pdf>.

Pagani, Fabricio. 2002. Peer Review as a Tool for Co-Operation and Change. *African Security Review* 15. https://doi.org/10.1080/10246029.2002.9628141.

Robert Goulder. 2021. How the OECD Inclusive Framework Shaped: A New World Tax Order. Forbes, December 29. https://www.forbes.com/sites/taxnotes/2021/12/29/how-the-oecd-inclusive-framework-shaped-a-new-world-tax-order/?sh=6ddaf11e33e7

Shaffer, Gregory C. and Mark A. Pollack. 2010. Hard vs. Soft Law: Alternatives, Complements, and Antagonists in International Governance. *Minnesota Law Review* 719.

United Nations. 2021. Introduction and overview. In *United Nations Handbook on the Avoidance and Resolution of Tax Disputes*, 3–10. New York: United Nations.

Vega, Alberto. 2012. International Governance through Soft Law: The Case of the OECD Transfer Pricing Guidelines. Max Planck Institute for Tax Law and Public Finance Working Paper (5 July 2012)

Chapter 11
Developing Protocols for Court-to-Court Communication in Transnational Insolvency Proceedings: A Limited Framework for Cooperation

Casey Watters

Abstract When global enterprises face insolvency, the expense of parallel insolvency proceedings in jurisdictions where the enterprises do business or have assets can deplete the funds available for distribution to creditors in a liquidation, or available for corporate restructuring. Recent trends show courts cooperating across jurisdictions to streamline the process and reduce costs. This trend has been facilitated by adoption of the UNCITRAL Model Law on Cross-Border Insolvency, and courts in different countries holding joint hearings. While cooperation and coordination are often necessary, courts in most jurisdictions are not authorised to discuss cases with external parties, including foreign courts, outside formal channels. To address this problem, the last few years have seen several courts adopt guidelines allowing parties to establish protocols that permit court-to-court communication. This chapter addresses the recent developments and challenges in facilitating cross-border judicial cooperation directed at reducing the costs of transnational insolvencies.

11.1 Introduction

Insolvency proceedings place a premium on cost effectiveness. However, the expense of parallel proceedings when a company engages in business or has assets present in multiple jurisdictions can deplete the amount available for distribution to creditors in a liquidation, or available to effectuate a restructuring. To streamline the process and reduce costs, the trend is for courts to cooperate across jurisdictions. This trend has been facilitated by countries adopting the UNCITRAL Model Law on Cross-Border Insolvency, and courts in different countries holding joint hearings. While cooperation and coordination are often necessary, courts in most jurisdictions are not authorised to discuss cases with external parties, including foreign courts, outside formal channels. To address this problem, recent years have seen several courts

C. Watters (✉)
Faculty of Law, Bond University, Gold Coast, Australia
e-mail: cwatters@bond.edu.au

U. Ghori et al. (eds.), *Globalisation in Transition*,
https://doi.org/10.1007/978-981-99-2439-4_11

adopt guidelines allowing parties to establish protocols that permit court-to-court communication. This chapter addresses the recent developments in judicial cooperation and continuing challenges to facilitating cooperation directed at reducing the costs of transnational insolvencies. This chapter first provides the legal framework for transnational insolvency, including the types of corporate insolvency and general approaches to cross-border proceedings. Part 3 then provides a history of modern protocols and their content, before discussing the establishment of the Judicial Insolvency Network and its protocol guidelines. Lastly, Part 4 addresses challenges to implementing protocols and provides a critique of the Judicial Insolvency Network Modalities ('the Modalities'), before concluding in Part 5.

The topic of empowering courts to communicate and cooperate in cross-border insolvency proceedings is fitting for a tribute to Professor Farrar not only because he is a company law scholar that has written broadly on insolvency[1] and the global economic crisis,[2] but due to his general interest in comparative law[3] and seeking equitable outcomes—one focus of modified universalism. John is a pioneer of corporate law scholarship through his academic roles in the United Kingdom, New Zealand and Australia, and has advanced the discipline through his student supervisions and generosity in mentoring students and junior colleagues.

11.2 Legal Framework

11.2.1 Types of Insolvency Regimes

When a company becomes insolvent, it needs to enter one of two types of proceedings; either a liquidation proceeding, also commonly referred to as a 'winding up', or a restructuring proceeding. Under a liquidation, the company ceases to operate, its assets are sold, and the proceeds are distributed to creditors, with secured creditors paid before junior categories of creditors. Jurisdictions may group all unsecured creditors together or may divide them into different levels. For example, some jurisdictions pay the claims of employees prior to those of trade creditors. After secured creditors are paid, many companies have no significant assets, and even those with assets may have little remaining for distribution to creditors after the cost of the liquidation procedure. As such, creditors ordinarily receive little, if anything, on their claims against the company.

Under a restructuring regime, also commonly referred to as 'corporate rescue', the company continues to operate and proposes a plan as to how the company will become profitable and repay its creditors. This plan is ordinarily presented to creditors for approval before being sanctioned by the court. Under a plan, the company ordinarily

[1] Farrar (2021), Farrar (1989a, b), Farrar and Tennent (2005).

[2] Farrar and Parsons (2012), Farrar (2010).

[3] See Farrar (1996–1997), Farrar (1989a, b), Farrar (2002).

proposes to pay creditors only a portion of the debts owed. However, creditors are often motivated to accept the plan because the company in operation will be able to pay a higher percentage of the debt owed than the creditor would receive upon liquidation. Purely from the creditor's perspective, a company should be restructured if the going concern value of the company is greater than the liquidation value.

Although the utility of insolvency proceedings is traditionally evaluated primarily on the preservation or creation of value for creditors, restructuring viable companies has other societal benefits. These include the retention of jobs for the employees and the protection of the local tax base. While it is important that non-viable companies exit the market, the societal benefits of restructuring have resulted in an increasing number of jurisdictions preferring restructuring over liquidation. Notable companies that have survived insolvency to become profitable include Marvel Entertainment and General Motors.

11.2.2 Approaches to Cross-Border Insolvency

When a company engages in business and has assets in more than one jurisdiction, the cross-border nature of the insolvency substantially complicates the process. Approaches to cross border insolvency exist on a spectrum with pure territorialism on one end, and pure universalism on the other.[4] This section introduces both frameworks in addition to the increasing trend of adopting a hybrid approach, known as modified universalism.

11.2.3 Territorialism

Territorialism is the traditional approach to cross-border insolvency and has often been dubbed as 'the grab rule', as courts only claim jurisdiction over assets they can seize within their territory and do not claim extraterritorial jurisdiction. Therefore, courts allocate assets to creditors according to the laws within each respective jurisdiction, without regard to parallel proceedings.[5] With respect to liquidation, territorialism has been criticised on multiple grounds, including the increased cost of parallel proceedings in each jurisdiction and the risk of unfair allocation. Under this approach, a full proceeding is necessary in every jurisdiction where the company has assets. These proceedings, through a combination of court costs and other legal fees, drain the assets of the insolvent company and thereby reduce the overall payout to creditors in addition to the burden on judicial resources.

Another criticism is the risk of inequitable distribution to creditors. As noted above, each jurisdiction has its own laws regarding the order in which types of

[4] Gopalan and Guihot (2016a, b); See also Symes and Duns (2012).

[5] Westbrook (1994), Ho (2016).

claims are to be paid. In a liquidation involving multiple jurisdictions, it is possible that some creditors would receive a higher percentage of their claim in a particular jurisdiction. As the allocation of the insolvent companies' assets is zero sum, if a large proportion of assets are present in a jurisdiction that favors a particular creditor, that creditor may receive a windfall to the detriment of the other creditors. This runs contrary to equitable principles that suggest similarly situated creditors of the same company should be treated equally when the company is liquidated. The possibility of unequal treatment also increases the risk of forum shopping, as the company may seek to transfer assets to a jurisdiction that favors certain creditors. For example, some jurisdictions subordinate the claims of related party creditors. Under territorialism, the company is likely to transfer assets out of these jurisdictions to locations where related party creditors would receive a distribution. It should be noted, however, that not all forum shopping is inherently negative.[6] In the context of restructuring, forum shopping may allow a company to successfully restructure in a jurisdiction that has more tools available in their restructuring regime, and thereby ultimately benefit all creditors. This benefit is why countries like the U.K., the U.S. and Singapore have become restructuring hubs.[7]

Territorialism is perhaps most problematic in the context of corporate rescue. Attempting to negotiate restructuring plans within multiple jurisdictions and to navigate the legal frameworks of multiple proceedings would deplete the resources that are necessary for restructuring for many otherwise viable companies. Additionally, a successful restructuring requires every jurisdiction where the company continues to conduct business or has significant assets to recognise and enforce the restructuring plan. If the court in one jurisdiction approves a restructuring plan, but another country permits creditors to seize assets that were necessary under the approved plan, the attempted restructuring may fail under territorialism. If a company believes it will be unable to have a plan accepted in one jurisdiction, it may seek to remove assets from the jurisdictions and cease operation where the restructuring plan is not enforced. While parallel proceedings are not necessarily a prohibitive obstacle in jurisdictions with similar legal systems, they may be difficult to conduct in jurisdictions with restructuring regimes that assign the company or creditors different rights or obligations.

This inefficiency of conducting proceedings in multiple jurisdictions also disincentivises creditors from participating in multiple proceedings, and therefore may reduce creditor oversight and the effectiveness of relying upon creditors to make informed and rational decisions with respect to approving a restructuring plan.

---

[6] Kannan (2017).

[7] Watters and Omar (2019), Watters (2017a, b), Wan et al. (2020).

11.2.4 Universalism

On the opposite end of the spectrum from territorialism is universalism, the approach by which an entire insolvency is dealt with in a single proceeding. By permitting a single court to have jurisdiction over the worldwide assets of the debtor, this approach removes the cost of multiple proceedings and ensures equal treatment of similarly situated creditors. While this theoretical approach addresses many of territorialism's shortcomings, it fails to recognise the sovereignty of each individual state. It is impossible for a single court to enforce its rulings over assets in multiple jurisdictions without the assistance of those jurisdictions. To embrace the benefits of universalism while recognising the need for judicial support in each jurisdiction where a company has assets or conducts business, the modern trend is toward a hybrid approach known as 'modified universalism'.

11.2.5 Modified Universalism and the UNCITRAL Model Law on Cross-Border Insolvency

Under modified universalism, a single proceeding is initiated in the company's center of main interest ('COMI').[8] This proceeding claims jurisdiction over all the company's global assets but relies on assistance from courts in other jurisdictions to assist the main proceeding and enforce its rulings. In the context of liquidation, ancillary proceedings, commonly referred to as 'non-main proceedings', often order the transfer of assets for distribution under the main proceeding. Courts may also assist in obtaining records and other information. In the context of restructuring, courts outside of the COMI may enjoin creditors from taking actions inconsistent with the court orders or a sanctioned plan from the main proceeding.

This approach has been adopted by most developed economies and is the approach enumerated in the UNCITRAL Model Law on Cross-Border Insolvency ('Model Law'). Unlike other approaches to cross-border harmonisation, such as the New York Convention, the Model Law is not a treaty, but a model text approved by the United Nations Commission on International Trade Law and recommended for adoption by individual nation states. While modified universalism provides increased opportunity for multinational companies to restructure, it is not without shortcomings. Due to the continued reliance on courts in multiple jurisdictions, some claim it is more appropriately characterised as 'modified territorialism'. As previously noted, approaches exist on a spectrum and jurisdictions vary greatly in the extent to which they embrace the principle of universalism.

Whether employing modified universalism or independent parallel proceedings, it is essential for courts to avoid issuing contradictory orders as these would prevent compliance by the relevant parties and may undermine attempts at corporate rescue.

---

[8] Westbrook (2005), Aitken (2015).

To ensure consistency, courts can establish protocols for court-to-court communication that permit judges in different jurisdictions to discuss an insolvency proceeding, or courts may employ technology to host joint hearings in multiple jurisdictions. This chapter focuses on the former.

11.3 Cooperation in Practice

11.3.1 Protocols for Court-to-Court Communication

Although there is evidence of bankruptcy protocols in Medieval Europe, modern protocols were first developed in the 1990's in the U.S., the first of which was employed in the *Maxwell* case.[9] The Maxwell Group was comprised of a British holding company owning multiple companies, with the majority of the assets located in the U.S.[10] Seeking to retain control of the company through Chapter 11's debtor-in-possession ('DIP') structure, the group sought to restructure in the New York Bankruptcy Court. However, creditors initiated an alternative proceeding in the United Kingdom, under which the court ordered the group's directors to dismiss the U.S. proceeding.[11]

Both courts claimed global jurisdiction over Maxwell's assets. Unable to satisfy inconsistent orders, the company and the British administrators entered a protocol permitting the two courts to coordinate and ultimately divide authority between the company and the administrators under the respective proceedings. The Maxwell protocol informed several other cases in the 1990's and, over time, protocols tended towards standardisation. This standardisation, and the resulting ability of practitioners to adopt protocols from previous cases, relieves the costs associated with drafting protocols, and should serve to reassure courts which may be hesitant to adopt a new protocol. One of the early protocols, and a significant case in expanding protocols to corporate group insolvency, was Lehman Brothers. In that case, the U.S. Bankruptcy Court judge urged the parties to establish a protocol. While this novel approach was significant in addressing the complex insolvency of the corporate group, the ability to propose court-to-court communication protocols is now a known practice, and protocols should no longer be initiated by the judiciary.

Cross-border insolvencies of financial institutions offer a greater complexity than those of most service or manufacturing companies, especially in the context of corporate groups. As the financial sector is highly regulated, rights and obligations can vary substantially between jurisdictions, and obtaining government approvals in each jurisdiction necessary for a successful restructuring can pose additional challenges. This is further complicated by the fact that some jurisdictions permit substantive

[9] Maltese (2013).

[10] In re Maxwell Communication Corporation, 170 B.R. 800 (Bankruptcy S.D.N.Y. 1994).

[11] Flaschen and Silberman (1998), Westbrook (1996).

consolidation, while others adhere to the principle that each company is a separate legal entity. The insolvency of banking behemoth Lehman Brothers became the model for using protocols to coordinate transnational financial group insolvency. The Lehman insolvency involved over 75 proceedings and more than 16 representatives to address the group's over USD 600 billion US in liabilities.[12] Although the protocol was first approved by Australia, Hong Kong, Singapore and the U.S., all common law jurisdictions, it was quickly adopted by civil law jurisdictions. As the Lehman Group was comprised of more than 650 companies,[13] determining the proper allocation of claims and assets was the primary challenge. To address the complexity of the claims, the protocol created procedures for resolving claims, including establishing a committee to develop accounting records for the group.[14]

The initial protocols were between western developed countries with similar legal systems, including Canada, the United Kingdom, and the U.S. These circumstances, like protocols or joint hearings between the Canadian and U.S. courts, or Australian and New Zealand courts, pose limited risk to parties due to the similarity of laws and high-quality judicial systems. However, the risks inherent in divergent legal systems and involving one or more jurisdictions in which parties may lack confidence should be considered when adopting systems to establish protocols and modalities of communication. Model systems and guides should account for these risks and further remove the risk of judicial pressure by requiring the parties to initiate the adoption of protocols.

In early cases, courts sometimes suggested protocols. However, with the contemporary availability of protocols, the initiative should now fall solely on the parties. Not only can rights and obligations vary between jurisdictions, but not all jurisdictions possess sophisticated judiciaries, and parties may not trust the integrity of some jurisdictions. The judiciary initiating the discussion of protocols, therefore, may place parties in a difficult position where their refusal might offend a court. Similar challenges have arisen in previous cases where courts are alleged to having pressured parties into settlement agreements.[15] However, if the company and creditors or their representative bring the protocol to the court, communications are facilitated while preserving the integrity of the process.

One argument in favour of courts initiating the adoption of protocols is the elevation of costs. However, the availability of multiple past protocols as models now reduces this cost. Additionally, great complexity is not a necessary. The success of protocols may often stem from their simplicity and flexibility.[16] However, the parties should always be involved in the adoption of the protocol and privy to all court communications to ensure the integrity of the proceedings.

---

[12] Kokorin (2020).

[13] Gopalan and Guihot (2016a, b).

[14] Maltese 2013 (above n 9).

[15] Welsh (2001).

[16] Wessels et al. (2009).

11.3.2 Content of Protocols

Although communication between courts is the focus of many protocols and an element that requires court approval, protocols often contain many aspects that are contractual in nature. Coordination is not limited to courts and often focuses on the roles of administrators, trustees, debtors-in-possession, or other court appointed representatives of the company. Protocols often detail how these parties will coordinate and may delineate the authority of each party in a global restructuring or liquidation. Additionally, protocols may extend to proceedings that adjust the debt of a company, removing insolvency as a requirement to adopting protocols.[17] The primary distinction between an agreement between the parties and a protocol is the role of the court. Courts cannot be parties to an agreement in the insolvency proceeding. However, they can issue an order adopting the terms of a protocol and take actions consistent with the protocol, including sharing information with other courts. The representatives of the debtor in the bankruptcy process, however, often have a more active role in managing the process under the supervision of the courts. As such, the scope of protocols often depends on the authority of the parties in their respective jurisdictions. The comparative prevalence of protocols in common law jurisdiction can be explained, at least in part, by the broad authority generally permitted courts and administrators under common law, in comparison to more prescriptive legislation in many civil law jurisdictions. Protocols adopted across common law and civil law jurisdictions therefore often adopt more flexible language to account for limitations in the discretion of the parties and courts, and often require parties to make best efforts in complying with delineated goals. This is common in the case of moratoriums. Ensuring moratoriums (often called stays) are in place in each jurisdiction is essential for a successful restructuring, and important in ensuring the equitable distribution of assets in a liquidation. However, moratorium laws vary between jurisdictions with some, such as the U.S., providing an automatic stay, some providing stays immediately upon application by the debtor, and some jurisdictions first requiring a hearing. Further, most jurisdictions limit the stay to the debtor. However, some jurisdictions, including Singapore, permit the extension of the moratorium to related companies under some circumstances to assist the insolvency procedure.[18]

Jurisdictional scope is one of the most significant issues to include in a protocol to avoid inconsistent orders. However, jurisdiction is a legal issue dictated by national laws, and not something that can be independently determined by the parties. Addressing jurisdiction therefore requires flexible language to convey the intent of the parties without risking clashing with national laws. This is another example of why courts must be careful in recognising protocols. If a party is successful on appeal in challenging the jurisdiction of a court in one country, the harm may be irreversible as courts in other countries will have relied on the initial orders in adjudicating their proceedings. Such concerns can, however, be addressed in protocols in several ways.

---

[17] Judicial Insolvency Network ('JIN'). 2019. Modalities of Court-to-Court Communication. P. 1, Para 3.

[18] Watters and Chang (2018), Watters (2017a, b).

First, the parties themselves may be permitted to waive rights of appeal directly or indirectly, by agreeing to the terms that could otherwise lead to an appeal. This approach should only be successful if the parties voluntarily negotiated the protocol and not where it is suggested by the court. Second, rulings could be conditional upon orders being entered in each jurisdiction consistent with the protocol. Under such an approach, a successful appeal in one jurisdiction may open all jurisdictions to relitigate. Due to the costs, this approach is only appropriate when dealing with a couple of jurisdictions. Finally, settling disputes with binding arbitration may assist in the risk of appeal. Protocols often contain provisions asking each jurisdiction to wait until disputes over claims are addressed, either through litigation in a particular jurisdiction, or through arbitration. For disputes that can be arbitrated, binding arbitration through the New York Convention reduces the risk of outcomes being challenged in most jurisdictions and limits the risk of appeal.

After moratoriums, perhaps the most important element in protocols is notice requirements. These provisions ensure that parties are informed of changes that impact them in any jurisdiction by prescribing notice responsibility to specific parties and may require all responsible parties to provide notice to parties of interest globally. However, another approach is to divide the work between jurisdictions. Under this approach, a representative in one jurisdiction would notify all parties of interest within their jurisdiction of any changes, and simultaneously notify the representatives in each corresponding jurisdiction who would take responsibility for notifying parties within their jurisdictions. Under this approach, representatives are providing notices for multiple proceedings. However, it reduces the complexity for creditors when notice is provided by one point of contact within their jurisdiction. When jurisdictions use different languages, this also has the benefit of the local representative being able to communicate more easily with creditors.

The UNCITRAL Model Law on Cross-Border Insolvency Article 9 permits an insolvency representative to appear in the recognising jurisdiction without being subject to the ordinary domestic requirements before that court. Importantly, this reduces the expense of additional attorneys, and removes licensing requirements which would ordinarily be prohibitively burdensome. For countries that have not adopted the Model Law, including such provisions in the protocol can reduce the costs of the proceedings. Such an agreement would be subject to court approval and may not be within the discretion of some courts, particularly in civil law jurisdictions. Nevertheless, any steps permitted to reduce procedural hurdles reduces the cost of the proceeding and thereby benefits all parties.

Along with content, timing is also important in adopting a protocol. In the context of restructuring, especially DIP restructuring, expedited recognition of proceedings and harmonising orders between jurisdictions may be essential for a business to continue operations and preserve value. Therefore, first-day orders submitted by the company may be beneficial in preserving the company and maximising creditor realisations. Speed is particularly important when protocols address issues such as moratoriums and the ability to transfer assets between jurisdictions to operate the company. Liquidations usually pose less urgency unless an operating portion of the company is being sold as part of the liquidation. Unlike restructuring, liquidation is a zero-sum game and courts should therefore undertake greater scrutiny when implementing protocols submitted by the debtor or only a subset of creditors.

11.3.3 Developments of the JIN

In 2017, the JIN promulgated guidelines for the establishment of court-to-court communication protocols in insolvency proceedings. The JIN was spearheaded by Singapore and held its inaugural meeting in October of 2016. It serves as a network of global insolvency judges, to address challenges to cross-border insolvency. The JIN has three stated objectives: 'judicial thought leadership in cross-border insolvency', establishing best practices in adjudicating insolvency proceedings, and increasing 'communication and cooperation amongst national courts in cross-border' insolvency proceedings.[19]

Initially, the JIN was comprised of only common law jurisdictions, with the inaugural meeting hosted by the Supreme Court of Singapore, attended by judges from Australia (the Federal Court and New South Wales), the British Virgin Islands, Canada (Ontario), the Cayman Islands, England & Wales, Hong Kong SAR (as an observer), Singapore and the U.S. (Delaware and the Southern District of New York).[20] However, subsequent to the creation of the Guidelines, they have also been adopted by the Seoul Bankruptcy Court and the Brazilian National Justice Counsel.[21]

The guidelines do not establish a substantive legal framework or a system of recognition and relief, instead focusing on communication and leaving the substantive provisions to the domestic law in each respective jurisdiction. However, apart from Bermuda, each territorial jurisdiction that adopted the guidelines had adopted the Model Law.

In addition to the preamble and introduction, the JIN Guidelines consist of fourteen guidelines and an annex addressing joint hearings. The guidelines are divided into five categories: adoption & interpretation (Guidelines 1–6), communication between courts (Guidelines 7–8), notification (Guidelines 9), appearance in court (Guidelines 10–11) and consequential provisions (Guidelines 12–14).

11.4 Modalities and Challenges to Implementation

In a recent article addressing judicially appointed mediators, something like protocols in that it incorporates judges into proceedings over which they do not preside, Professor Jacoby identified issues of judicial ethics and structural constraints that

[19] JIN.JIN, 2018. About Us. http://jin-global.org/about-us.html. Accessed 1 February 2022.

[20] Watters (2017a, b).

[21] National Justice Counsel (2021).

are challenged when additional judges are incorporated into proceedings.[22] Ethical issues include impartiality, *ex parte* communication, public commentary and extra-judiciality. Although the structural constraints in the article focus on the U.S. court system, the significance of separation of powers is core to the liberal common law system, at the foundation of most countries currently adopting protocols or the JIN Guidelines. As Jacoby notes, 'the prevailing oversight mechanisms [...] work more effectively for formal court acts creating a record in a particular case than for activities that happen behind the scenes'.[23] As these guidelines and modalities are not legislation, regulation, or common law in the traditional sense, and because they are established through cross-border negotiation, not traditionally the purview of the judicial branch, the establishment of protocols has been dubbed by some scholars as judicial diplomacy.[24] The lack of oversight in an area not traditionally the role of the judiciary necessitates caution in establishing and implementing protocols.

11.4.1 Problems with the Modalities

11.4.1.1 Ex Parte Communications

Although the JIN Guidelines state that '[i]n the normal case, parties may be present',[25] this is undercut by the Modalities which allows the parties to request the judge contact a judge in parallel proceeding 'or the Initiating Judge may seek it on his or her own initiative'[26] and communicate with the other judge 'without the necessity for the participation of counsel or the parties'.[27] The Modalities further allow the appointment of non-judge court officials as 'facilitators' to establish the communication process. This poses an additional risk as the actions of these facilitators may not be properly documented and it is unclear if mistakes by court personnel aside from the presiding judge are a basis for appeal. Even if administered carefully, adding a third party without the consent and presence of the parties risks undermining the perception of the process. Far from seeking the consent of the parties, the Modalities empower judges to 'require the parties over whom he or she exercises jurisdiction to obtain the identity and contact details of the Facilitator of the other court'.[28] This risk can be reduced if all communications through facilitators are in writing or recorded with records available to all parties. The suggestion that courts publish the contact details

[22] Jacoby (2022).

[23] Ibid., 43.

[24] Law (2015), Lee and Ip (2020); see generally, Nicola and Davies (2017).

[25] JIN. 2016. Guidelines for Communication and Cooperation Between Courts in Cross-Border Insolvency Matters 8(i).

[26] JIN Modalities. 2019. (above n 17) 1, para 3.

[27] Ibid., 4, para 15.

[28] Ibid., 2, para 8.

of facilitators on court websites[29] can help facilitate this by limiting contact channels to those which can be recorded and notifying parties that all communications will be publicly available.

Judges are ordinarily prohibited from commenting publicly on a pending case to avoid prejudicing a party or even the appearance of prejudice.[30] However, communicating with courts administering parallel proceedings inherently impacts those proceedings. If impacted parties provide consent by initiating a protocol, concerns are minimised. Even with respect to procedural matters, the court must ensure 'no party will gain a procedural, substantive, or tactical advantage as a result of the *ex parte* communication'.[31] Absent the voluntary consent of the parties, ensuring that communications will not provide an advantage to one party whether procedural, substantive, or tactical, is nearly impossible as it requires the judge to be knowledgeable of the procedural and substantive laws in the jurisdiction of the parallel proceeding. The risk is substantially higher where jurisdictions have dissimilar legal systems or linguistic barriers. Indeed, courts in similar jurisdictions such and Canada and the U.S.,[32] and Australia and New Zealand,[33] have already held successful joint hearings, and the success of the protocols amongst the jurisdictions that have already adopted the Guidelines, all of which have mature legal systems with sophisticated judiciaries, should be applauded. However, it is essential to examine the risks in adopting this approach with all jurisdictions.

11.4.1.2 Confidentiality

Courts should also account for the privacy rights of the parties. In some countries, only final judgments are available to the public with other court filings treated as confidential or limited to parties. However, other jurisdiction may deem communications with the court or foreign facilitator as subject to freedom of information requests. Such risks should be disclosed at this stage and will be decreased by only commencing communication if the parties initiate the adoption of the protocol and, contrary to the Modalities which only require judges to follow adopted protocols 'as far as possible', judges should restrain communication to comply with the terms of the protocol. In circumstances where jurisdictions are developed and have similar legal system, as with the JIN states, there is nothing to prevent parties from adopting protocols that give wide discretion to judges in communicating, to limit the administrative burden. However, judges should not exceed the authority afforded them by the parties to discuss a pending case with external entities.

---

[29] Ibid., 2, para 6.

[30] See Code of Conduct for U.S. Judges, Cannon 3(A)(6).

[31] Code of Conduct for U.S. Judges, Cannon 3A(4)(b).

[32] Peacock (2015), Pottow (2017).

[33] Apathy (2019), Pelly (2019).

11.4.1.3 Translations

The significance of the precise language used in statutes, cases, contracts, and other evidence cannot be overstated, and courts in jurisdictions with different languages pose an additional threat to harming the interests of parties. The JIN Modalities state that 'appropriate arrangements shall be made, as agreed by the courts' to address translation or interpretation. The modalities, however, do not address the protection of the rights of parties. Translations or interpretations should be addressed specifically in any protocol, and such protocol should be initiated by the parties. In the absence of such a provision, the court should provide sufficient time for parties to review translations and object to any language before sending it to the other court. At no point should the courts require parties to provide translations for a foreign proceeding unless the parties freely consent to such a provision in the protocol. To do otherwise would require the parties to bear an expense outside the scope of the proceeding.

11.4.1.4 Lack of Oversight and Separation of Powers

The judicial diplomacy undertaken to establish the JIN Guidelines has provided an important foundation to facilitate coordination and reduce the procedural costs of parallel insolvency proceedings. Nevertheless, restrictions are necessary to protect the parties. Diplomacy is traditionally the purview of the executive, as it is limited by the legislature and executives are subject to democratic removal. The judiciary, however, is limited to the disputes brought before it, and must operate within the statutes provided by the legislature.[34] The enforcement mechanism to address both procedural and substantive errors and the redress for abuse is appeal to a higher court. However, sharing information with other jurisdictions without the consent of parties undercut this. The point of sharing information is coordination, but what if a party appeals a decision in one jurisdiction? If the courts communicate to ensure consistency, the ability to effectively redress the courts' errors may forever be lost as assets are dispersed and orders entered in multiple jurisdictions. Information may also be shared that is not admissible in another jurisdiction. As some jurisdictions assign criminal penalties to director and officer behaviour during periods of insolvency, sharing of information may threaten a party's due process rights. Even asking the parties to establish a protocol may harm the interests of a party that refuses, as the refusal risks insulting a court. Court-to-court communication is often beneficial to the parties by reducing overall costs and risk of inconsistent orders. However, to ensure the interests of parties are protected, the court should require all impacted parties freely consent by first proposing a protocol to the court, and the authority of the court to communicate should be strictly limited by the terms of the protocol. In many cases, parties will likely give courts wide discretion in communicating. However, requiring

[34] Although common law jurisdictions produce judge-made law within spaces not occupied by legislation.

the parties consent ensures the protection of the parties, removes the risk of insult to a less mature jurisdiction, and ensures the integrity of the judicial process.

11.5 Conclusion

Since the establishment of the Model Law on Cross-Border Insolvency 25 years ago, the trend towards universalism facilitated greater cooperation between jurisdictions and thereby reduced the expense of insolvency proceedings to the benefit of both creditors and debtors, as well as employees and other stakeholders. To this end, protocols that permit court-to-court communication are a powerful tool, but one that must be used carefully. Courts initiating communication without the consent of parties or pressuring parties may undermine the judicial process. Generally, protocols and modalities should be calibrated to protect rights, especially with the participation of jurisdictions with less sophisticated judiciaries and those with laws or procedures that may prejudice non-local parties to the current proceeding. The jurisdictions having adopted the JIN Guidelines and Modalities, although not homogeneous, all have mature legal systems with sophisticated judiciaries, in which parties can have a high level of confidence. However, as more jurisdictions adopt these frameworks, risks will increase, and the frameworks need to ensure that courts are not sharing information with other jurisdictions where a risk exists to the parties. The best means of ensuring the protection of the parties is to rely on parties to propose protocols and limit all communications to situations where the parties are present. This includes a limitation on providing any translations until all interested parties have reviewed the translations and had an opportunity to object to any wording.

If countries have similar laws and legal systems, more flexible methods of establishing protocols can be established through bilateral agreements through the traditional diplomatic channels, approved by the national legislatures, and be subject to judicial interpretation and due process rights. Global diplomacy is not the traditional domain of the judiciary and, despite the many advantages of court-to-court communication in parallel insolvency proceedings, modalities should be carefully tailored to protect the parties and maintain the separation of powers.

References

Aitken, L. 2015. Modified Universalism: Confined or Confirmed. *Australian Bar Review* 41:27.

Apathy, Paul. 2019. Classic Cross-Border Cooperation: Joint Court Hearing in the Halifax Insolvency. Herbert Smith Freehills https://www.herbertsmithfreehills.com/latest-thinking/classic-cross-border-cooperation-joint-court-hearings-in-the-halifax-insolvency

Farrar, John and Doug Tennent. 2005. The Unfitness of Directors, Insolvency and the Consequences - Some Comparisons. *Canterbury Law Review* 11:239.

Farrar, John and Louise Parsons. 2012. Globalisation, the Global Financial Crisis and the Reinvention of the State. *Singapore Academy of Law Journal* 24(2):367–401.

Farrar, John. 1989a. The Responsibility of Directors and Shareholders for a Company's Debts.4 *Canterbury Law Review* 12.
Farrar, John. 1989b. Harmonisation of Business Law between Australia and New Zealand. *Victoria U Wellington L Rev* 19:435.
Farrar, John. 1996–1997. The Duty of Care of Company Directors in Australia and New Zealand. *Canterbury Law Review* 6:228.
Farrar, John. 2002. Developing Corporate Governance in Greater China. *UNSWLJ* 25:462.
Farrar, John. 2010. The global financial crisis and the governance of financial institutions. *Australian Journal of Corporate Law* 24(3):227–243.
Farrar, John. 2021. Directors' Duties and Corporate Governance in Troubled Companies. *Canterbury Law Review*. 8(1):99–112.
Flaschen, E., and R. Silberman. 1998. Cross-Border Insolvency Cooperation Protocols. *Texas Int'l Law Journal* 33:587.
Gopalan, S. and M. Guihot. 2016a. *Cross-Border Insolvency Law*. LexisNexis Butterworths.
Gopalan, S., and M. Guihot. 2016b. Cross-Border Insolvency Law and Multinational Enterprise Groups: Judicial Innovation as an International Solution. *Geo. Wash. Int'l L. Rev.* 48:549, 602.
Look Chan Ho. 2016. *Cross-Border Insolvency: Principles and Practice.* Sweet and Maxwell.
Jacoby, M. 2022. Other Judges' Cases. NYU Annual Survey of American Law 72 (forthcoming).
Kannan, Ramesh. 2017. The 'Gibbs principle': A tether on the feet of good forum shopping. *Singapore Academy of Law Journal* 29(1):42–74.
Kokorin, I. 2020. Conflicts of Interest, Intra-Group Financing and Procedural Coordination of Group Insolvencies. *International Insolvency Review* 29(1):32.
Law, D. 2015. Judicial Comparativism and Judicial Diplomacy. *University of Pennsylvania Law Review* 163:1004, 1023.
Lee, E., and E. Ip. 2020. Judicial diplomacy in the Asia-Pacific: theory and evidence from the Singapore-initiated transnational judicial insolvency network. *Journal of Corporate Law Studies* 20:2, 389–420.
Maltese, M. 2013. Court-to-Court Protocols in Cross-Border Bankruptcy Proceedings: Differing Approaches Between Civil Law and the Common Law Legal Systems. Thesis p. 11–12 FN 30. https://www.iiiglobal.org/sites/default/files/media/maltese_michele%20submission.pdf
National Justice Counsel. 2021. *Justiça internaliza tratado de comunicação em insolvência internacional.* May 18 https://www.cnj.jus.br/justica-internaliza-tratado-de-comunicacao-em-insolvencia-internacional/
Nicola, F., and B. Davies. 2017. Judges as Diplomats in Advancing the Rule of Law: A Conversation with President Koen Lenaerts and Justice Stephen Breyer. American University Law Review 66:1159.
Peacock, L. 2015. A Tale of Two Courts: The Novel Cross-Border Bankruptcy Trial. *American Bankruptcy Institute Law Review* 23: 543–570.
Pelly, Michael. 2019. Judge Paves Way for Trans-Tasman Court over Broker Collapse. Financial Review https://www.afr.com/companies/professional-services/judge-paves-way-for-trans-tasman-court-over-broker-collapse-20190829-p52lup
Pottow, J. 2017. Two Cheers for Universalism: Nortel's Nifty Novelty. Univ. of Michigan Law & Econ Research Paper No. 15-020 https://papers.ssrn.com/sol3/papers.cfm?abstract_id=2697095
Symes, C. and J. Duns. 2012. *Australian Insolvency Law.* LexisNexis Butterworths.
Wan, Wai Yee, Casey Watters, and Gerard McCormack. 2020. Schemes of Arrangement in Singapore: Empirical and Comparative Analysis. *American Bankruptcy Law Journal* 94(3):463.
Watters, C., and K. Chang. 2018. The Common Law Principle of Universality Extended in the Wake of Hanjin Shipping's Insolvency. *Insolvency Law Journal* 26(3):158.
Watters, C. and P. Omar. 2019. The Evolution of Corporate Rescue in Singapore. *Insolvency Law Journal* 27(1):18.
Watters, Casey. 2017a. Singapore Amends Companies Act to Strengthen its Role as a Regional Restructuring Hub. *Company Lawyer* 38(9):293.

Watters, C. 2017b. Guidelines for Cooperation and Communication Between Courts in Cross-Border Insolvency Matters: Too Far or Not Far Enough. *Company Lawyer* 38(6):169–171.
Welsh, N. 2001. The Thinning Vision of Self-Determination in Court-Connected Mediation: The Inevitable Price of Institutionalization? *Harvard Negotiation Law Review* 6:1.
Wessels, B., B. Markell, and J. Kilborn. 2009. *International Cooperation in Bankruptcy and Insolvency Matters* p. 188. Oxford University Press.
Westbrook, J. 1994. A More Optimistic View of Cross-Border Insolvency. *Washington University Law Quarterly* 72:947.
Westbrook, J. 1996. The Lessons of Maxwell Communications. *Fordham Law Review* 64:2531.
Westbrook, J. 2005. Chapter 15 at Last. *American Bankruptcy Law Journal* 79:713, 716.

Chapter 12
Central Banks in Crisis Times: Mandates in Crisis?

Louise Parsons

Abstract Although monetary policy has historically been the primary focus of central banks, after the GFC there was broad (although not complete) consensus that central bank mandates also included a mandate for financial stability. During the COVID-19 pandemic, the financial stability mandate of central banks has again been reaffirmed. Similarly, central bank initiatives in the fight against climate change are also justified under their responsibility for financial stability. This chapter examines the governance of central banks in light of the fact that central bank mandates have significantly evolved and enlarged in the twenty-first century, mostly without any statutory change. The expanding missions reflect a growing notion that central banks have a social responsibility mandate—albeit poorly defined—that is broader than their statutory mandate. Questions that arise include legitimacy of decisions and accountability in light of a potential democratic deficit. Globalisation has increasingly connected not just financial markets, institutions and systems, but also regulators, regulatory institutions and public institutions, including central banks, and crisis responses by central banks have pushed them into increasingly new territory; expectations of what central banks should turn their attention to, have changed. Central banks themselves have enlarged their missions and taken more initiative by reframing their missions; external parties have also called for more action from central banks in certain areas. Interpreting the mandate of a central bank too broadly increases the scope of its responsibility in an unreasonable manner. When a central bank is responsible for combatting a wide range of social ills, it loses its focus. Moreover, adequate measures should be in place for the accountability and governance of central banks as public institutions through alignment between their de facto missions and statutory mandates.

L. Parsons (✉)
Faculty of Law, Bond University, Gold Coast, Australia
e-mail: lparsons@bond.edu.au

U. Ghori et al. (eds.), *Globalisation in Transition*,
https://doi.org/10.1007/978-981-99-2439-4_12

12.1 John Farrar—A Scholar and a Gentleman

I met John Farrar at Bond University when the first tremors of the Global Financial Crisis (GFC) were felt all over the world. We were both fascinated by the extraordinary events, and the impact these had on the roles of the regulators, central banks, governments and international organisations. Discussions over coffee led to a jointly authored journal article on the regulatory response to the GFC, one of the first comprehensive reviews of the topic. Collaboration on this and a few subsequent works also led to an ongoing friendship. John became a mentor and was also the guiding light and saving grace in my Ph.D. candidature, during which we further debated central bank mandates and central bank governance. Our professional ties were deepened by a shared connection as immigrants to Australia and connections to South Africa, my country of origin. The debt and gratitude I owe to John are immense. His integrity, deep respect for knowledge, and limitless generosity are legendary and inspirational. Thank you, John, for being so much more than a colleague, an inspiring mentor and a true friend.

12.2 Of Missions and Mandates: The Role of the Central Bank as a Statutory Body, Public Institution and Functionary of the State, yet also an Independent Bank and Regulator

Central banks are unique institutions. They are created by the State, typically through legislation, and perform public functions in the national interest. They are nevertheless independent of government. The independence of central banks is rooted in their role in currency stability and protecting the internal and external value of the domestic currency, a task that should be done without political interference. Central banks have a variety of other roles, including acting as the lender of last resort for banks and financial institutions with liquidity problems, issuing and managing the banknotes and coins in the national currency, providing and overseeing payment systems, and performing final settlement functions for banks and financial institutions. Some central banks are also the prudential supervisors of banks and financial institutions. The roles a central bank plays are generally provided for in the statute creating the central bank, often formulated as a mandate. Some central banks have a statutory charter, some have statutory objectives, and some have specified powers. The founding statutory framework of a central bank is therefore both empowering but also a limitation on the scope of the central bank's powers and operations.

Central banks are impacted by current events, and crises may propel central bank operations into unchartered territory. Central banks are often metaphorical firefighters in crises, especially in financial crises. In this role, they respond with actions to ameliorate the situation and abate or resolve the crisis. Their mission may become fighting the present crisis. In this manner, central banks frame and reframe their mission[1]—their objective or raison d'être—in a manner that responds to the crisis. Their crisis responses may not fall squarely within their express statutory mandates, and through crisis responses, their missions evolve and sometimes expand, mostly without any statutory changes to their formal mandates.[2] For example, in the Global Financial Crisis (GFC) central banks—even those without statutory financial stability mandates—argued that financial stability was one of the mandates of a central bank. Crisis responses also often draw central banks away from their national focus. Multiple central banks in different jurisdictions may adjust or expand their missions at the same time and in a similar manner, and although central banks are typically nationally focused, they may collaborate and coordinate their actions despite not having any express authority to do so.[3]

Central bank mandates are important. By virtue of being included in a legal instrument, mandates encapsulate what the central bank is formally authorised and also required to do by the authority (the State) by which it is created. Mandates, therefore, have two purposes—providing and restricting authority and power. Mandates give legitimacy to central banks as institutions, particularly through their actions, and regulate the roles of central banks in society vis-à-vis citizens. However, because central banks redefine their missions based on circumstances and through an interpretation of what can be a broadly-phrased mandate, misalignment between central bank formulated missions and parliament-formulated mandates may occur. Central bank formulated missions are current and situation-based; parliament-formulated mandates are often historical and even outdated.

Historically, central banks are predominantly monetary policy authorities, with their independence linked to their role in monetary policy.[4] In the midst of multiple crises in 2022, President of the European Central Bank (ECB), Christine Lagarde, confirmed that defeating inflation is the 'mantra, mission and mandate' of the central bank.[5]

Through recent crisis response, the missions of central banks are enlarging to encompass more. This chapter examines how central-bank formulated missions in

---

[1] In this chapter, central bank 'missions' will be construed to be what the central bank considers its role to be and what it considers it is required to do in particular circumstances.

[2] See for example Michele Bullock's references to 'interpretations' of the RBA's mandate, through phrases such as: 'In practice, we interpret this to mean that the Bank should ...': Michele Bullock, 'Policymaking at the Reserve Bank' (Speech delivered at the AFIA Annual Conference, Sydney, 18 October 2022) https://www.rba.gov.au/speeches/2022/sp-dg-2022-10-18.html; and the phrase 'we haven't changed the way we interpret our mandate ...': Michele Bullock, 'Has the Way We Look at Financial Stability Changed Since the Global Financial Crisis?' (Speech, Bloomberg Breakfast, Sydney, 14 March 2017) https://www.rba.gov.au/speeches/2017/sp-ag-2017-03-14.html.

[3] International collaboration and the making of international agreements may be political decisions that may sit best with the government of the day.

[4] See Goodhart and Lastra (2018).

[5] Christine Lagarde, Governor of the ECB, stated in an interview that 'defeating inflation is our mantra, our mission, our mandate'. See Zoe Schneeweiss, 'ECB's Lagarde Says Beating Inflation Is Mission, Mantra, Mandate' (Bloomberg, 29 October 2022, Webpage) https://www.bloomberg.com/news/articles/2022-10-29/ecb-s-lagarde-says-beating-inflation-is-mission-mantra-mandate?leadSource=uverify%20wall.

response to various crises are placed vis-à-vis the central bank's formal mandate and demonstrates that contrary to the affirmation of Lagarde and others, central bank missions have not remained static but have been broadened in light of recent crises, and concerns of mission-creep and increased legitimacy and accountability deficits, are not unfounded. The impact of globalisation and more recent shifts away from globalisation are also visible.

12.3 Broadening of the Mission as a Crisis Response

Recent events have impacted central banks and have led to an expansion of their missions.

12.3.1 The Global Financial Crisis and the Development of the Central Bank's Financial Stability Mandate

The responses of central banks to the GFC in 2008 reflected a shift in their general modus operandi and in how central banks perceived or articulated their missions. Some of the actions of central banks post-GFC signalled a departure from the pre-GFC so-called 'New Consensus', in which central banks adopted a framework with three key pillars: Independence, price stability and inflation targeting.[6] For example, little attention was paid to financial stability in the mandate of the ECB when the ECB was created in 1998,[7] before the GFC. However, the rather singular focus of central banks pre-GFC on inflation soon became a somewhat singular focus on financial stability in the GFC and its aftermath. The GFC marked the end of the so-called 'golden age' of central banking[8] and the end of the 'Great Moderation'.[9] The GFC was also a crisis for central banks, who acted as firefighters—proverbial first responders to the crisis.[10] Central banks resorted to unprecedented coordination and several central banks lowered interest rates at virtually the same time within the first two weeks of October 2008. 'In the global financial crisis some of the notions of

[6] Vallet (2021).

[7] Wilsher expresses surprise at this state of affairs. See Wilsher (2013).

[8] See Gerlach et al. (2009).

[9] A period (mid 1980s to 2007) in which macroeconomic volatility decreased. See Federal Reserve, 'History of the Federal Reserve The Great Moderation, (Webpage, 22 November 2013) https://www.federalreservehistory.org/essays/great-moderation#:~:text=During%20the%20Great%20Moderation%2C%20the,after%20the%20economist%20John%20B.

[10] See for example Martin Marcussen, The Triumph and Despair of Central Banking (Routledge, 2013).

central bank independence became strained as collaborative actions between central banks clearly pointed to political, or political-economic, objectives'.[11]

The pursuit of financial stability may not have been an express mandate for central banks at the time of the GFC, but it has been recognised by some academics and central bankers as one of the general missions of a central bank. For example, according to Allen and Lastra, central banks always had a financial stability mandate before the GFC, but it was 'rediscovered' in the GFC.[12]

The actions of central banks in response to the GFC demonstrate a broadening of mandate, that is reflective of a broader economic or even more general social purpose. A broadening of scope was proposed by both central banks and commentators.[13] Vallet points out that events such as the GFC and also the COVID-19 pandemic.[14]

> ...would incentivize central banks to redefine and broaden their mission in a way that better reflects the societal consequences of their actions in an increasingly complex economic context. It is not only a matter of "technical" purposes (how to build new models with the existing tools, such as interest rates models) but also to consider new transmission channels of monetary policy and redesign the role of central banks toward society. The recent two crises exemplify this, through the need for a more complete understanding of crises, from their roots to their management and their prevention.[15]

The redefining of the role of the central bank as being responsible for financial stability, even over and above the monetary policy mission, because of the central bank's unique balance sheet, has important consequences. Allen and Lastra point out that, unlike monetary stability, financial stability is not national in nature[16]:

> What is clear, though is that financial stability complicates border problems because it transcends institutional mandates and geographical boundaries, thus further challenging the traditional notion of sovereignty. Financial stability is indeed a national, regional and international goal; episodes of instability, like tsunamis and epidemics, do not respect territorial boundaries.

Nevertheless, this expansion of missions beyond the formal mandates of central banks[17] was not reflected in mandate changes, with perhaps the exception of the Bank of England and the South African Reserve Bank. Despite the impact of the GFC and the work of bodies such as the Financial Stability Board, very little formal change was effected to the mandates of central banks after the GFC.[18]

---

[11] Farrar et al. (2009).

[12] Allen and Lastra (2020).

[13] Vallet (2021).

[14] Ibid.

[15] Ibid.

[16] Allen and Lastra, n 12, 525 (footnotes omitted).

[17] On the expansion of central bank mandates following the GFC, see Goodhart and Lastra, n 4, 65.

[18] See Parsons (2018); see also Louise Parsons, 'Developments in central banking after the GFC: central banks, the state, globalisation and the GFC' in Farrar and Mayes (2013).

12.3.2 *A Global Health Crisis: Responding to the Impact of Public Health Measures During the COVID-19 Pandemic*

The responses of central banks to the impact of the global financial crisis caused by the COVID-19 pandemic demonstrated high levels of coordination and reaffirmed the extent to which cross-border cooperation and synchronisation and alignment of purpose and action had become entrenched. On 11 March 2020, the World Health Organisation declared the novel coronavirus COVID-19 a global pandemic.[19] Although governments in different countries adopted different ideological approaches,[20] the measures they used were often identical, for example, restriction of movement, including national and international border closures, quarantine and isolation, lockdowns, mandatory testing and vaccinations and density restrictions. Businesses were often restricted in whether and how they could operate; employment losses occurred especially where working from home was not possible. Financial problems in this crisis included domestic and international liquidity issues, serious recessions, sovereign debt defaults and the like. Some governments, like the Australian federal and state governments, provided financial support for impacted individuals and businesses. However, the result was a 'global financial crisis once most countries locked down their economies'.[21]

Fiscal measures by governments were complemented by central bank action. Although central banks and monetary authorities 'have generally followed the global financial crisis playbook, the scope, size, and speed of the policy responses to the pandemic have been unprecedented',[22] and described as extraordinary. [23] Central banks responded by lowering interest rates (i.e. used monetary policy) in an attempt to mitigate the financial impact of the pandemic. With interest rates in many countries already being low, and monetary policy tools having limited effect, central banks also resorted to quantitative easing (QE). QE entails the central bank purchasing longer-term financial assets,[24] often government bonds, to inject liquidity into the system.[25] In addition, forward guidance was a further new tool of monetary policy used by

---

[19] WHO Director-General, Opening Remarks at the media briefing, 11 March 2020 https://www.who.int/director-general/speeches/detail/who-director-general-s-opening-remarks-at-the-media-briefing-on-covid-19---11-march-2020.

[20] Some countries aimed at eradication, others at aggressive suppression. Later in the pandemic, some countries maintained a 'COVID-zero' policy, whilst others adopted a 'living with the virus' approach.

[21] Bordo (2021).

[22] United Nations Department of Economic and Social Affairs, 'Economic Analysis UN DESA Policy Brief No. 129: The monetary policy response to COVID-19: the role of asset purchase programmes' (9 February 2022) https://www.un.org/development/desa/dpad/publication/un-desa-policy-brief-no-129-the-monetary-policy-response-to-covid-19-the-role-of-asset-purchase-programmes/.

[23] Ibid.

[24] Ibid.

[25] QE was also used in the GFC.

many central banks. Although these measures helped protect and restore financial markets, '[t]he speed at which these tools were deployed and scale of their usage have been unprecedented'.[26]

The responses by central banks also involved significant central bank cooperation.[27] Central banks cooperated in 'lender of last resort actions; the sharing of information and techniques of central banking and the discovery of common problems'.[28] The coordination involved 'policy actions formally agreed upon and taken by groups of policy makers to achieve beneficial outcomes for the international monetary system as a whole'.[29] Post-pandemic, central banks have also raised interest rates in the same manner as a new era of high inflation took hold, and the IMF has pointed out that '[t]he monetary policy cycle is now increasingly synchronized around the world'.[30]

12.3.3 The Climate Crisis and the Development of 'Green Central Banking'

Although the climate crisis has been developing over many years and is the result of decades of human impact on the planet, it has reached a level of mainstream recognition and a truly meaningful commitment to action on the part of governments with the signature of the Paris Agreement which entered into force on 4 November 2016.[31] 'There is now increasing recognition around the world that climate change is a global emergency, and that building green objectives into COVID-19 recovery packages is a priority. Importantly, sustainable policies also need to make economic sense, and

---

[26] Christian Vallence and Peter Wallis, 'The Response by Central Banks in Advanced Economies to COVID-19' (RBA Bulletin, 10 December 2020) https://www.rba.gov.au/publications/bulletin/2020/dec/the-response-by-central-banks-in-advanced-economies-to-covid-19.html.

[27] Basel Committee on Banking Supervision Governors and Heads of Supervision, 'Governors and Heads of Supervision commit to ongoing coordinated approach to mitigate Covid-19 risks to the global banking system and endorse future direction of Basel Committee work' (November 2020) https://www.bis.org/press/p201130.htm. As referred to in: FSB, COVID-19 support measures Extending, amending and ending (6 April 2021).

[28] Bordo (2021).

[29] Ibid.

[30] IMF, 'Central Banks Hike Interest Rates in Sync to Tame Inflation Pressures' (Blog, International Monetary Fund, 10 August 2022) https://www.imf.org/en/Blogs/Articles/2022/08/10/central-banks-hike-interest-rates-in-sync-to-tame-inflation-pressures.

[31] UNFCC, The Paris Agreement—United Nations Framework Agreement on Climate Change, (Adopted by Decision 1/CP.21November 2015 at COP 21, signed on 22 April 2016) https://unfccc.int/documents/184656. Also note James Martin, Deputy Director of Operations, of the Office of Financial Research, US Department of Treasury, described climate change as 'a frontier risk borne by changes in the physical environment as well as regulatory changes to address those challenges'. James Martin (Speech delivered on 18 November 2022 at the Financial Stability Conference: Frontier Risks, A New Normal, And Policy Challenges) https://www.financialresearch.gov/from-the-director/2022/11/18/remarks-by-james-martin-fin-stab-conference/.

financial institutions will be important in financing the investments required for green transition'.[32]

Although climate change is recognised as a global emergency, it differs from other crises. It has had a much longer build-up, is ideologically highly divisive (not everyone accepts the science of climate change), evidence of its existence is harder to identify, reversal or resolution is much more difficult and perhaps even impossible, and it will take much longer to resolve. Further, those nations, peoples and generations most affected by climate change are generally not those most responsible for climate change.

Some of the consequences of the climate crisis have a financial impact, and responding to the climate emergency involves more than remediation but also fundamental changes in how things are done, which resources are used, and replacing existing climate-unfriendly technologies with strategies that will prevent further climate change and even reverse the damage that has been done. Giving effect to net-zero emissions targets will involve transition risks and financial risks for example through stranded assets.

Although central banks and monetary authorities worldwide are not the key 'needle-movers' in the climate wars, central banks are preparing their financial systems for a smooth 'net-zero transition'.[33]

Around the time of signing the Paris Agreement in 2015, the then Governor of the Bank of England and Chairman of the Financial Stability Board, Mark Carney, delivered a highly influential speech on the importance of addressing climate change.[34] It was a form of call-to-arms for central banks who have responded in a novel way. the Network for Greening the Financial System (NGFS) was created as 'a global group of central banks, acknowledging that climate-related risks will have consequences for the economic outlook, for the financial system in which central banks operate and, thus, for the conduct of monetary policy'.[35] The NGFS now has more than 120 members.[36] The extent to which central banks have cooperated with each other and even moved into a quasi-political sphere is evidenced in the Joint COP26 Statement issued on 3 November 2021, in conjunction with the Coalition of Finance Ministers

---

[32] Berger et al. (2021).

[33] Ravi Menon, chair of the Network for Greening the Financial System, has warned: 'A disorderly transition is thought to be potentially destabilising for the financial system, as banks and investors could struggle to keep pace with changes in policy, technology or consumer behaviour. They may also find themselves exposed to firms with business models not built around the economics of an accelerated low carbon transition'. See David Clarke, 'Ukraine crisis puts world in disorderly climate transition scenario, says NGFS's Menon' Network for Greening the Financial System, Monetary Authority of Singapore, European Central Bank (Webpage, 2021 Green Central Banking), https://greencentralbanking.com/2022/08/17/ukraine-disorderly-climate-transition-scenario-ravi-menon/.

[34] Mark Carney, Breaking the tragedy of the horizon - climate change and financial stability, Speech delivered at Lloyds of London, 29 September 2019 https://www.bis.org/review/r151009a.htm.

[35] See Wall Street Journal 24 March 2021 Central Bank Group: Climate Change a Risk to Monetary Policy Execution https://www.wsj.com/articles/central-bank-group-climate-change-a-risk-to-monetary-policy-execution-11616620574.

[36] As at 3 October 2022, there were 121 members and 19 observers. NGFS, 'Membership' (Webpage, NGFS, 10 April 2022) https://www.ngfs.net/en/about-us/membership.

for Climate Action.[37] Central banks are also using tools such as ESG requirements (environmental, social and corporate governance requirements) for securities to be used in repo transactions, and in collaboration with supervisory and prudential authorities, requirements are set for commercial banks. Central banks are also working on assessing climate risks and 're-orienting investments towards green projects in anticipation of future green projects'.[38] Whilst access to credit for green projects is important to meet net-zero emissions targets, central banks still have to ensure financial stability.

Climate change risks could be considered to be financial stability risks, and therefore fall within the mandate of central banks with financial stability mandates. For example, in November 2020, the Federal Reserve recognised climate change as a financial stability risk, and in December 2020 the Federal Reserve joined the NGFS.[39] Mitigating climate risks may or may not fall within a financial stability mandate. Central banks may however include those as part of their mission, whether or not actions in support of the fight against climate change fall within their legal remit.[40] For example, the Federal Reserve Bank is somewhat restricted in its actions concerning climate change because of limitations on its legal powers[41]:

> To date, the U.S. Congress has not legislated a climate mandate for the Fed, or adopted policies requiring that businesses abandon carbon-rich activities. So it could very well be costly to democratic values were the Fed to sidestep the legislative process with measures to deter the banks that it oversees from lending to brown businesses or households. Such action could be perceived as state action toward picking winners and losers with regulation.[42]

Other central banks may find themselves in a similar position.

In the case of the Reserve Bank of Australia (RBA), for example, its enabling legislation includes the requirement that the RBA's decisions are to be directed to the 'greatest advantage of the people of Australia',[43] in respect of the stability of the currency, full employment in Australia, and also 'the economic prosperity and welfare of the people of Australia'.[44] The latter could be interpreted to be wide enough

---

[37] The Coalition of Finance Ministers for Climate Change, 'Joint COP Statement with the NGFS Chair', (3 November 2021) https://www.financeministersforclimate.org/news/coalition-chairs-release-joint-cop26-statement-ngfs-chair.

[38] Berger et al. (2021). 'Many banks have signed green pledges to reduce their lending to fossil-fuel-friendly industries and promote lending to new low-climate-risk energy firms. So far, there has not been convincing data that they have turned these words into actions, but all indications are that the secular pressures will increase. In the post-COVID world, impact and implications of these developments for the banking industry will be an interesting topic of future research'.

[39] Hilal Atici, 'The Fed recognises climate change as financial stability risk' (Webpage, Greencentralbanking.com, November 2021) https://greencentralbanking.com/2020/11/09/fed-recognises-climate-change-as-financial-stability-risk/.

[40] See Skinner (2021).

[41] Ibid. Skinner argues that 'many aspects of climate change sit outside the Fed's legal remit today', while investigating 'the limits of the Fed's mandates to address climate change and how far.. the Fed [can] press beyond those mandates to make the economy greener' (see abstract)."

[42] Ibid., 1354.

[43] Section 10(2), Reserve Bank of Australia Act (1959).

[44] Ibid.

to encompass a climate change objective, but given that these objectives come under the umbrella of the 'monetary and banking policy' of the RBA, an express objective referencing the 'management of climate-related risks and opportunities'[45] would be preferred.[46]

Not everyone is enthusiastic about the role adopted by central banks or proposed for central banks in response to the climate crisis, because doing so would amount to pursuing a mission that strays from the state-sanctioned legislative mandate. Jens Weidman, President of Deutsche Bundesbank, is of the view that central banks should not be making up for a lack of effective political climate policies (even if they may be critical of political action). In his opinion, 'price stability is the best contribution monetary policy can make to overall welfare'.[47] For others, however, the decisions of central banks 'in favour of low-carbon industries' … 'is not a value judgement but a prudential judgement'.[48] Vallet is of the view that:

> '[a] "precautionary approach" (Chenet, Ryan-Collins, and van Lerven, 2019, 2021) is required since it seeks to have a distributive impact benefitting the common good. In other words, the environmentally unequal distributive impact of monetary policy serves the people'.[49]

Nevertheless, many central banks and prudential regulators currently maintain a climate change mission. For example, the RBA and prudential regulator (APRA) published a joint statement[50] on how they intended to deal with climate change and affirmed that they would also share the outcome of their work with other central banks.[51] This is a clear expression of how these institutions have formulated their mission. The RBA and APRA also consider climate action as part of their mandates,[52] but state that climate change is 'related to' their mandates (not 'within'). They note

---

[45] Toby Phillips, It's time to add climate change and net-zero emiissions to the RBA's top 3 economic goals'. (Webpage, The Conversation, 21 November 2022). This recommendation was made by the Centre for Policy Development.

[46] See for example the recommendations of the Centre or Policy Development, 'Submission to the Review of the Reserve Bank of Australia: Equipping the RBA for a dynamic climate risk and transition response', https://cpd.org.au/wp-content/uploads/2022/11/Equipping-the-RBA-for-a-dynamic-climate-risk-and-transition-response-5-1.pdf.

[47] Jens Weidmann, 'Bundesbank chief: How central banks should address climate change' (Financial Times, 19 November 2020) https://www.ft.com/content/ed270eb2-e5f9-4a2a-8987-41df4eb67418.

[48] Vallet (2021), 29.

[49] Ibid.

[50] APRA and RBA, 'NGFS Pledge – Combined Statement from APRA and the RBA', 4 November 2021, https://www.apra.gov.au/ngfs-pledge---combined-statement-from-apra-and-rba.

[51] Uribe (2021).

[52] APRA and RBA, n 50. In the Preamble APRA and the RBA state: 'Climate change directly affects the economy and the financial system, and is therefore closely related to the mandates of the Australian Prudential Regulation Authority (APRA) and Reserve Bank of Australia (RBA). APRA is tasked to ensure the financial safety of individual financial institutions and to promote the stability of the Australian financial system, and the RBA is mandated to implement monetary policy to achieve price stability and maintain financial stability. The physical impact of climate change, and the global transition to a lower emissions economy, will affect economic output, prices and

'[c]limate change directly affects the economy and the financial system and is therefore closely related to the mandates of the Australian Prudential Regulation Authority (APRA) and the Reserve Bank of Australia (RBA)'. [53] Whether this reframing of a mandate as a mission is simply a matter of interpretation of a mandate or amounts to mission creep,[54] remains to be seen.

12.3.4 Geopolitical Crises of War, Peace and Disrupted Supply Chains: Central Bank Responses to the New War on Inflation

The financial crisis caused by the COVID-19 pandemic has been exacerbated by supply chain disruptions caused by geopolitical tensions. In February 2022, Russian troops invaded Ukraine in what is described by Russia as a 'special military operation'.[55] From the Ukrainian perspective, it is however an invasion and war. Although the Russian-Ukranian conflict has not involved other nations at the time of writing, Ukraine has received assistance and support from the international community. NATO has formally condemned the invasion, and there have been many calls to end the invasion and recall Russian troops from Ukraine. There were several sovereign responses including the imposition of various economic sanctions against Russia. The conflict has critically impacted the provision of commodities, including wheat and gas.

Central bank responses to the Ukrainian war have been both direct and indirect. For example, in the first week of March 2022, the European Commission took the decision to disconnect seven Russian banks from SWIFT, the Belgium-based Society for Worldwide Interbank Financial Telecommunication.[56] This move was only taken after significant deliberation and consideration, and endorsement was sought from

employment. Climate change will be a driver of change in the value of certain assets and income streams, and therefore poses a risk to financial institutions and financial stability.'

[53] APRA and RBA, NGFS Pledge—Combined Statement by APRA and RBA, Preamble Statement, (4 November 2021) https://www.apra.gov.au/ngfs-pledge-%E2%80%93-combined-statement-from-apra-and-rba.

[54] Merryn Somerset Webb, 'Central Banks Need To Stop The Mission Creep', (Financial Times, Online, 28 August 2021). Webb cites Former Governor of the Bank of England, Mervyn King's warning that centra lbanks are moving into the political arena. He also criticises Christine Lagarde' defense of a liberal interpretation of the ECBs mandate as not 'mission creep, but rather an acknowledgement of reality.

[55] Vladimir Putin, Speech on 24 February 2022 as reported by Andrew Osborn and Polina Nikolskaya, 'Russia's Putin authorises 'special military operation' against Ukraine (Reuters, 24 February 2022) https://www.reuters.com/world/europe/russias-putin-authorises-military-operations-donbass-domestic-media-2022-02-24/.

[56] SWIFT is a significant messaging service facilitating large volumes of cross-border payments. See Robert Greene, 'How Sanctions on Russia Will Alter Global Payments Flows' (Webpage) (4 March 2022) Carnegie Endowment for International Peace, https://carnegieendowment.org/2022/03/04/how-sanctions-on-russia-will-alter-global-payments-flows-pub-86575.

leaders in countries such as the United States, the United Kingdom, and Japan.[57] Following the invasion and spikes in oil and natural gas prices, inflationary pressures rose worldwide, and central banks started tightening monetary policy. It is interesting to note that the Russian central bank, in the position where the value of its domestic currency, the rouble, has been damaged as a result of sanctions, has taken steps to significantly raised the interest to protect the value of the domestic currency.[58] The geopolitical crisis will impact investors, which could be felt all over the world, as Russia has taken steps to not repay investors in retaliatory measures.[59] The geopolitical uncertainty that coincides with rising inflationary pressure also creates additional challenges for central banks.

12.3.5 A Potential Cyber Crisis: Novel Approaches in the Foreshadowing of a Potential Cyber Crisis

Although not a crisis (yet), central banks all over the world must deal with the threats posed by cryptocurrencies and crypto assets more generally.[60] Cryptocurrencies and crypto assets used as payment mechanisms pose problems for payment systems and can be threats to fiat currencies. For example, in the Russian-Ukrainian conflict, cryptocurrencies have been used to transfer funds directly to the impacted areas when the regular payment channels were disabled/not available.[61] Non-governmental payment mechanisms (private 'money' or barter instruments) were used in the conflict with relative ease.

---

[57] See Greene, n 56.

[58] Reuters, 'Russian central bank hikes rate to 20% in emergency move, tells firms to sell FX' (Webpage, 24 February 2022) https://www.reuters.com/business/finance/russia-hikes-key-rate-20-tells-companies-sell-fx-2022-02-28/.

[59] Some investors will not get payment on their Russian investments as Russia reciprocates. "The Russian government has made a list of unfriendly countries, which includes all EU members, the US, Canada, South Korea, Australia, the United Kingdom, Monaco, New Zealand, Norway, Switzerland, Japan, and others. We expect there will be numerous cases of investors not receiving any payments on their Russian risk assets. So, this will mean technical default which may turn to real default and legal actions after the grace period." Egor Federov, Timothy Rahill, Oleksiya, Soroka, Nadège Tillier, Jeroen van den Broek, 'The credit reaction to the Ukraine-Russia crisis', (Webpage article, 8 March 2022) https://think.ing.com/articles/the-credit-reaction-russia-ukraine-crisis.

[60] See Steven Maijoor, 'Public trust: the litmus test of financial innovation' (Speech at the Institutional Digital Assets and Crypto Regulation Symposium 17 November 2022) https://www.dnb.nl/en/general-news/speeches-2022/speech-steven-maijoor-into-the-unknown-decision-making-in-uncertain-times/.

[61] Elizabeth Gail, 'What the Russia-Ukraine war has revealed about crypto' (Webpage, Cointelegraph, 28 October 2022) https://cointelegraph.com/news/what-the-russia-ukraine-conflict-has-revealed-about-crypto.

Cyberspace and in particular cybercurrencies and crypto assets have been flagged by Allen and Lastra as a potential looming crisis. [62] There are three areas in which cryptocurrencies and crypto assets challenge the current roles of central banks and monetary and prudential authorities. When cryptocurrencies function as money, they pose a 'direct challenge to the monetary sovereignty of central banks in their money creation role',[63] they also create a challenge for central banks acting as supervisory and prudential authorities in their oversight roles, [64] and lastly, through 'conceptual challenges to definitions (i.e. of categories such as 'money,' 'currency,' and 'security') that are presupposed in the distribution of regulatory competence, but are, both as a matter of legal and economic theory, contentious'. [65] Allen and Lastra 'argue that sovereign states still have a unique and irreplaceable role in guarding financial stability, which must be reflected in the law of Internet jurisdiction: an emerging lex cryptographica financiera'.[66] Because fiat money (central bank money) and private 'money' issued by private entities 'form part of an integrated, hierarchical money system, both domestically and globally',[67] the roles of central banks as monetary authorities, payment system regulators and financial stability regulators, are challenged. Both through joining the cryptocurrency sphere through possible central bank digital currencies (CBDCs) or regulating private cryptocurrencies, central banks may be acting beyond their mandates, and they may be crossing over the so-called 'third border'[68] between the current physical world and cyberspace. In this space too an international response will be required, which will push central banks beyond their normal national focus.[69]

12.4 Legislative Mandate of a Central Bank—Role and Importance

The legislative mandate of a central bank is important and it cannot be treated as a mere formality. Firstly, from a practical perspective, a central bank should be able to draw on its formal mandate for clarity as to its obligations and roles. A clear legal

[62] Allen and Lastra, n 12.

[63] Rosa Mara Lastra and Jason Grant Allen, Virtual Currencies in the Eurosystem: Challenges Ahead, (2019) (52) 2 The International Lawyer; Chicago, 177–232.

[64] Ibid.

[65] Ibid.

[66] Allen and Lastra, n. 12, 531.

[67] Ibid, 530.

[68] See Allen and Lastra, n 12.

[69] For example, Steven Maijoor of the FSB encouraged central bankers to look outward and collaborate: 'Regulators and supervisors will not only need to work together across borders, but also *across sectors.*' Steven Maijoor, 'Public trust: the litmus test of financial innovation' (Speech at the Institutional Digital Assets and Crypto Regulation Symposium 17 November 2022) https://www.dnb.nl/en/general-news/speeches-2022/speech-steven-maijoor-into-the-unknown-decision-making-in-uncertain-times/.

mandate will inform the central bank's decisions and direction, and the durability that comes from the legislation will be an advantage. The impact will extend beyond operational issues such as resource allocation. Secondly, the legitimacy of central banks is important. Chief Justice Murray Gleeson characterised that which is not legitimate, as arbitrary. In light of its role, importance and impact, a central bank should never be perceived as 'arbitrary'. Formal and societal legitimacy should be protected by the product of formal democratic processes, i.e. legislation through Parliament. When the actions of a central bank are aligned with the roles given to the central bank through the formal democratic processes in Parliament, its formal and societal legitimacy will be protected. This requires clear legislative/statutory expression.

Further, central banks are accountable not only to Parliament but to the electorate. Accountability is only truly effective if the requirements that have to be met by the public institution are clear enough. Legitimacy and accountability are important components of public institutions in a democratic society. Leading experts in central banking law, Charles Goodhart and Rosa Lastra, have emphasised that 'the legal interpretation of whether a central bank is abiding by the mandate or exceeding its powers, are fundamental issues in a democratic system'. Similarly, Paul Tucker, formerly from the Bank of England, has pointed to the extent to which central banks benefit from 'unelected power' and as such, their legislative mandate and legal architecture should balance out the potential negative consequences of their independence. Getting the legislative framework of the RBA and other central banks right, is therefore important.

Globalisation has increasingly connected not just financial markets, institutions and systems, but also regulators, including central banks. Simultaneously, over the past 20 years, crisis responses by central banks have pushed them into increasingly new territory, and expectations of what central banks should turn their attention to, have changed. Central banks themselves have enlarged their missions; external parties have also called for more action from central banks in certain areas. Central banks have also taken more initiative (sometimes when political will was lacking, for example in relation to climate change) and have broadened their scope to take into consideration more international priorities. The risk of interpreting the mandate of a central bank too broadly is that the scope of its responsibility may extend beyond its capabilities. When a central bank is responsible for combatting a wide range of social ills, it loses its focus. To be effective in public policy implementation, the number and alignment of policy objectives and tools should be carefully considered. Central banks should not be 'one-stop policy shops'. Moreover, '[i]t is important to have in place adequate mechanisms to 'guard the guardians' of monetary and financial stability'.

References

Jason Grant Allen and Rosa María Lastra, Border Problems: Mapping the Third Border, 2020 (83) 3 The Modern Law Review, 505–538, 525.

Allen N Berger, Asli Demirgüç-Kunt, Fariborz Moshirian and Anthony Saunders, 'Editorial: The way forward for banks during the COVID-19 crisis and beyond: Government and central bank responses, threats to the global banking industry' (2021) 113 Journal of Banking and Finance, 1–4, 4.

Michael David Bordo, 'Monetary Policy Cooperation/Coordination and Global Financial Crises in Historical Perspective' (2021) 32 Open Economies Review 587–611, 588. https://doi.org/10.1007/s11079-020-09611-5

John H Farrar and David Mayes (eds), *Globalisation, the Global Financial Crisis, and the Reinvention of the State* (Edgar Elgar, 2013).

John H Farrar, Louise Parsons and Pieter J. Joubert, 'The Development of an Appropriate Regulatory Response to the Global Financial Crisis' 2009 21(3) Bond Law Review, 1, 13.

Stefan Gerlach, Alberto Giovannini, Cédric Tille, and José Viñals, "Are the Golden Years of Central Banking Over? The Crisis and the Challenges," (2009) Geneva Reports on the World Economy 10.

Charles Goodhart and Rosa Lastra, 'Populism and Central Bank Independence' (2018) 29 Open Economic Review 49–68, 65. DOI https://doi.org/10.1007/s11079-017-9447-y.

Louise Parsons, 'Domestic regulatory architecture for the protection of financial stability after the GFC: Global order or disorder', in Danielle Ireland-Piper and Leon Wolff (eds), *Global governance and regulation: Order and disorder in the 21st century* (Routledge, 2018).

Christina Parajon Skinner, 'Central Banks and Climate Change' (2021) (74)5 Vanderbilt Law Review, 1301 – 1364).

Alice Uribe, 'Australia's Central Bank, Prudential Regulator Step Up Climate-Change Analysis; The central bank plans to conduct analysis that monitors the implications of climate change and related mitigation policies', Wall Street Journal, 4 November 2021.

Guillaume Vallet, 'Great Power, Great Responsibility: Addressing the Underestimated Issue of Central Bank's Social Responsibility' (2021) (3) Journal of Central Banking Theory and Practice, pp. 23–39, 24. DOI: https://doi.org/10.2478/jcbtp-2021-0022

Daniel Wilsher, Ready to Do Whatever it Takes? The Legal Mandate of the European Central Bank and the Economic Crisis. (2013) Cambridge Yearbook of European Legal Studies, 15, pp. 503–536, 507. DOI: https://doi.org/10.1017/S1528887000003141

Chapter 13
Moral Virtue and Corporate Law

Mary Hiscock

Abstract The scholarly work of John Farrar has demonstrated two major areas of concentration: the relationship of law and morality, and the analysis and development of corporate responsibility and corporate governance. This work has moved way beyond the historic debate of corporate responsibility as against individual responsibility of those engaged in the process of corporate governance. The twenty-first century has seen a rise in the scope of obligations imposed on corporations and their sources. The concept of stakeholder has been extended as has the range of interests and values to be managed. This chapter examines these issues in the context of two Australian situations: the governance effects of the destruction of an historic sacred site by Rio Tinto; and the reaction of the Australian government to the modern phenomenon of corporate slavery. In each case there are cross-border implications: the significance of the size and nature of Rio Tinto, and the extent to which Australia is only one of many governments seeking to remedy the situation by legislation and regulation. The outcomes are not finally resolved.

13.1 Introduction

"Every act and every enquiry, and similarly every action and pursuit, is thought to aim at some good".[1] In the long and productive scholarly career of my friend and colleague, John Farrar, two constant themes are discernible. The first is the centrality of moral virtue to his concept of law. His work, Legal Reasoning,[2] studied by generations of law students, begins with a simple question—'is a course of action, right?'—a question we sometimes vary to ask—'is a course of action ethical?' As he explains, the English word 'ethical' derives from the Greek word 'ethos'—which means character and traditions. The Oxford English Dictionary defines ethics as

[1] Aristotle (2001).

[2] Farrar (2010).

M. Hiscock (✉)
Faculty of Law, Bond University, Gold Coast, Australia
e-mail: mhiscock@bond.edu.au

U. Ghori et al. (eds.), *Globalisation in Transition*,
https://doi.org/10.1007/978-981-99-2439-4_13

principles of human duty. Morality derives from the Latin 'mos', meaning custom. Aristotle says that "moral virtue comes about as a result of habit, whence its name (ethike) is formed by a slight deviation from the word ethos (habit)".[3] Cicero believed that Roman law, including its commercial law, reflected moral obligations.[4] These are ancient concepts coming to us from the classical world of Greece and Rome. There are parallel developments in Judeo-Christian morality, found also in Islam, that are still part of contemporary law, such as the prohibition of usurious dealings. Ethics and morality are not hollow antiquarian notions for the commercial lawyer.

The second aspect of his body of work is corporate law, especially corporate governance. His mastery of this area has been demonstrated in numerous editions of his work in multiple jurisdictions.[5] For him, corporate governance is not just about good housekeeping and orderly administration. John has analysed the evolution of the demands that society puts on the modern corporation. The expression of these is no longer reflected only in law, whether legislative or judicial. Increasingly, the opinions of investors and, sometimes, an even wider public group have bearing.[6] It is here that the junction, or perhaps collision, of law and morality are most evident.

> If we adopt the position that corporate governance is about the legitimacy of corporate power, corporate accountability and the standards by which the corporation is to be governed, and by whom, it is obvious that the concept transcends legal standards and liability, perhaps reflecting the fact that the law deals with a minimal morality of obligation rather than a morality of obligation.[7]
>
> The basic questions of corporate governance are these: in whose (various) interests should a corporation operate and, where those interests diverge, what laws, rules, structures and processes are most likely to support a fair and efficient resolution of that divergence.[8]

This is not a view peculiar to Australia or even to common law systems. John Kaeser, the Chief Executive of Siemens, the German mega-corporation, when interviewed about the rise of right-wing populism in Europe and why few of his peers would, as he did, speak against it, said:

> For all companies, there is often a conflict between values and interests. In this case [speaking out], this was a unique case where both correlated. Before, you had to consider customers, employment, and shareholders. Now there is a fourth consideration: Society.[9]

Contemporary corporate governance has cast the responsibilities of directors wider and wider.[10] Some recent areas of growth include the environmental context of

---

[3] Aristotle (n 1) Book II, 1.

[4] Cicero (1991).

[5] These include Australia, England and Wales, and New Zealand.

[6] See Ehrlich (1936). "The centre of legal gravity of legal development... from time immemorial has not lain in the activity of the state, but in society itself, and must be sought there at the present time."

[7] Farrar (1993).

[8] Farrar and Hanrahan (2017).

[9] Kampfner (2020).

[10] Farrar and Hanrahan (above n 8), 128 (n 8), 551 (note 10), 553, Fig. 32.3.

corporate activities and the Modern Slavery legislation.[11] Both areas require proactive responses by corporations and reflect a growing synergy between what is legal and what is morally right.

13.2 A Contemporary Example

Rio Tinto Ltd. (Rio Tinto) is a corporation listed on the Australian Stock Exchange, but it is managed from London. It operates 60 mining sites in 35 countries. In 2021, its net profits were USD 21.4 billion, having paid royalties and taxes of USD 13 billion.[12] This was an increase over the previous year of 60%, and it paid the highest ever dividends to shareholders. It has a complex structure, built around the major products it mines and sells: Iron Ore, Aluminium, Copper and Diamonds, and Minerals and Energy. Each Division is autonomous, with relatively little control from the central executive, the Executive Committee, and the Board, which are physically based in England. The Executive Committee includes the Chief Executive, the heads of the four product divisions and of Human Relations, the Chief Legal Officer, the Chief Corporate Officer, the Chief Financial Officer, the head of a collective of growth, innovation, health, and safety, and of corporate relations. This last remit includes external affairs, sustainability, communications generally and specifically with Indigenous Relations, Research, Media, Government and Employees. A parallel management structure in Australia reports to an Australian head, who then reports to the global head. This structure isolates the product divisions from the cross-over responsibilities, notably indigenous relations. Its priorities would always be relative to the other activities in the collective, and the time constraints of senior management.

In 2020, Rio Tinto demolished an ancient indigenous sacred site, the Juukan Caves, in Western Australia, to enlarge an existing mine and to reach AUD 132 million worth of ore beneath. The ore was particularly rich and was needed to mix in with other ore to reach the standard of "Pilbara" ore. There were other ways that the ore could have been reached without the demolition. It was a lawful act under Western Australian law.[13]

Rio Tinto had established, years before, a formal indigenous liaison with the *Puutu Kinti Karama* and *Penikura* (PKKP), the traditional owners of the land, but had failed to use it to seek consensus on this action. The site had a history of 46,000 years of spiritual use and occupation. The PKKP, to whom the site belonged and was held sacred by, protested publicly at the time. But the PKKP had agreed to a "gag" clause in their original agreement with the company, which had dealt with several matters including finance, employment, and education. Rio Tinto admitted that immediately before the demolition, it had specifically taken legal advice on what measures it could use to stop PKKP protesting and/or going to court. This whole process was rushed

[11] *Modern Slavery Act 2018* (Cth).

[12] Rio Tinto. (2021). Annual Report.

[13] By licence granted under the *Aboriginal Heritage Act 1972* (WA).

because the Head of Corporate Relations, based in London, had only become aware of the demolition and its possible consequences some three days before it occurred in Western Australia.

This whole course of conduct was, however, so strongly and widely condemned by the shareholders and by the public that within a year, the Chief Executive Officer of the company, Jean-Sebastien Jacques, and the managers of corporate affairs and of public affairs resigned. In a notice to the Australian Stock Exchange (ASX) it reported that the chief executive of the Iron Ore Product Division would also leave the company.[14] Initially, the company had publicly apologised and stripped the responsible executives of millions of dollars of bonuses. There was significant directorial breast beating. But this served only to exacerbate the corporate scandal.

A federal Parliamentary Inquiry was established and published a Final Report in October 2021.[15] Its work was substantially delayed by the COVID-19 pandemic, and particularly the restrictions caused on travel. Some recommendations are formally tabled. The Report usefully sets out a full statement of the facts that led to the decision to demolish the site. The governance structure of the corporation, which impeded knowledge and discussion of the proposed action until it was imminent, and the corporate culture which deterred lower-level management pursuing issues unlikely to be welcomed higher up the chain, were contributing factors. The dominant consideration was the commercial value of ready access to the ore.

The Chair of the Parliamentary Inquiry stated in the opening paragraphs of the Report[16]:

> Lawmakers and corporations alike must consider the relevance of the United Nations Declaration on the Rights of Indigenous Peoples (UNDRIP) to the social, cultural economic realities of Aboriginal and Torres Strait Islander peoples and review that relationship in light of these realities.

He also thanked "Rio Tinto which, perhaps in contrition for its error, has been forthcoming with evidence—not always to its advantage".

As part of its public reaction and to ameliorate the reputation of Rio Tinto, a number of actions were taken. Three months after the demolition, Hamersley Iron Pty Ltd. and the PKKP Corporation reached a funding agreement "to address the moral obligations of Rio Tinto to the PKKP and to support the repair of a meaningful relationship". Rio Tinto published a formal document under the signature of the Chief Executive, Jakob Stausholm.[17] It republished the formal apology and committed to a new structure which would enable its capacity to "Listen, hear, and show greater care". It undertook over time to improve its engagement with Indigenous and First Nations Communities globally. In the document, it acknowledged that its publication was a result of pressure from its major global investors. It bravely engaged to seek feedback on its proposals from the PKKP, and to publish this with the report. It did so.

---

[14] Hopkins and Kemp (2020).

[15] Joint Standing Committee on Northern Australia. (2021).

[16] Ibid., xii.

[17] Rio Tinto. (2021).

The gist of the feedback by the PKKP was that there was no recognition or acceptance that the issues arose only partly because of the governance structure, but that there was also a major issue of corporate culture which had neither been acknowledged nor tackled. This was reflected in several ways—the existence of a "glass ceiling" for indigenous employees so that they did not reach a significant level of corporate decision making, a highly legalistic approach demonstrated using corporate lawyers, always remote from the site of the issues, and a continuing attitudinal problem of some longstanding staff members who resisted change.

Rio Tinto agreed to substantial compensation for the damage to this sacred site and promised physical remediation as far as possible. It is estimated by some that the final amount of compensation over time could be USD 250 million. The accounts of the PKKP Aboriginal Corporation, the group that represents the owners of the native title, show that it spent USD 300,000 in employing a lead mediator and that their legal expenses over the first year since the offer of compensation were AUD 325,000, AUD 85,000 on media and communication expenses, AUD 70,000 on travel costs, and AUD 113,840 on external administration costs.

Analysis of areas of societal concern show a continuing linkage and growth between them and the responsibilities of corporations, boards, and directors. It is a move from passive observance of established rules to managed values—the broadening of the interests of corporations.

13.3 Modern Slavery Legislation

One aspect of globalisation is a contemporaneous reaction to a particular issue in various jurisdictions. There may not be an exact replication of the response, but a broad pattern can emerge and there can be a synthesis and harmonious result despite the cross-border nature of the issues. This is what has happened with "modern" slavery.

In the case of the modern slavery legislation,[18] the responsibilities of the corporation through its board extend to enquiries, not only of its direct operations but also of its supply chains of materials and products, despite their possibly remote connection with the territorial activities of the corporation. There is a duty to report annually to ASIC (the corporation's regulator) and results are placed in a public register kept by the Australian Border Force. This legislation follows a model from the European Union, and national legislation in the United Kingdom and in the Netherlands. The proactive stance required is a substantial addition to the responsibilities of corporations and of individual directors. So, what has led to this comparatively recent change?

Slavery is an institution which has existed at least as long as recorded history. Its core is the ownership of a human being by another human being, with all the various entitlements that ownership brings. These have varied from society to society

[18] *Modern Slavery Act 2018* (Cth).

and reflect the perceived needs of the time. Slavery survived the radical attitude of Christianity to the equality of human beings. In the central question of a relationship to God, a slave might be socially diminished in terms of status in civil society, but not otherwise. As Paul writes in his Letter to the Colossians,[19] "There is no longer Greek and Jew…slave and free."

The common law first tackled the issue of slavery in the eighteenth century. In 1772, in *Somerset v Stewart*,[20] a writ of *habeas corpus* was filed on behalf of an African slave, James Somerset. He had been brought to England and then detained on a vessel with the intent to transport him for sale in Jamaica. There was protracted argument by counsel. Lord Mansfield urged the parties to settle for the sake of clarifying the status of some 15,000 slaves residing in England. The parties could not agree.

In his judgment, Lord Mansfield stated:

> The state of slavery is of such a nature, that it is incapable of being introduced on any reasons, moral or political; but only positive law, which preserves its force long after the reasons, occasion, and time itself from whence it was created, is erased from memory: it's so odious, that nothing can be suffered to support it, but positive law. Whatever inconvenience, therefore, may follow from a decision, I cannot say this case is allowed or approved by the law of England; and therefore the black must be discharged.[21]

In subsequent English decisions, it was clear that the decision had limited application, not affecting slaves outside the jurisdiction, and applying only to slaves being detained against their will. But there was a growing anti-slavery movement from that time onwards led by William Wilberforce MP, himself a former slave trader.[22] He argued that slavery was immoral and contrary to the tenets of the Established Church of England, and that it was oppressive and cruel.

As the result of the untiring efforts of the Abolitionists, in 1807, *the Slave Trade Abolition Act 1807* (U.K.) was passed,[23] which prohibited British subjects from engaging in the slave trade or importing slaves into a British colony. In 1833, Parliament passed the *Slavery Abolition Act 1833* (U.K.), which abolished slavery in all British colonies, plantations, and possessions. An interesting characteristic of this legislation is that the owners of slaves were compensated handsomely, as they would have been for the expropriation of any other property right. Slaves were business assets. Ironically, many former slave owners used these funds to purchase plantations in Queensland, and then managed them with "indentured labourers".[24] Although this practice was never held to be slavery, the repatriation of any remaining

---

[19] The Bible. Epistle to the Colossians. 3:10.

[20] *Somerset v Stewart* (1772) 98 ER 499.

[21] Ibid., 510.

[22] Hague (2007).

[23] *Slave Trade Abolition Act 1807* (U.K.).

[24] Sanders and Saunders (2022) Kidnapping and Slavery in Queensland: The Jason and The Hopeful. Presented at Selden Society Seminar, Supreme Court of Queensland, 18 August 2022.

indentured labourers was a condition of Queensland entering the Federation of the Commonwealth of Australia.[25] The repatriation was accomplished in 1906–7.

In 1860, the southern states of the U.S., where slavery was legal and endemic, seceded from the union, leading to the commencement of a civil war in April 1861. On 1 January 1863, President Lincoln issued the Emancipation Proclamation which declared that all slaves residing in the southern Confederate States "henceforward shall be free".

The modern trigger for this striking example of a global feeling of social responsibility for modern slavery was the Rana Plaza disaster in Bangladesh in 2013. Factories containing garment workers caught fire. The buildings had no appropriate fire escapes and all the doors were locked and the windows barred.

As a result, more than 1100 workers perished in the fire. The garments being made were to be on sold to major Western retailers, including many major fashion houses. The NGO Oxfam in its 2017 Report, "What She Makes: Power and Poverty in the Fashion Industry" estimated that only 4% of the price of garments sold in Australia is paid to the factory workers who made them.[26] In the situation in Bangladesh, this is only 2%, far below a wage that would cover shelter and food.

This tragic fire led to the Bangladesh Accord on Fire and Building Safety.[27] The parties to the Accord included several hundreds of major global fashion brands and relevant workers' unions. The Accord covers 2.5 million workers in ready-made garment factories. It contains a series of obligations requiring the fashion retailers to help contractors eliminate fire and safety hazards. So far, it is estimated that more than 90% of identified hazards have been eliminated.

The Accord contains an arbitration clause to enable disputes over any breach of the Accord to go to arbitration before The Permanent Court of Arbitration in the Hague. There has already been one arbitration, which was settled by the parties before the decision of the tribunal was given.[28] The brands remain anonymous, but if they supply Australian retailers, it would be a breach of the *Modern Slavery Act 2018* by the corporation and its directors, if there had not been careful enquiry and attempts to remediate the hazard and any risks. Such a breach must be reported to ASIC and then publicly reported by it. At present, there is no penalty prescribed for the corporation or the directors, but this is a possible result of a review of the operation of the legislation to be conducted within the next year.

The *Modern Slavery Act 2018* defines and regulates modern slavery for Australian entities and businesses with Australian operations having a minimum consolidated revenue of AUD 100 million. It includes eight types of serious exploitation, including trafficking in persons, slavery, or servitude, forced marriage, forced labour, debt bondage, deceptive recruiting for labour and services and child labour involving slavery, servitude or extreme danger.

[25] *Pacific Islands Labourers Act 1901* (Cth).

[26] Oxfam Australia. (2017).

[27] Accord on Fire, Buildings and Safety. 2013. Subsequently updated as the New Bangladesh Accord. 2018.

[28] Permanent Court of Arbitration Case Nos 2016-36, 2016-37.

The Act requires entities to submit an annual statement. This has certain mandatory elements covering those entities owned or controlled by the reporting entity. These include the risks of modern slavery in its operations or supply chains, the methods of assessment of risk and of control of risk, including due diligence and remediation. The report must estimate effectiveness of its actions and any process of consultation undertaken.

Those consulted include employees, unions, joint ventures, and key suppliers.

These tasks fall on the principal governing body of the entity. Usually this will be the board. The report must be signed by a responsible member of the board. This task cannot be delegated. The board must be able to demonstrate that it is actively involved, calling for monitoring and review. Drafting codes of conduct and compliance terms is not sufficient. The penalty currently is the naming of the entity.

Many Australian entities, such as Telstra and Rio Tinto, have also to comply with similar but not identical requirements of the U.K. and the U.S. legislation. The details of these are given in the full annual report to shareholders.

13.4 Penalties

The trend towards increased penalties reflects the changing attitudes towards corporate behaviour.[29] There is, however, a problem. How far can concepts and ideas developed for natural persons be applied to corporate legal persons? A company was once described by Lord Thurlow as having neither a body to be kicked nor a soul to be damned.[30] Penalties could be financial, which were an ineffective deterrent when the corporation made a profit from the criminal behaviour. In extreme cases, the company could be dissolved, but that often only penalised shareholders who may have had little direct involvement in the crime. Therefore, the only persons involved usually were the directors of the corporation. Thankfully, in this regard, part of the great corporate legal revolution was transferring economic power from those who controlled or managed the company to those who owned the company shares themselves.

The alternative strategy to punishment is inducement to comply. A penalty of "naming and shaming" feeds off a general sentiment of disapproval within the community: "the pub test".

An economic equivalent is to accept that good corporate behaviour is good business practice. This was firmly accepted by Lord Mansfield as the basis of commercial law when he merged it into the common law in the eighteenth century. Adam Smith in "The Wealth of Nations",[31] a work of enormous influence published in 1776, said that "business is predicated or based on the rational pursuit of self-interest in a

[29] There is presently before the Australian Parliament a Bill to do this, Treasury Laws Amendment (More Competition, Better Prices) Bill 2022.

[30] Coffee (1981).

[31] Smith (1776).

market situation".[32] He went on to say, "this leads as if by an invisible hand to the common good". Many people who rely on "The Wealth of Nations" as a handbook of great status often overlook the companion volume that Smith wrote, "The Theory of Moral Sentiments". This book develops the idea that our moral ideas and actions are the product of our very nature as social creatures and that this is a better guide to moral action than is reason. Although we have our self-interest to uphold, we must learn to live with others without doing harm. This is a minimum requirement for the preservation of society. If we go further and do positive good, that is beneficence. However, justice demands rules, again for the preservation of society. Constant moral standards lead to a truly virtuous person, showing prudence, justice, beneficence, and self-command in their actions. For Smith, reciprocity of conduct is a prerequisite for a market to exist.

When Smith speaks of reciprocity in the context of corporations, does this call for social responsibility on the part of the corporation exercised by the directors?[33] Milton Friedman said that "business does not have a duty to exercise social responsibility". Rather, Friedman states "it has a duty not to have an eye to social responsibility; the business of business is to make profits".[34]

However, many now point out that a market is only a system of information. It does not determine ends or goals. So, the discussion turns to the question whether good ethics or behaviour on the part of a corporation are good for business. The duties of a director in Australia are defined under the general law derived from common law and equitable principles, but now in statutory form as having a duty of loyalty and good faith towards the company and a duty to act in good faith in the interests of the corporation and to use its powers for a proper purpose.[35] These duties are supplemented by more specific obligations. These basic duties, if breached can be met by civil penalties. In this respect, Australia is much stricter than other common law countries such as England, Canada, New Zealand, and the U.S.

There is a general legal expectation in Australia now that directors and officers of a corporation will take responsibility for the culture, conduct and behaviour of the corporation.[36]

There is an intrinsic hesitancy in framing uncertain obligations in the common law system. But leading judges since the days of Lord Mansfield have sought to dispel this. The Chief Justice of the Federal Court of Australia said:

> Certainty is a quality sometimes posited as a reason for removing from the expression of rules to govern conduct (in particular in regard to commercial conduct) standards, values and norms that lack precise definition, or that involve the application of values, or that apply or operate in contestable fields or with contestable results. But no sophisticated legal system,

---

[32] Ibid., 423.

[33] Farrar and Hanrahan (n 8) 432.

[34] Friedman (1970).

[35] Farrar and Hanrahan (n 8) ch 12.

[36] Baker McKenzie. (2021); Farrar and Hanrahan (n 8) ch 15, 15.2.

or society, seeks intellectual refuge in the proposition that rules alone are the guardians of the security of certainty.[37]

Non-fiscal penalties are not imposed for failure to comply with the reporting requirements of the *Modern Slavery Act*. That may change with the review of the impact of the Act on the behaviour of entities, as there is evidence of weak compliance.[38] The research collective of several NGOs, the University of NSW and the University of Melbourne analysed the reports of entities in the first year of submission, looking for quality as well as extent of reporting.

> Less than a fifth of companies (19%) disclose procedures to ensure responsible purchasing practices. Just 14% of companies express a commitment to ensuring workers in their supply chains are paid a living wage. Only 13% of companies describe processes for ensuring that workers are not being charged recruitment fees. Only 34% of companies disclose collaboration with key stakeholders such as trade unions, migrant worker groups, or civil society organisations, with just 13% demonstrating evidence of stakeholder consultation in developing or reviewing relevant policies.[39]

The consequences of this failure to comply with reporting requirements, which call for proactive response from those charged with this responsibility, indicate that substantial penalties may be called for. There has been a major increase in many corporate penalties, both legislated and imposed by regulators, this year.

13.5 Globalisation and Transition

John Farrar used this expression to refer initially to the "dismantling" of the post-World War II rules-based international legal order.[40] But he turned the focus to "globalisation" and expanded its scope. As he concluded, this is not a new term, although it has been used more extensively in this century. Its novel aspect is the increased speed of development of new technologies, and the impact of this on corporate finance and the spreading of risks in investment. It refers to complex phenomena in flux.[41]

However, the more critical question is "Transition to What?".[42] As in the example of modern slavery, globalisation now properly refers to a contemporaneous response to concerns over environmental, social and governance (ESG) issues. It is not always the same response. The understanding of moral virtue and the place of the State is always local as it inevitably reflects the balance of history, social and economic pressures.

---

37 *Paciocco v Australian and New Zealand Banking Group Limited* [2015] FCAFC 50, [266] (Allsop CJ, Besanko J and Middleton J agreeing).

38 Sinclair and Dinshaw (2022).

39 Ibid., 2–3.

40 Farrar and Hanrahan (n 8) pp 594–595; Farrar and Parsons (2019).

41 Farrar and Parsons (2012).

42 Ibid., 35.8.

This concern is clearly reflected in the complexities of supply chains.[43] The development of State power to impose thematic or autonomous sanctions can be directed against trade in goods or investment by parties involved in behaviour regarded as unacceptable, for example, the transport of goods produced by modern slavery or forced labour.

This trend is not yet as intrusive in Australia as it is in the U.S.[44] That may change with the review of the impact of the *Modern Slavery Act* on the behaviour of entities, as there is evidence that they are not in full compliance.[45]

This pattern of intervention is not new. It was part of the GATT 1947, which embodied State practice going back to the 1920s. States could act against other States permitting prison labour as an exception to the general principle of free trade. It is also within the WTO that the relationship between the demands of free trade and environmental sustainability are being negotiated. The COVID-19 pandemic has significantly changed all forms of international discussion and cooperation, but global debate is resuming. International bodies such as the UN, the WTO and the G20 have formulated principles on various aspects of desirable behaviour which will scaffold developments but not necessarily determine outcomes. The outcomes of application of debated general principles must be shaped locally to reflect appropriate understandings of moral virtue.

References

Aristotle 2001. *Nichomean Ethics, Book I*. Trans. W.D. Ross. In *The Basic Works of Aristotle*, ed. Richard McKeon. New York: Random House

Baker McKenzie. 2021. Duties and Liabilities of Directors of Australian Companies. https://www.bakermckenzie.com/-/media/files/insight/guides/2021/duties-and-liabilities-of-directors-of-australian-companies-oct-2021.pdf

Cicero. 1991. *On Duties*. Edited by MT Griffin and EM Atkins. Cambridge (U.K.): Cambridge University Press, 118–9.

Coffee Jr, John C. 1981. "No Soul to Damn: No Body to Kick: An Unscandalized Inquiry into the Problem of Corporate Punishment. *Michigan Law Review* 79:386.

Ehrlich, E. (1936). *Fundamental Principles of the Sociology of Law* (p. 390). Harvard University Press.

Farrar, J. (1993). Corporate Governance, Business Judgment, and the Professionalism of Directors. *Corporate and Business Law Journal, 6*, 1.

Farrar, J. (2010). *Legal Reasoning* (p. 431). Thomson Reuters.

Farrar, J., & Parsons, L. (2012). Globalisation, the Global Financial Crisis, and the Reinvention of the State. *Singapore Academy of Law Journal, 24*(367), 400.

Farrar, John and Pamela Hanrahan. 2017. *Corporate Governance*. Chatswood: Lexis-Nexis, 3.

Farrar, John and Louise Parsons. 2019. Financial Stability After the Global Financial Crisis: Globalisation, Nationalism, and the Potential Demise of a Rules-Based Order. In *Scholarship, Practice*

[43] Hudson (2022).

[44] *Tariff Act 1930* 19 U.S.C. 4 (U.S.).

[45] Sinclair and Dinshaw, above n 38.

and Education in Comparative Law: A Festschrift in Honour of Mary Hiscock, eds. John Farrar, Vai lo Lo and Bee Chen Goh, 81–111. Singapore: Springer.
Friedman, Milton. 1970. A Friedman Doctrine – The Social Responsibility of Business is to Increase Profits. New York Times Magazine. https://www.nytimes.com/1970/09/13/archives/a-friedman-doctrine-the-social-responsibility-of-business-is-to.html.
Hague, W. (2007). *William Wilberforce: The Life of the Great Anti-Slave Trade Campaigner*. Harper Collins.
Hopkins, Andrew and Deanna Kemp. 2020. Corporate Dysfunction on Indigenous Affairs: Why Heads Rolled at Rio Tinto. *The Conversation*. https://theconversation.com/corporate-dysfunction-on-indigenous-affairs-why-heads-rolled-at-rio-tinto-146001
Hudson, Andrew. 2022. The Rise of ESG Issues in the Supply Chain. Rigby Cooke Lawyers. rigbycooke.com.au/the-rise-of-esg-issues-issues-in-the-supply-chain/
Joint Standing Committee on Northern Australia. 2021. A Way Forward. Parliament of Australia. https://parlinfo.aph.gov.au/parlInfo/download/committees/reportjnt/024757/toc_pdf/AWayForward.pdf;fileType=application%2Fpdf
Kampfner, J. (2020). *Why the Germans Do it Better*. Atlantic Books.
Oxfam Australia. 2017. What She Makes: Power and Poverty in the Fashion Industry. https://www.oxfam.org.au/what-she-makes/
Rio Tinto. 2021. Communities and Social Performance Commitments Disclosure: Interim Report. file://datatwo/13566922$/Profile/Downloads/RT-CSP-commitments-disclosure-interim-report-2021.pdf.
Sanders Andrew and Kerry Saunders (2022) Kidnapping and Slavery in Queensland: The Jason and The Hopeful. Presented at Selden Society Seminar, Supreme Court of Queensland, 18 August 2022.
Sinclair, Amy and Freya Dinshaw. 2022. Paper Promises: Evaluating the Early Impact of Australia's Modern Slavery Act. Human Rights Law Centre. https://www.hrlc.org.au/reports/2022/2/3/paper-promises-evaluating-the-early-impact-of-australias-modern-slavery-act.
Smith, Adam. 1776. *An Inquiry into the Nature and Causes of the Wealth of Nations*. The Stand: W. Strahan and T. Cadell.

Chapter 14
Concluding Thoughts on Globalisation and the Contributions of Emeritus Professor John Hynes Farrar

Umair Ghori, Mary Hiscock, Louise Parsons, and Casey Watters

As John Farrar enters his ninth decade of age, one can truly say that he has sampled and shone in every aspect of law. He has completed studies with distinction at every level of academic performance; was a law clerk in a globally eminent law firm; has been solicitor and partner in a national firm; but, most notably, he is an academic leader, legal scholar, and a generous teacher.

He has been a professor for several decades, a dean more than once, and a vice-chancellor. John has the hint of ruthlessness that is needed for administrative responsibilities, but mostly he assumed these duties for a purpose, tempered with a kind and empathetic heart. These included expanding the role of indigenous students and law in New Zealand; and at Bond the preservation of a newly-created private law school within a university seeking to embody the intellectual values of integrity and independence. John has worked across several countries: Australia, England, Wales, New Zealand. If one adds the many occasions of being a productive and generous visitor, the list expands dramatically in terms of countries, continents, and of legal systems. His colleagues, Laurence Boulle, Ian Edwards,[1] and Douglas Branson[2]

U. Ghori (✉) · M. Hiscock · L. Parsons · C. Watters
Faculty of Law, Bond University, Gold Coast, Australia
e-mail: ughori@bond.edu.au

M. Hiscock
e-mail: mhiscock@bond.edu.au

L. Parsons
e-mail: lparsons@bond.edu.au

C. Watters
e-mail: cwatters@bond.edu.au

[1] Boulle, L. and I. Edwards 'John Farrar and his /juːˈbɪkwɪti/ in Legal Education' (Chap. 8).

[2] Branson, D. 'John Farrar: Leading Expert and Scholar in Company Law and Corporate Governance' (Chap. 2).

U. Ghori et al. (eds.), *Globalisation in Transition*,
https://doi.org/10.1007/978-981-99-2439-4_14

have elaborated these progressions in time and space. Esposito's tribute is a voice for many former students.

We chose to honour John by editing this volume. The contributors come in several guises—former students, colleagues, mentees—all friends. All of us have been affected by John. We have chosen to write in areas and ways that reflect his influence and interests. The glue is John. Each of us has reflected the comments above about him as a person, a scholar and a colleague and friend, and our chapters draw on his work.

14.1 Emerging Themes

We have two major conceptual foci in globalisation: its human and economic elements.[3] The range of discussion around these is very broad, covering the past, the present, and most importantly—the future and how better things can be brought about.

We see the world as being in a profound state of change—beset by a pandemic, enduring a proxy global war on the ground and in cyberspace, suffering the direct and indirect effects of climate change, demographic changes in the movement of peoples and the composition of the population: and the consequent economic and social disruption brought about by all these factors. This is amplified in its effect on the public by the speed and immediacy of exchange of visual and textual information. Globalisation is inherently in a condition of flux. It is always in transit, but to where?

14.2 The Role of Government

Inevitably there is a changing role for governments worldwide and of all descriptions—in the formulation of policy, the content and means of regulation and the management of expectations. The scope of the challenges is unexpected, but the events are foreseeable. The earlier pattern of globalisation through interconnectedness and the role of international and cross-border institutions has had a kaleidoscopic change. What is constant is the push–pull of social consequences and economic imperatives, of the moral issues of accessibility and inequality.

Bonython and Arnold draw attention to the supply chain and accessibility issues for the drugs and medical equipment needed to treat COVID-19.[4] Bonython and Arnold astutely observe that global health systems (a product of globalisation) have resulted in the subjugation of the public health bodies. The COVID-19 pandemic has

[3] Ghori, U. et al. 'Human and Economic Perspectives of Globalisation: An Introduction' (Chap. 1).

[4] Bonython, W., and B. Arnold 'Transition up to Best Practices, or Down to the Bar Minimum? Global Harmonisation of Regulation of Therapeutic Goods' (Chap. 5).

highlighted the vulnerabilities which must be carefully considered in the quest for harmonisation of health, patent, and safety standards.

Globalisation has also resulted in the emergence of new trends. Ghori's contribution touches upon the intrusion of globalisation into the domestic domain where non-institutional actors in an exporting country are now dictating the behaviour of the importers, even after the conclusion of the transaction.[5] Ghori posits that export oriented industries favour certainty over the current norm-driven regulation by invisible custodians using social licences. Ghori has further highlighted that the issuance of social licences is no longer limited to the immediate communities but as seen in the case of animal welfare, can be done by diverse range of welfare groups.

Welfare and morality are now emerging as key themes of globalisation. In many ways the emphasis of moral actions by the corporations, welfare of the people it engages with, care of animals, the natural environment and steps against climate change are now driving the transition of globalisation away from its traditional mercantilist incline. Hiscock's contribution illumines the reporting of modern slavery in supply chains of goods and services.[6] Corporate policies require proactive responses that reflect a synergistic links between the legal actions of a body corporate and its morality. Both precepts can no longer be divorced and in the current socio-economic milieu would be dangerous to be ignored by any multinational corporation that is partaking in the fruits of globalisation.

Welfare and humanity in immigration and labour policies is another aspect touched upon in this book. Judge Spiller's insightful contribution highlights the need for empathy in dealing with the vulnerable and the weak.[7] The emphasis on sensitivity becomes an important factor when dealing with the cross-border movement of people, especially in economies witnessing labour shortages, negative population growth and the unwillingness of the locals to engage in menial occupations.

Parsons's contribution highlights the importance of keeping public institutions, such as central banks, accountable, especially when under the forces of globalisation, and in light of historical transitions marked by crisis, they themselves redefine their missions. Responses to crises by central banks worldwide can often result in changes in their operations that are not reflected in statutory mandates. As central banks are independent from government, the democratic deficit is at risk of increasing in light of new global challenges.[8]

There is a universal recognition of problems and issues, and frequently and not surprisingly similar solutions, with sporadic co-operation and responses. Many institutions and organisations in the legal order are based on government and nation state membership and control and are beset by outmoded technology and patterns of commercial interactivity. Therefore, there is a perceptible movement towards informal coalitions of government and non-government bodies to work out solutions

---

[5] Ghori, U. 'Calculated Compliance in a Globalised World: The response to Social Licence compulsions by the Australian Live Export Sector' (Chap. 9).

[6] Hiscock, M. 'Moral Virtue and Corporate Law' (Chap. 13); see also Kumar (2020).

[7] Judge Spiller 'Globalisation in the Immigration Context' (Chap. 3).

[8] Parsons, L. 'Central Banks in Crisis Times: Mandates in Crisis?' (Chap. 12).

to restrictions holding over from the nineteenth and twentieth centuries, such as the global patent system, the territoriality of debt but the prevalence of multinational corporation that become insolvent. The contribution by Watters underscores the need for insolvency courts to be more flexible and operate with enhanced communication to resolve the complications associated with corporate insolvencies.[9] In continuation of the corporate theme, Markham's contribution explains the mismatch of earnings of corporations and their responsibility to pay taxes where they earn their profits.[10] Markham's analysis is a thematic extension of the chapter by Watters. Cooperation among the regulators, tax authorities and the courts are essential in the new era of globalisation. The public bodies cooperating with each other enables them to protect their own interests as well as to achieve a greater public good—one that is both efficient and moral. Multilateral cooperation enables countries to assure their tax sovereignty, and this collaboration defines the adoption of a new inclusive framework that will see large multinationals being held to account for their actions overseas.

The transition within globalisation should not be viewed as natural and automatic. The transition process itself brings a cacophony of its winners and losers, its proponents and enemies, amid a plethora of analysis praising and warning about the changes ahead. The problems within the realm of globalisation have proven to be stubborn and politically difficult to resolve, but in the last few years co-operation has produced some commendable results. Global cooperation on climate change is one category that can be considered as a success. The fact that irreconcilable countries from the global North and South have set aside their ideological differences and agreed that the effects of climate change are not only economically undesirable but also as threatening to human life and dignity, is by no means an easy feat. It is a sign that the next phase of globalisation will be defined by cooperation. If that is achieved, it will bring immense benefits across the developmental divide. If it fails, the results will be in nobody's favour.

14.3 Globalisation Versus State Sovereignty

The concept of place has been irreversibly changed by globalisation. As a matter of law, sovereignty is essentially territorial. Sovereignty and globalisation are frequently described in media as in antithesis. There is a call to revive sovereignty in the belief that it brings control, in the face of some panic and increasing frustration. But economic activity and information exchange are not so restricted. An example is the universal problem of disruption of supply chains extending over more than one state, particularly affecting the medical infrastructure of the pandemic response

[9] Watters, C. 'Developing Protocols of Court-to-Court Communication in Transnational Insolvency Proceedings: Limited Framework for Cooperation' (Chap. 11); see also Wan and Watters (2021), Watters (2020).

[10] Markham M, 'Towards More Effective and Inclusive Globalisation Strategies in International Tax: The Use of Peer Reviews in Evaluating Tax Treaty Dispute Resolution Mechanisms' (Chap. 10).

(highlighted in Bonython and Arnold's chapter).[11] The existing institutional response is inadequate although globally agreed only some thirty years ago, and already tested by HIV-Aids.

14.4 Advancement of Scientific and Technological Knowledge and Capabilities

The edges of human knowledge are constantly being pushed out through scientific research and experimentation. No area is immune to the change. The contributions by Lo[12] and Lupton[13] touch upon the age-old quest of human immortality. The theme of ageing of the human population is well-covered in this book by these two outstanding contributions. An ageing population in the global North affords new economic opportunities in medical research and the international health sector. The global South can be considered as a readily available source for meeting the demands in the developed market. However, cultural, social, and politico-economic barriers may prevent a wholesale integration.

The ageing of the world's population has been a major target of all manner of research whether medical or cosmetic. The population has grown with increasing speed, and this has led to the changing size and nature of the workforce, with both human and economic consequences. This generates major moral and economic questions posed in Lo's chapter: Who supports whom? Who gets to live longer? What is the infrastructure of a better or longer life?

14.5 Migration

The ageing of the population several developed nations, accompanied by negative population growth has also resulted in an increased demand for labour. Migration is an off-the-shelf solution to meet labour shortages. However, migration brings with itself major social and economic issues. The issue of refugee relief has been conflated with the need of people to move to find work and meets the push–pull of economies needing workers with various skills. We find ourselves drawn to Judge Spiller's insights in resolving some of the complicated problems associated with the cross-border movement of people.[14] Even though, the role of the unskilled worker has been restricted to agricultural and construction jobs, a globalised world must adapt

[11] Bonython W & B. Arnold 'Transition up to Best Practices, or Down to the Bar Minimum? Global Harmonisation of Regulation of Therapeutic Goods' (Chap. 5).

[12] Lo V., 'The Criss-Cross of Ageing and Globalisation' (Chap. 6); for more on ageing and the law see Ryan and Bonython (2018).

[13] Lupton M, 'A Peek Behind the Curtain of Anti-Aging Science' (Chap. 7).

[14] Judge Spiller 'Globalisation in the Immigration Context' (Chap. 3).

to multi-ethnic and multicultural groups, usually with different levels of education and social advantage. In there are immeasurable advantages for both the destination countries and the migrants.

14.6 First Nations and Post-colonialism

Even though migration brings certain advantages to the destination countries, the results can sometimes be catastrophic for those groups that are already vulnerable and marginalised. The waves of migration emphasise the position of the first inhabitants, who may also have migrated but, as in the case of Australia, tens of thousands of years ago. Bedford's contribution[15] touches upon the colonialism of the last millennium which led to the forceful imposition of foreign laws and structures of power in every continent, save Antarctica. Its intrinsic aspect of exploitation of foreign resources to benefit a colonial power was efficiently achieved, albeit sometimes with mixed motives. Post-colonial consequences are both economic and social, often disruptive to the point of violence.

14.7 The Cost of Economic Change

Throughout there is a hard economic edge. Ideology, whether political, social, or economic, has been set aside to deal with the practical consequences of the pandemic—the loss of jobs, businesses, and lives (highlighted in the chapter by Parsons).[16] In Australia, this has had a ripple effect together with the effects of climate change and the widespread extreme weather events of fire and flood. The shift in monetary policy has led to direct and indirect support for a wider class of "the vulnerable", and governments of whatever complexion have managed to change law, policies, and expectations. The moral arguments for accessibility and equality of support have been more public and stronger. Global and institutional co-operation on these matters seems a lot closer than it did earlier this century.

Each of these issues underlines the importance of the question—if globalisation is not dead but in transition, where is it going? Each of the contributors has tackled that question in their own context. It is not surprising that there is no unanimous conclusion, but more informed material to continue the debate.

---

[15] Bedford, N, 'Comparative First Nations Treaty Experience Across the Tasman' (Chap. 4); see also Taylor and Bedford (2022), Bedford et al. (2021).

[16] Parsons L, 'Central Banks in Crisis Times: Mandates in Crisis?' (Chap. 12).

References

Bedford, N., McAvoy, T., & Stevenson, L. (2021). First Nations Peoples, Climate Change, Human Rights and Legal Rights. University of Queensland Law Journal, 40(3), 371–401. https://doi.org/10.38127/uqlj.v40i3.6125

Kumar, K. (2020). Discussion on the paper by Bernard W Silverman on "Multiple-systems analysis for the quantification of modern slavery: classical and Bayesian approaches". Journal of the Royal Statistical Society. Series A: Statistics in Society, 183(3), 724. https://doi.org/10.1111/rssa.12505

Ryan, T., & Bonython, W. E. (2018). Whose Fault in an Aging World?: Comparing Dementia-Related Tort Liability in Common Law and Civil Law Jurisdictions. Washington International Law Journal, *27*(2), 407–448. https://digitalcommons.law.uw.edu/wilj/vol27/iss2/4

Taylor, A., & Bedford, N. (2022). Submission to Senate Standing Committee on Legal and Constitutional Affairs: Application of the United Nations Declaration on the Rights of Indigenous Persons in Australia.

Wan, W. Y., & Watters, C. (2021). Mandatory disclosure in corporate debt restructuring via schemes of arrangement: A comparative approach. *International Insolvency Review, 30*(S1), S111–S131. https://doi.org/10.1002/iir.1425

Watters, C. G. (2020). Cross-Border Insolvency in East Asia: Cooperation and Convergence. In D. Arner, W. Y. Wan, A. Godwin, W. Shen, & E. Gibson (Eds.), *Research Handbook on Asian Financial Law* (pp. 257–272). Edward Elgar Publishing. https://doi.org/10.4337/9781788972208.00023

MIX
Papier aus verantwortungsvollen Quellen
Paper from responsible sources
FSC® C105338

If you have any concerns about our products, you can contact us on
ProductSafety@springernature.com

In case Publisher is established outside the EU, the EU authorized representative is:
Springer Nature Customer Service Center GmbH
Europaplatz 3, 69115 Heidelberg, Germany

Printed by Libri Plureos GmbH
in Hamburg, Germany